SOUTHERN ENGINES OF GLOBAL GROWTH

UNU World Institute for Development Economics Research (UNU-WIDER) was established by the United Nations University as its first research and training centre and started work in Helsinki, Finland, in 1985. The purpose of the institute is to undertake applied research and policy analysis on structural changes affecting developing and transitional economies, to provide a forum for the advocacy of policies leading to robust, equitable, and environmentally sustainable growth, and to promote capacity strengthening and training in the field of economic and social policymaking. Its work is carried out by staff researchers and visiting scholars in Helsinki and via networks of collaborating scholars and institutions around the world.

United Nations University World Institute for Development Economics Research (UNU-WIDER)
Katajanokanlaituri 6 B, FIN-00160 Helsinki, Finland
www.wider.unu.edu

Southern Engines of Global Growth

Edited by

AMELIA U. SANTOS-PAULINO AND GUANGHUA WAN

A study prepared for the World Institute for Development
Economics Research of the United Nations University
(UNU-WIDER)

OXFORD
UNIVERSITY PRESS

OXFORD
UNIVERSITY PRESS

Great Clarendon Street, Oxford OX2 6DP

Oxford University Press is a department of the University of Oxford.
It furthers the University's objective of excellence in research, scholarship,
and education by publishing worldwide in

Oxford New York

Auckland Cape Town Dar es Salaam Hong Kong Karachi
Kuala Lumpur Madrid Melbourne Mexico City Nairobi
New Delhi Shanghai Taipei Toronto

With offices in

Argentina Austria Brazil Chile Czech Republic France Greece
Guatemala Hungary Italy Japan Poland Portugal Singapore
South Korea Switzerland Thailand Turkey Ukraine Vietnam

Oxford is a registered trade mark of Oxford University Press
in the UK and in certain other countries

Published in the United States
by Oxford University Press Inc., New York

© United Nations University—World Institute for Development
Economics Research (UNU-WIDER) 2010

The moral rights of the authors have been asserted
Database right Oxford University Press (maker)

First published 2010

British Library Cataloguing in Publication Data
Data available

Library of Congress Cataloging in Publication Data
Library of Congress Control Number: 2009943751

Typeset by SPI Publisher Services, Pondicherry, India
Printed in Great Britain
on acid-free paper by
MPG Books Group, Bodmin and King's Lynn

ISBN 978–0–19–958060–6

3 5 7 9 10 8 6 4 2

To our families, for their support

Foreword

ANTHONY SHORROCKS

Director, UNU-WIDER

Discussion of economic development issues has been dominated recently by the global economic crisis and the associated challenges for policymakers and regulators worldwide. A consensus seems to be emerging for action aimed at reducing the negative impact of economic vulnerability on the real economy, particularly in the world's poorest countries.

This volume presents a valuable selection of historical, empirical, and case studies on the development experience in large emerging economies, particularly China, India, Brazil, and South Africa—referred to here as the 'Southern Engines'. The key role and the potential impact of these countries in trade, capital flows, official financial and technical assistance, and opportunities for investments are increasingly significant.

Development, particularly its financing, is no longer confined to the old North–South paradigm. The increasing contribution of these emerging countries to trade and financial flows creates opportunities for a broader and more inclusive framework for international cooperation and global decision-making. Capital markets in the Southern Engines are attracting massive flows of foreign investment. The major attractions for investors are the sheer size of these economies and their large populations, translating into a potentially vast domestic market, progressive infrastructure (particularly in China), and straightforward trade and exporting platforms. Adding to these attractions are the political and economic reforms which have facilitated stability and consistent growth, and their record of achievement in upgrading production and trade from commodities to manufacturing and on to high-technology advanced services.

Despite rapid growth and successful trading and financial systems, deep concerns remain about the continued high rates of poverty in the Southern Engine countries. More than one-third of the world's poor live in China and India and other developing giants. Economic growth in these countries will therefore contribute significantly to global poverty reduction. These topics are examined in the present volume by prominent economists from the perspectives of economics, politics, and governance. China and India are two of the world's oldest civilizations, home to an ancient tradition of culture, commerce, and imperialism. This economic and cultural legacy endures in the new era of globalization and conveys a symbolic message of evolving political and economic ideas. The Southern Engines are driving a shift in the balance of power from North to South, forging a new global economic and political landscape in the process.

These are hugely important contemporary topics, which will continue to attract significant research and attention. There is a widespread belief that the world's future lies in the hands of China and India—particularly China. This book will therefore interest anyone concerned about global prosperity in the next few decades, particularly scholars and students of politics and economics, and policymakers in both developed and developing countries.

Acknowledgements

This volume is the outcome of the UNU-WIDER research project 'Southern Engines of Global Growth', directed by Amelia U. Santos-Paulino and Guanghua Wan. The chapters of this book were selected from the UNU-WIDER Conference on Southern Engines of Global Growth: China, India, Brazil, and South Africa, held 7–8 September 2007 in Helsinki. We express our gratitude to all the conference participants who contributed as presenters, session chairs, and discussants. Special thanks are due to Tony Shorrocks, Augustin Fosu, Deepak Nayyar, José R. Sánchez-Fury, numerous colleagues, and anonymous referees, for helpful guidance, comments, and suggestions.

UNU-WIDER staff provided excellent support. We are most grateful to the project assistant Janis Vehmaan-Kreula and to Barbara Fagerman for their effective editorial and administrative assistance during the project's activities. Sean Crowley, Ara Kazandjian, Liisa Roponen, and Lisa Winkler also contributed to the volume and the project's activities. Thanks are also due to Adam Swallow and Neha Mehrotra for their support during the publication process. Finally, we would like to thank our families for supporting and encouraging our work on this volume.

UNU-WIDER thanks the Finnish Ministry of Foreign Affairs for its support to this project, and gratefully acknowledges the financial contributions to the research programme by Denmark's Royal Ministry of Foreign Affairs, Finland's Ministry for Foreign Affairs, the Swedish International Development Cooperation Agency (Sida), and the United Kingdom's Department for International Development.

A.U.S.-P.
G.W.
Helsinki
2009

Contents

List of Figures

List of Tables

List of Abbreviations

ACFTA	ASEAN and China free trade agreement
ADF	augmented Dickey–Fuller [test]
ADR	American depositary receipts
AfrIPANet	African Investment Promotion Agency Network
AFTA	Asian Free Trade Area
AGOA	African Growth Opportunities Act
APEX-Brasil	Agência Brasileira de Promoção de Exportação e Investimentos [Brazilian Trade and Investment Promotion Agency]
BDR	Brazilian depositary receipts
BEEPS	Business Environment and Enterprise Performance Survey
BRIC	Brazil, Russia, India, and China
CAL	capital account liberalization
CC-5	Carta-Circular no. 5
CCES	China Center for Economic Studies
CE	common era
CEPII	Centre d'études prospectives et d'informations internationales
CGE	computable general equilibrium
CIBS	China, India, Brazil, and South Africa
CIPS	coordinated investment portfolio survey
CISA	China, India, and South Africa
DI	domestic investment
EBA	'Everything but Arms' [Agreement]
ECM	error correction model
EDB	Economic Development Board
EPZ	export processing zone
ETDZ	economic and technology development zone
FAPESP	Fundação de Amparo à Pesquisa do Estado de São Paulo [Foundation for Research Support of the State of São Paulo]
FCAC	fuller capital account convertibility
FDI	foreign direct investment
FIEs	foreign-invested enterprises

Fiex	Fundos de Investimento no Exterior [special investment funds abroad]
FMCG	fast-moving consumer goods
FTA	free trade agreement
GCF	gross capital formation
GDP	gross domestic product
GDS	gross domestic saving
GIDD	global income distribution dynamics
GIO	[monthly] gross industrial output
GTAP	Global Trade Analysis Project
IBSA	India, Brazil, and South Africa
ICOR	incremental capital:output ratio
ICT	information and communication technologies
IDA	Industrial Development Agency
IIP	international investment position
IMF	International Monetary Fund
IPA	investment promotion agency
IPI	industrialized products tax
IT	information technologies
LDC	least-developed country
L-M	P. Lane and G. M. Milesi-Ferretti (2006) 'The External Wealth of Nations Mark II: Revised and Extended Estimates of Foreign Assets and Liabilities, 1970–2004'. IMF Working Paper WP/06/69 (Mar.) (Washington, DC: IMF).
m km^2	million square kilometres
M&A	mergers and acquisitions
MDG	millennium development goal
MFN	most-favoured nation
MNC	multinational corporation
MNE	multinational enterprise
MOST	Ministry of Science and Technology
NBS	National Bureau of Statistics
NEC	new engineering contract
NEPAD	New Partnership for Africa's Development
NERC	National Engineering Research Centre
NPL	non-performing loan

NSF	[American] National Science Foundation
NSI	National System of Innovation
OFC	offshore financial centre
OFDI	outward foreign direct investment
PPP	purchasing power parity
PTI	process theory of internationalization
RENAI	Rede Nacional de Informações sobre o Investimento [National Network of Investment Information]
RoW	rest of the world
S&T	science and technology
S&T&I	science, technology, and industry
SADC	Southern African Development Community
SEBI	Security Exchange Board of India
SEZ	special economic zone (China) / zones (India)
SSA	sub-Saharan Africa
TFP	total factor productivity
TNC	transnational corporation
TRIPS	trade-related intellectual property rights
TWMNE	third world multinational enterprise
USBTA	bilateral trade agreement with the United States
USITC	United States International Trade Commission
VAT	value added tax
WIR	(UNCTAD) World Investment Report
WTO	World Trade Organization

List of Contributors

Mariana Corrêa Barra studied Economics at Universidade Estadual Paulista Júlio de Mesquita Filho (UNESP), and obtained an MSc in Science and Technology Policy at Universidade Estadual de Campinas (Unicamp). She also works as a researcher in a project on policies of foreign direct investment attraction in R&D. She specializes in industrial economics focused on venture capital, R&D investment decisions, and location choice.

Henri Bezuidenhout, PhD is a Senior Lecturer at the North-West University (Potchefstroom campus) in South Africa. He has a background in development economics and international trade. His current research interests include regional integration and international factor movements such as foreign direct investment, aid, migration, and remittances.

Maurizio Bussolo is currently at the World Bank where he has been working on quantitative analyses of economic policy and development. He previously worked at the OECD, at the Overseas Development Institute in London, and at Fedesarrollo and the Los Andes University in Colombia. He has published in numerous international journals and one of his most recent works, co-edited with François Bourguignon and Luiz Awazu Pereira da Silva, is *The Impact of Macroeconomic Policies on Poverty and Income Distribution: Macro-Micro Evaluation Techniques and Tools* (Houndmills: Palgrave Macmillan, 2008). He holds a PhD in Economics from the University of Warwick.

Edilaine Camillo graduated in Economics at Universidade Estadual Paulista Júlio de Mesquita Filho (UNESP) and holds an MSc in Science and Technology Policy from Universidade Estadual de Campinas (Unicamp), where she is currently a PhD student. She has experience in industrial economics focused on industrial and technology policies, foreign direct investment attraction in R&D, and industrial development, telecoms, and energy sectors.

Flávia Pereira de Carvalho holds a BA in Economics from Universidade Estadual de Campinas (Unicamp), an MA in Science and Technology Policy from the Science and Technology Policy Department, Universidade Estadual de Campinas (Unicamp), and is currently a PhD student at the UNU-MERIT Innovation Studies and Development programme in Maastricht. Her main research areas include international business and emerging multinationals; economics of innovation; microeconomics of innovation; and firm capabilities.

Pollyana de Carvalho Varrichio studied Economics at Universidade Estadual Paulista Júlio de Mesquita Filho (UNESP) and holds an MSc in Science and Technology Policy from Universidade Estadual de Campinas (Unicamp). She is currently a PhD student in the same institution and works as a researcher at the Instituto de Pesquisas Tecnológicas (IPT) do Estado de São Paulo. She has experience in industrial economics focused on industrial and technology policies, foreign direct investment attraction in R&D, and industrial development.

Jean-Raphael Chaponnière graduated from L'École Supérieure d'Électricité and has been an Economist in the Asian Department of Agence Française de Développement (AFD) since 2005. He was previously a researcher at the Centre National de la Recherche Scientifique (CNRS) and an economic counsellor for the French Ministry of Finance in Korea (1998–2000) and Turkey (2000–3). He has been conducting research on Asian economies since 1980.

Jean-Pierre Cling holds a PhD in Economics from Université Paris-Dauphine. He is also a graduate of L'École Nationale de la Statistique (ENSAE), Paris and an administrator of L'Institut National de la Statistique et des Études Économiques (INSEE). He has been working in Hanoi as a senior researcher for L'Institut de Recherche pour le Développement (IRD) since 2007. His research focuses on trade and development and employment issues.

Lord Meghnad Desai is Emeritus Professor of Economics at the London School of Economics (LSE), where he was on the faculty between 1965 and 2003. His work has encompassed applied econometrics, macroeconomics, and monetary theory; development economics; and economic history. His academic work can be seen in *The Selected Essays of Meghnad Desai*, 2 vols (Cheltenham: Edward Elgar, 1995). Recent publications include *Marx's Revenge: The Resurgence of Capitalism and the Death of Statist Socialism* (London: Verso 2002); *The Route to All Evil: Political Economy of Ezra Pound* (London: Faber, 2006); *Rethinking Islamism: The Ideology of the New Terror* (London: Tauris, 2006); and *The Rediscovery of India* (New Delhi: Penguin India, forthcoming).

Ricardo Gottschalk is senior lecturer at Middlesex University. Previously he was a Research Fellow at the Institute of Development Studies and Convenor of the new MA programme, Globalisation and Development. He is currently working on: capital flows to developing countries; Basel II and its impacts on financial inclusion; growth policies in Angola; the macroeconomic content of poverty reduction strategy papers (PRSPs); the sequencing of capital account liberalization; and China's impacts on other developing countries and their macroeconomic policy responses. He has worked as consultant to the European Commission, G24, UNCTAD, UNDP, UNRISD, and the governments of various sub-Saharan African countries.

John Henley is Emeritus Professor of International Management, University of Edinburgh Business School. He was principal consultant to the team that carried out and wrote the UNIDO Africa Foreign Investor Survey 2005. He has published widely on foreign direct investment in emerging markets and the relations between host governments and foreign investors, particularly in China, India, and Africa.

Rafael E. De Hoyos is currently the Chief of Advisers to the Under-Minister of Education in Mexico. Before joining the Ministry of Education, he was a researcher in the Development Prospects Group of the World Bank. He holds a PhD in Economics from the University of Cambridge and his main research focus is the economics of income inequality and how this links with the process of globalization.

Stefan Kratzsch has been a consultant to the Investment Promotion Unit in the United Nations Industrial Development Organization (UNIDO) since 2005. He worked on UNIDO's African Investment Promotion Agency Network and was instrumental in structuring the analyses of the UNIDO Africa Foreign Investor Survey 2005. He holds a degree in Business Engineering from the Technical University, Karlsruhe. While working for UNIDO he is also enrolled in a PhD programme at the Vienna University of Economics and Business Administration.

Mithat Külür is Chief of the Investment Promotion Unit at the United Nations Industrial Development Organization (UNIDO), where he has worked on issues of development since 1981. In Africa he developed programmes for promoting industrial investment projects; facilitating technology transfer; and training local professionals in industrial investment project formulation, appraisal, and promotion. He initiated the establishment of the UNIDO–Africa Investment Promotion Agency Network (AfrIPANet), which is a platform for monitoring foreign direct investment flows into African countries and formulating investment promotion strategies based on surveys of foreign investors. Mr Külür has degrees in Engineering and Development Economics from the University of Leeds, Cornell University, and Columbia University.

Denis Medvedev is an Economist with the West Africa Poverty Reduction and Economic Management department at the World Bank, where he uses general equilibrium and micro-simulation modelling tools to inform and motivate policy discussions with member governments. Before joining the Africa region department, he worked in the Development Prospects Group of the World Bank. He holds a PhD in Economics from the American University, Washington, DC.

Dominique van der Mensbrugghe is a Lead Economist with the Development Prospects Group of the World Bank and holds a PhD in Economics from the University of California, Berkeley. His main research focus has been the effects of globalization on developing economies, particularly as shaped by international trade and migration policies. His more recent work concentrates on the economics of climate change.

Wim Naudé is Senior Research Fellow and Project Director at UNU-WIDER in Helsinki. A widely published researcher focusing on spatial economics, entrepreneurship, trade, and African development, he graduated in Development Economics from the University of Warwick. Previously he has been research officer at the University of Oxford, a member of St Antony's College, and research director at North-West University, South Africa. He also served on the council of Statistics South Africa.

Deepak Nayyar is Professor of Economics at Jawaharlal Nehru University, New Delhi. He has taught at the University of Oxford, the University of Sussex, the Indian Institute of Management, Calcutta, and the New School for Social Research, New York. He was Vice Chancellor of the University of Delhi. He also served as Chief Economic Adviser to the Government of India. His research interests are primarily in the areas of international economics, macroeconomics, and development economics. Globalization and development are areas of focus in his present research.

Marion Pircher is currently employed at the On-site Banking Inspections Division of Oesterreichische Nationalbank. She holds a doctoral degree in Economics from Universität Wien (University of Vienna). She has formerly been a teaching assistant at Libera Università di Bolzano (Free University of Bolzano). Her research interests are international economics and emerging market finance.

Amelia U. Santos-Paulino is Research Fellow at UNU-WIDER and was previously a Research Fellow at the University of Sussex Institute of Development Studies and visiting scholar at the University of California, Davies. She specializes in trade, macroeconomics, and development issues and her work has been published in academic journals including *Economic Journal, Manchester School*, and *World Development*. She holds a PhD in Economics from the University of Kent.

Cecilia Azevedo Sodré is a Special Adviser at Instituto Jones dos Santos Neves (IJSN), Governo do Estado do Espírito Santo, Brazil. She currently oversees and conducts research projects undertaken through partnership between Instituto de Pesquisa Econômica Aplicada (IPEA) (Institute of Applied Economic Research) and IJSN. Her research interests include capital flows to developing countries, financial crises in emerging market economies, money, credit, and banking. More recently, she has been involved in research focused on poverty reduction, inequality, and growth in Latin America and issues concerning urban and regional dynamics in Brazil.

Eduardo Strachman graduated in Economics at Universidade Estadual de Campinas (Unicamp). He also holds an MSc and PhD in Economics from the same university. Since 2003, Dr Strachan has been Assistant Lecturer in the Department of Economics of Universidade Estadual Paulista Júlio de Mesquita Filho (UNESP) and in 2007 was appointed Coordinator of Postgraduate Studies in Economics. His research is in industrial economics (industrial and technology policies, transnational corporations and foreign direct investment, and sectoral studies, including banks), macroeconomics, and monetary economics.

Tamer Tandogan works on planning and implementation projects, investment surveys, and analysis and research on investment and technology promotion at the United Nations Industrial Development Organization (UNIDO). He holds degrees in Management and in Economics from Boğaziçi Üniversitesi (Bosphorus University), Istanbul and an MBA in Organizational Behaviour from Marmara Üniversitesi, Istanbul. He is currently a doctoral student in Management at Universität Wien (University of Vienna).

Guanghua Wan is a Senior Economist at the Asian Development Bank. Previously he was Senior Research Fellow and Project Director at UNU-WIDER. He is Honorary Professor at several leading universities in China and a prolific researcher, having published over fifty analytical papers in refereed journals and more than ten academic books. He is a pioneer in developing regression-based decomposition techniques for inequality and poverty accounting.

Mariana Nunciaroni Zanatta graduated in Economics at Universidade Estadual Paulista Júlio de Mesquita Filho (UNESP) and holds an MSc and PhD in Science and Technology Policy from Universidade Estadual de Campinas (Unicamp). Dr Zanatta currently works as a researcher at the Instituto de Pesquisas Tecnológicas (IPT) do Estado de São Paulo. Her research focuses on industrial economics focused on industrial and technology policies and foreign direct investment attraction in R&D.

Jun Zhang is Cheung Kong Professor of Economics at Fudan University, Shanghai where he serves as Director of the China Centre for Economic Studies. He is a member of the editorial board for, amongst others, *Journal of the Asia Pacific Economy, China Economic Journal,* and *China Economic Quarterly.* He publishes extensively and is one of the editors of *Economic Transitions with Chinese Characteristics,* 2 vols (Montreal and Kingston: McGill–Queen's University Press, 2008).

Bin Zhou holds a BA from Shanghai University of International Studies and Masters degrees in Economic Governance and International Affairs from Institut d'Études Politiques, Paris.

1

Introduction: Southern Engines of Global Growth

Amelia U. Santos-Paulino and Guanghua Wan

The exceptional economic performances of China, India, Brazil, South Africa (CIBS), and other southern economies is changing the socio-economic landscape of the world, with profound implications for international politics and global governance. These economies' performances reflect, inter alia, their active roles in global markets, which are echoed in their rapidly growing trade and capital flows. The increasing engagement in global trade and financial activities is also a manifestation of CIBS's opening to global trade and investment. This has led to the evolution of the countries' comparative advantages, by experiencing technical upgrading and the diversification of their production and trade capabilities, although with diverse degrees of success (Hausmann, Hwang, and Rodrik 2007; Guariglia and Santos-Paulino 2008).

While worldwide media audiences are being deluged by reports on some of the emerging countries, systematic analyses of these growing economies are relatively scarce, causing considerable misperception, ambiguous debate, and sometimes costly misguidance. The historical roots of the countries' development experiences, their growth outlook, and the role of capital flows, mostly in the form of foreign direct investment (FDI), are exhaustively studied in this volume.

AN OVERVIEW OF THE BOOK

This volume analyses the prospects of major southern economies by exploring the trends, sources, and consequences of economic growth in these countries. It also identifies the challenges that the economies face, and discusses the implications for the global development outlook. The role of FDI as a major indicator of globalization, its determinants and connectivity with other economic variables, is a central topic in the volume. The book is composed of three sections.

In Part I, Deepak Nayyar and Meghnad Desai explore the rise of the Southern Engines (the CIBS) considering historical, economic, and political elements. Nayyar and Desai examine the likely impacts of CIBS rapid growth on industrialized and developing countries. These effects could be complementary or competitive and, on balance, positive or negative. The main transmission mechanisms identified are international trade, investment, finance, and migration. Rapid growth in China has already proven to be positive on other countries, primarily by providing a market for exports. India and Brazil have the potential to provide similar support. But, according to Nayyar, South Africa does not yet exhibit that capability. These countries also supply resources for investment and technologies for enhancing productivity, notably India. The insights provided in this section of the volume also imply that the transformation and catching-up processes in the Southern Engines and the global economy could span at least five decades.

Rapid growth in these large emerging economies is already beginning to change the balance of economic power in the world, and particularly the shape of multilateral financial and trade institutions. But their sustained growth cannot be taken for granted. Each country needs to pursue policies that will lead to overcoming internal and external bottlenecks—mostly inequalities of wealth and lifetime opportunities—that could hinder sustained growth and hence their potential role in the global economy.

Part II focuses on the development approaches and growth paths of China, India, and Vietnam. Jun Zhang; Maurizio Bussolo, et al.; and Jean-Raphael Chaponnière, et al. evaluate the trajectories and institutional reforms in China's and India's economic successes and on the global distribution of wealth. Rapid growth in China and India is a key driver behind the expected convergence of per capita incomes at the national level and internationally. This has also prompted what is coined as a rapidly emerging global middle class, defined as a group of people who can afford the standards of living previously only accessible for higher income groups or more advanced countries. Still, fast growth might widen income distribution within countries, and that should not be overlooked.

Finally, Part III deals with the role of capital flows, FDI, and trade in the Southern Engines' economic success. Five chapters by Ricardo Gottschalk and Cecilia Azevedo Sodré; Marion Pircher; John Henley, et al.; Mariana Zanatta, et al.; and Henri Bezuidenhout and Wim Naudé study the distribution of capital and investment flows across regions and country groups, and what opportunities they bestow for developing countries. A noteworthy determinant of foreign capital and investment relocation is the liberalization of the capital account in CIBS and other developing countries, which in turn has facilitated investment flows. The chapters also examine the choice of location; the determinants of FDI; the impact on the host economy; the links between foreign and domestic investment; the relationship between FDI and trade; and national policies for attracting FDI—particularly in knowledge and technology intensive activities such as research and development (R&D). The following section focuses on the academic literature that studies the role of FDI and its impact on growth and development.

FOREIGN AND DOMESTIC INVESTMENT

Foreign investment largely originated from developed countries, and has increased rapidly across the world in recent years, outgrowing other capital flows to developing countries. Academic and policy studies recognize the positive externalities that FDI can generate for the host country. FDI is expected to boost economic growth via technological upgrading and knowledge spillovers in the long run, while in the short run FDI's impact depends on the degree of complementarity and substitution between domestic and foreign investment. FDI could also increase the existing stock of knowledge in the recipient economy through labour training and skill acquisition, as well as the introduction of alternative management and organizational practices (Grossman and Helpman 1991; De Mello 1999). Foreign investment also generates backward linkages to domestic suppliers and local activities. The linkages have beneficial impacts on the host country, as new inputs may become available, or the quality of existing inputs may improve substantially.

However, FDI's merits in enhancing the host country growth performance are increasingly under debate. Recent empirical evidence suggests that the effects of FDI on the host country are ambiguous at both the micro and the macro levels (Hanson 2001; Blomström and Kokko 1998; 2003; Alfaro, Kalemli-Ozcan, and Sayek 2008). These studies show that spillovers are not automatic, as local conditions—that is, the host country's absorptive capacity—have a non-trivial impact on a firm's exposure to foreign technologies and skills. This partly explains why different countries have had diverse degrees of success in attracting FDI.

Particularly, FDI inflows tend to be higher in countries with better governance and institutions. The level of investment inflows is determined by a country's physical and financial infrastructure, as well as by human capital and institutional capabilities. Alongside active policies for promoting and attracting FDI, the degree of openness to international trade is an important factor, particularly in outward-oriented developing countries (Balasubrama-nyam, et al. 1996).

The interface between private domestic and foreign investment is a key issue in studying FDI's externalities in the recipient economy, as FDI tends to crowd out private investment in a number of developing economies. Both FDI and domestic investment are essential for economic growth. But the challenge for developing countries is to devise an FDI strategy that can foster both economic growth and domestic investment by contributing to the development of new skills, technology, or products to the host country.

THE SOUTHERN ENGINES, LOOKING AHEAD

This volume shows that the increasing economic, social, and political linkages between developing countries involves resources mobilization in the areas of trade, finance, and the provision of development and technical assistance. Southern economic giants, notably China, India, Brazil, and increasingly South Africa, are contributing to these developments. CIBS and other fast growing developing countries are important sources of investments. Southern multinational corporations, notably from China and increasingly India, are also becoming providers of capital and technology to developing economies.

South–South capital flows are progressively critical for international develop-ment, but international trade remains the strongest and most direct channel through which southern leading economies impact on other countries—mostly their developing partners (Winters and Yusuf 2007). In addition to financial integration, reflecting current account surpluses and financial inflows, emerging markets—predominantly China—currently hold significant foreign reserves, changing the traditional international debt-holding patterns between rich and developing nations. This development can be regarded as a stabilizing weight to financial openness (Obstfeld 2009).

There are still many issues to be understood. However, these topics are potentially fruitful for international development. As this collection reflects, the Southern Engines are endowed with significant resources and powerful international institutions that could contribute to improve international policies and cooperation.

REFERENCES

Alfaro, L., S. Kalemli-Ozcan, and S. Sayek (2008) 'Foreign Direct Investment, Productivity, and Financial Development: An Empirical Analysis of Complementarities and Channels', *World Economy* (forthcoming). Special Issue 'Foreign Direct Investment and Multinational Economic Activity'.

Balasubramanyam, V., M. Salisu, and D. Sapsford (1996) 'Foreign Direct Investment in EP and IS Countries', *Economic Journal*, 106: 92–105.

Blomström, M., and A. Kokko (1998) 'Multinational Corporations and Spillovers', *Journal of Economic Surveys*, 12: 247–77.

——(2003) 'The Economics of Foreign Direct Investment Incentives', NBER Working Paper 9489.

de Mello, L. R. (1999) 'Foreign Direct Investment-led Growth: Evidence from Time Series and Panel Data', *Oxford Economic Papers*, 51: 133–51.

Grossman, G. M., and E. Helpman (1991) *Innovation and Growth in the Global Economy*. Cambridge, Mass.: MIT Press.

Guariglia, A., and A. U. Santos-Paulino (2008) *Export Productivity, Finance, and Economic Growth: Are the Southern Engines of Growth Different?*, UNU-WIDER Research Paper No. 2008/27.

Hanson, G. H. (2001) 'Should Countries Promote Foreign Direct Investment?', G-24 Discussion Paper 9.

Hausmann, R., J. Hwang, and D. Rodrik (2007) 'What You Export Matters', *Journal of Economic Growth*, 12: 1–25.

Obstfeld, M. (2009) 'International Finance and Growth in Developing Countries: What Have We Learned?', *NBER Working Paper*, 14691 (Cambridge, Mass.).

Winters, L. A., and S. Yusuf (2007) *Dancing with Giants: China, India and the Global Economy*. Washington, DC and Singapore: World Bank/Institute of Policy Studies.

Part I

Historical, Economic, and Political Contexts

2

China, India, Brazil, and South Africa in the World Economy: Engines of Growth?

Deepak Nayyar[1]

INTRODUCTION

The object of this chapter is to analyse the economic implications of the rise of China, India, Brazil, and South Africa, situated in the wider context of the world economy. The structure of the chapter is as follows. The first section sketches a profile of China, India, Brazil, and South Africa in the world economy. It sets the stage by outlining the broad contours of their significance in the past, present, and future. The next section asks whether these countries could be the new engines of growth for the world, beginning with history and statistics to touch upon the underlying economic causation. The third section examines the possible impact of rapid growth in the four economies on the world economy, the industrialized countries, and the developing countries. The penultimate section considers the main forms of engagement and channels of interaction for these countries with the world economy, with a focus on international trade, international investment, international finance, and international migration. The final section discusses the potential influence of China, India, Brazil, and South Africa on institutions in the global context, which would obviously extend beyond economics into politics and range from bilateralism through plurilateralism to multilateralism.

CHINA, INDIA, BRAZIL, AND SOUTH AFRICA IN THE WORLD ECONOMY

The significance of China, India, Brazil, and South Africa (CIBS) in the global context has changed over time. The discussion in this section provides a

[1] The author would like to thank Ananya Ghosh-Dastidar for valuable assistance.

historical perspective of the past, a snapshot of the present, and an extrapolated scenario for the future.

The past

The emerging significance of CIBS in the world economy must be situated in historical perspective. Table 2.1, which is based on estimates made by Angus Maddison, presents evidence on the shares of CIBS in world population and in world income for selected years during the period 1820–2001. It shows that in 1820 CIBS accounted for 57 per cent of world population and almost 50 per cent of world income. There was a dramatic change in the next 150 years. In 1973, the share of CIBS in world population was significantly lower, at about 40 per cent, but their share in world income collapsed to less than 11 per cent, which was a small fraction when compared with 150 years earlier. The next thirty years witnessed some recovery. While the share of CIBS in world population remained in the range of 40 per cent, their share in world income rose to almost 21 per cent in 2001. These aggregates reveal the essential contours, but also conceal some aspects of the story. There are

Table 2.1. *China, India, Brazil, and South Africa in the world economy: share in world population and world GDP, 1820–2001*

Year	China	India	Brazil	South Africa
	Percentage share of world population			
1820	36.6	20.1	0.4	0.1
1870	28.1	19.9	0.8	0.2
1913	24.4	17.0	1.3	0.3
1950	21.7	14.2	2.1	0.5
1973	22.5	14.8	2.6	0.6
2001	20.7	16.5	2.9	0.7
	Percentage share of world income			
1820	32.9	16.0	0.4	0.1
1870	17.1	12.1	0.6	0.2
1913	8.8	7.5	0.7	0.4
1950	4.5	4.2	1.7	0.6
1973	4.6	3.1	2.5	0.6
2001	12.3	5.4	2.7	0.5

Notes: The percentages in this table have been calculated from estimates of population and GDP in Maddison 2003. The data on GDP are in 1990 international Geary-Khamis dollars, which are purchasing power parities used to evaluate output that are calculated based on a specific method devised to define international prices. This measure facilitates inter-country comparisons over time.

Source: Maddison 2003.

similarities between China and India, just as there are similarities between Brazil and South Africa; however, there are significant differences between the two sets of countries. For much of the time, China and India had dominant shares.[2]

Beginning in 1820, the share of China and India in world population declined steadily until 1973 but over the same period the decline in their share of world income was considerably more pronounced. Consequently, during the period 1820–1973 there was a sharp increase in the asymmetries, or disproportionalities, between the shares of China and India in world population and in world income. The partial recovery in their share of world income during the period 1973–2001 has reduced the asymmetry but the disproportionality remains significant. For much of the time, the shares of Brazil and South Africa were far smaller. However, there were also other important differences: the shares of Brazil and South Africa in world population and in world income increased, even if slowly for some of the time throughout this period; the shares of Brazil and South Africa in world population and in world income were symmetrical and proportional throughout this period.

The present

It is possible to juxtapose this past with the present. Table 2.2 outlines a profile of GDP, population, and GDP per capita in CIBS in 2000 and 2005, as compared with developing countries, industrialized countries, and the world. It shows that the population of the world is more than 6 billion, of which slightly fewer than 1 billion are in the industrialized countries, somewhat more than 5 billion are in the developing countries, and more than 2.5 billion are in CIBS. Thus, 40 per cent of the population in the world and 50 per cent of the population in developing countries live in CIBS. There are two sets of figures on GDP and GDP per capita: at constant prices with market exchange rates, and in terms of purchasing power parities.

At market exchange rates, between 2000 and 2005, the share of CIBS increased from 7 per cent to 9 per cent of world GDP and from 39 per cent to 43 per cent of GDP in developing countries. Over the same period, at market exchange rates, GDP per capita in China was about the same,

---

[2] The dominance was even greater earlier. During the period from 1000 to 1700, China and India, taken together, accounted for 50 per cent of world population and 50 per cent of world income. Two thousand years ago, in 1 AD, China and India accounted for almost 60 per cent of world population and world income. For a more detailed discussion, see Nayyar 2008b.

Table 2.2. *GDP, population, and GDP per capita: China, India, Brazil, and South Africa, 2000 and 2005*

| | GDP | | | | Population | | PPP-GDP | | | |
| | ($ billion) | | ($ per capita) | | (million) | | ($ billion) | | ($ per capita) | |
Country	2000	2005	2000	2005	2000	2005	2000	2005	2000	2005
China	1,198	1,890	949	1,449	1,263	1,305	4,973	7,842	3,939	6,012
India	460	644	453	588	1,016	1,095	2,402	3,362	2,364	3,072
Brazil	602	670	3,461	3,597	174	186	1,251	1,393	7,193	7,475
South Africa	133	160	3,020	3,406	44	47	386	463	8,764	9,884
Total	2,393	3,364			2,496	2,632	9,011	13,061		
Developing countries	6,058	7,813	1,191	1,440	5,085	5,427	18,818	25,322	3,701	4,666
(CIBS as percentage of)	(39.5)	(43.1)			(49.1)	(48.5)	(47.9)	(51.6)		
Industrialized countries	24,542	27,148	27,304	29,251	899	928	25,157	27,898	27,988	30,058
World	31,756	36,352	5,241	5,647	6,060	6,438	45,144	54,573	7,450	8,477
(CIBS as percentage of)	(7.5)	(9.3)			(41.2)	(40.9)	(20.0)	(23.9)		

Notes: GDP and GDP per capita are measured in constant 2000 US$. PPP-GDP and PPP-GDP per capita are measured in constant 2000 international dollars.

Source: World Bank 2007.

GDP per capita for India was less than half, while GDP per capita in Brazil and South Africa was more than double the average GDP per capita in developing countries. It is worth noting that CIBS are far below GDP per capita in the industrialized countries and significantly below GDP per capita in the world as a whole. The picture is somewhat different if the comparison is in terms of purchasing power parities. Between 2000 and 2005, the CIBS share increased from 20 per cent to 24 per cent of world purchasing power parity (PPP)-GDP and from 48 per cent to 52 per cent of the PPP-GDP of developing countries. It would seem that, for CIBS, taken together, these shares in world income are now much more symmetrical with their share in world population. Over the same period, in PPP terms, GDP per capita in China moved ahead of GDP per capita in developing countries, whereas GDP per capita in India was about two-thirds of GDP per capita in developing countries. In contrast, GDP per capita in Brazil and South Africa was more than double the GDP per capita in developing countries and close to the world average.

This snapshot situates CIBS in the world economy at the present juncture. However, the observed reality has been shaped by their economic performance in the past. Table 2.3 sets out rates of growth in CIBS GDP and GDP per capita during the period 1951–80 and 1981–2005 in comparison with regions within the developing world, the developing countries, the industrialized countries, and the world economy.[3]

It is worth noting that time-series data on GDP and GDP per capita for the entire period from 1951 to 2005 are not available from a single source. The figures for the period 1951–80 are based on the Maddison data, as United Nations data are not available before 1971. The figures for the period 1981–2005 are based on United Nations data because Maddison data are not available after 2001. These two sources are not strictly comparable. However, it is possible to resolve the problem, as data are available from both sources for the period 1981–2000. To facilitate a comparison, Table 2.3 also presents figures on growth rates during 1981–2000, computed separately from Maddison data and United Nations data. A comparison of the two sets of growth rates during the period 1981–2000, for which both sources are available, shows that the numbers correspond closely, except in the figures for China, where UN data suggest much higher growth rates than Maddison data. Even so, it is reasonable to infer that the growth rates for the periods 1951–80 and 1981–2005, even if computed from different sources, are comparable, with the exception of China. In interpreting the data on China, where the step-up in

[3] The evidence in Table 2.3, and the discussion that follows, draw upon earlier work by the author. See Nayyar 2008c.

Nayyar

Table 2.3. *Growth performance of China, India, Brazil, and South Africa, 1951–80 and 1981–2005: comparison with regions and country-groups (percentage per annum)*

	Maddison data		United Nations data	
	1951–80	1981–2000	1981–2000	1981–2005
	GDP			
China	5.0	7.4	9.8	9.7
India	3.6	5.7	5.5	5.8
Brazil	6.8	2.1	2.0	2.0
South Africa	4.5	1.5	1.6	2.0
Asia	6.3	4.0	3.9	4.1
Latin America	4.7	2.0	2.1	2.3
Africa	4.1	2.4	2.6	3.0
Developing countries	4.8	2.7	2.7	3.0
Industrialized countries	4.4	2.6	2.6	2.5
World	4.8	2.6	2.7	3.0
	GDP per capita			
China	3.0	6.0	8.5	8.5
India	1.4	3.6	3.5	3.8
Brazil	3.9	0.3	0.2	0.3
South Africa	1.9	−0.3	−0.6	0.0
Asia	2.9	1.6	1.4	1.6
Latin America	2.1	0.2	0.2	0.4
Africa	1.7	−0.2	−0.1	0.4
Developing countries	2.2	0.4	0.4	0.8
Industrialized countries	3.5	2.0	2.1	2.0
World	2.4	0.7	0.7	1.0

Notes: The growth rates for each period are computed as geometric means of the annual growth rates in that period. The Maddison data and the United Nations data on GDP and GDP per capita are not strictly comparable. The Maddison data on GDP and GDP per capita, which are in 1990 international Geary–Khamis dollars, are purchasing power parities used to evaluate output which are calculated based on a specific method devised to define international prices. This measure facilitates inter-country comparisons. The United Nations data on GDP and GDP per capita are in constant 1990 US dollars. The figures in this table for the world economy cover 128 countries, of which 21 are industrialized countries and 107 are developing countries. Latin America includes the Caribbean.

Sources: Maddison 2003, United Nations 2006b, 2006c.

growth rates between these two periods is probably overstated, some downward adjustment might be needed.

A study of Table 2.3 clearly shows that growth in GDP and GDP per capita during 1981–2005 was much slower than during 1951–80. This was so for the world economy, for industrialized countries, and for developing countries. Almost everywhere, growth in GDP was in the range of 4 per cent to 5 per cent per annum during 1951–80 and in the range of 2 per cent to 3 per cent per annum during 1981–2005, except in Asia, where it was 6 per cent and 4 per cent per annum, respectively. Growth in GDP per capita slowed down considerably, even in the industrialized countries, from 3.5 per cent per annum to 2 per cent per annum, but the slowdown was more pronounced for developing countries, from 2.2 per cent per annum to 0.8 per cent per annum. In Latin America and Africa during 1981–2005 growth in GDP per capita was less than 0.5 per cent per annum, while Asia fared better at more than 1.5 per cent per annum.

The economic performance of China, Brazil, and South Africa presents a mixed picture, which does not quite conform to the trends observed in the aggregate. The most striking contrast is that China and India were the clear exceptions to this worldwide slowdown in growth. In both countries, growth rates in the second period were much higher than the perfectly respectable growth rates in the first period. So much so that, between 1951–80 and 1981–2005, average annual growth in GDP per capita almost trebled in both China and India. This was attributable, in part, to higher GDP growth rates and lower population growth rates. Unlike China and India, however, Brazil and South Africa were a part of the worldwide slowdown in growth. In both countries, growth rates in the second period were much lower than the impressive growth rates in the first period. So much so that, during 1981–2005, average annual growth in GDP per capita was almost negligible in both Brazil and South Africa. However, it is also worth noting that during 1951–80 average annual growth in GDP and GDP per capita in Brazil was significantly higher than that in China and India. The growth performance of South Africa during 1951–80 was also better than that of India, although it did not quite match that of China. This suggests that during the period 1981–2005 growth performance in China and India may have been better, in part, because their growth was on a lower base than that in Brazil and South Africa.

It might also be worthwhile comparing the growth performance of CIBS with the growth performance of other latecomers to industrialization, such as Japan and Korea, at comparable stages of development. Figure 2.1 attempts such a comparison. It shows the GDP growth trajectories in China (starting in 1979), India (starting in 1980), Brazil (starting in 1964), and South Africa (starting in 1990), compared with Japan (starting in 1960) and Korea (starting in 1965). The selected years coincide, as far as possible, with points at which rapid economic growth began in these countries. In Japan, rapid growth started around the mid-1950s but comparable data for the period before 1960 are not available. In South Africa, it is not possible to discern any turning-point in economic growth, but 1990 may be the most appropriate choice as the economic and political situation stabilized around that time. It is worth noting that in Figure 2.1 the year of origin for each country is different, which makes it possible to compare their growth trajectories at similar stages of development. It would seem that China's growth performance is discernibly better, while India's growth performance is roughly comparable with that

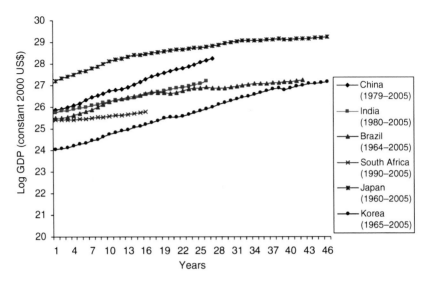

Figure 2.1. *GDP growth trajectories in China, India, Brazil, and South Africa compared with Japan and Korea*

Source: World Bank 2007.

of Japan and Korea. Brazil's growth performance, until about 1980, was also broadly comparable with that of Japan and Korea at similar stages but lagged behind thereafter. South Africa, it would seem, is the exception in so far as its growth performance is simply not comparable with that of other latecomers to industrialization. Interestingly, a comparison of growth in exports of goods and services, shown in Figure 2.2, reveals that export performance in China (beginning in 1979), India (starting in 1980), and Brazil (beginning in 1964 but only until 1980) was roughly comparable with that in Japan (beginning in 1960) and Korea (starting in 1965), although export growth in Japan and Korea was discernibly higher in the first decade. Once again, South Africa does not fit into this picture.

The future

Most growth scenarios for the future are based on an extrapolation of growth from the past. In attempting such projections, most exercises assume that growth rates in China and India, as also in the industrialized countries, would remain at levels observed in the recent past, while growth rates in Brazil would step up once again. Of course, it is Russia, rather than South Africa, that is an

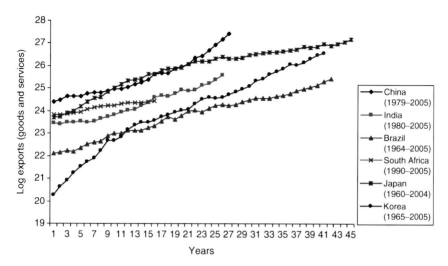

Figure 2.2. *Export growth in China, India, Brazil, and South Africa compared with Japan and Korea*

Source: World Bank 2007.

integral part of projections for, and scenarios in, 2050. And even if South Africa has some potential it is not yet on a trajectory of rapid economic growth.

The construction of future scenarios began with the Goldman Sachs study, which attempted to project levels of GDP and GDP per capita for Brazil, Russia, India, and China (BRIC) in 2050.[4] The exercise is based on a simple model of capital accumulation and productivity growth combined with demographic projections. The broad conclusions of the study[5] are that in 2000 the GDP of these four economies was less than 15 per cent of the GDP of the G6: US, Japan, Germany, UK, France, and Italy. By 2025, in terms of GDP, BRIC would be more than 50 per cent of the G6. And, in 2040, BRIC economies together would have a larger GDP than the G6. In terms of GDP, each of the BRIC economies would overtake each of these G6 economies, except the USA, by 2040. And, by 2050, of the G6, only the USA and Japan would remain among the six largest economies in the world. It is estimated that about two-thirds of the increase in BRIC GDP, measured in US dollars, would come from real growth, while the remaining one-third would be attributable to currency appreciation. BRIC catch-up is expected to be at its

---

[4] See O'Neill, et al. 2004.
[5] For a discussion of the methodology, assumptions, and conclusions, see Wilson and Purushothaman 2004.

most dramatic until 2030. Thereafter, BRIC growth would also slow down and only India might have growth rates higher than 3 per cent per annum in 2050. The catch-up would be less marked in terms of GDP per capita. On average, with the exception of Russia, BRIC citizens are likely to be poorer than citizens in the G6. It must be stressed that the projected BRIC growth path, even in the Goldman Sachs study, depends on critical assumptions about policies and institutions, and also the capacities of these countries to resolve their problems: outcomes are therefore neither predictable nor certain.[6]

In a more sophisticated exercise for China and India that uses simple convergence equations, Robert Rowthorn (2006) projects that, in 2050, at PPP, per capita income in China would be 63 per cent of per capita income in the USA, while per capita income in India would be 45 per cent of per capita income in the USA. It is also projected that both China and India should comfortably overtake the USA in GDP measured at PPP. This catch-up is not confined to PPP-GDP comparisons. The Rowthorn projections show that, even at market exchange rates, by 2050, total output in China would be 60 per cent larger than in the USA, while total output in India and the USA would be roughly equal.[7]

It must be said that these projections suggest broad orders of magnitude rather than precise predictions. Even so, such projections highlight the power of compound growth rates—for growth rates do, indeed, matter. If GDP grows at 10 per cent per annum, national income doubles in seven years. If GDP grows at 7 per cent per annum, national income doubles in ten years. If GDP per capita grows at 5 per cent per annum, per capita income doubles in fourteen years. Growth rates in China and India have been in this range for some time. Also, growth rates in India have accelerated during the early 2000s. Growth rates in Brazil were also in this range during the period 1951–80 and could return to that path once again. If such growth rates are sustained, their cumulative impact over time is no surprise. However, growth is not simply about arithmetic. In fact, it is about more than economics. Therefore, it is necessary to consider the economic determinants of growth.

In principle, China and India might be able to sustain high rates of economic growth for some time to come for several reasons. Brazil might also be able to attain high rates of growth for similar reasons, although their relative importance could be different. First, the population in these countries

---

[6] The authors recognize this limitation to state: 'there is a good chance that our projections are not met, either through bad policy or bad luck' (Wilson and Purushothaman 2004: 25).

[7] For a detailed discussion, see Rowthorn, who explains the methodology underlying these projections (Rowthorn 2006 appendix 1: 17–18).

is large and income levels are low. Second, their demographic characteristics—in particular, the high proportion of young people in the population, which would mean an increase in the workforce for some time to come—are conducive to growth. Third, in China and India, more so than in Brazil, wages are significantly lower than in the world outside, while there are large reservoirs of surplus labour. Fourth, emerging technological capabilities have the potential to support an increase in productivity. In practice, however, China, India, and Brazil might not be able to sustain their high rates of growth because of constraints that are already discernible. In China, the declining productivity of investment at the margin and the sustainability of the political system are both potential constraints. In India, the crisis in agriculture, the bottlenecks in infrastructure, and the limited spread of education in society are potential constraints. In Brazil, the level and the productivity of investment, both of which are low, constrain growth at a macro level. Of course, these constraints are illustrative rather than exhaustive. And there are many other problems in these countries that could slow down the process of growth. Even if growth slows, however, a catch-up scenario is plausible, but it would require a greater length of time.

ENGINES OF ECONOMIC GROWTH IN THE WORLD

Globalization is associated with increasing economic openness, growing economic interdependence, and deepening economic integration in the world economy. In such a world, growth prospects would be significantly influenced, if not shaped, by the growth performance of lead economies. The discussion that follows asks whether CIBS could be new engines of growth, to consider the underlying causation and mechanisms.

Engines of growth

History provides obvious examples. Britain in the nineteenth century and the USA in the twentieth century were engines of growth for the world economy. Statistical analysis for the period since the early 1960s provides confirmation.[8] It is widely accepted that GDP growth in the USA leads GDP growth in the world. A statistical analysis of long-term trends in economic growth for the

---

[8] For a more detailed discussion on the statistical evidence and analysis cited in this paragraph, see United Nations 2006a.

period 1963–2001, with five-year moving averages for both sets of growth rates, yields a correlation coefficient of 0.82, while a simple lead–lag analysis shows that the US economy leads the world economy by one year. Evidence available also reveals that developing countries, excluding China, follow the trends in world economic growth and, hence, trends in the economic growth of the USA. It is worth noting that economic growth in developing countries follows economic growth in the USA with a lag, but with more pronounced swings in cyclical ups and downs.

In reflecting on the future, is it possible to think of CIBS as engines of growth for the developing world, even if not for the world economy? The answer depends, in large part, on the size of the four economies and their rates of growth. There are some pointers in recent experience. Statistical analysis shows that, since 1980, the Chinese economy has also led world GDP, with a lag of one or two years, although the correlation coefficient is much smaller than that for the USA.[9] This is not surprising: consider that, in 2005, China accounted for 5 per cent of world GDP at market exchange rates and 14 per cent of world GDP in PPP terms. Also, GDP growth in China has been at approximately 9 per cent per annum for twenty-five years. By these criteria, India is not an engine of growth—at least, not yet. This is also not surprising. In economic terms, it is smaller than China and its growth rate is not as high. For example, in 2005, India accounted for only 2 per cent of world GDP at market exchange rates and 6 per cent of world GDP in PPP terms. Additionally, GDP growth in India has been in the range of 6 per cent per annum for twenty-five years. Even so, India is a potential engine of growth in terms of both attributes. Brazil presents a mixed picture. Its economic size is significant. In 2005, Brazil accounted for 2.5 per cent of world GDP both at market exchange rates and in PPP terms. However, GDP growth has been just 2 per cent per annum for the past twenty-five years. Brazil has the economic size to exercise some influence on, even if it cannot drive growth in the world economy, but it does not have the growth rate to do so. South Africa provides a sharp contrast. In 2005, it accounted for only 0.6 per cent of world GDP at market exchange rates and 0.8 per cent of world GDP in PPP terms, and GDP growth has only been at 2 per cent per annum for the past twenty-five years. Clearly, South Africa meets neither criterion, whether size or growth. Of course, given their economic size in relation to most developing countries, taken together, CIBS could be a possible engine of growth for the developing world, but that would depend on the degree and nature of linkages.

[9] See United Nations 2006a: 22–3.

Rapid economic growth in lead economies drives economic growth elsewhere in the world by providing markets for exports, resources for investment, finances for development, and technologies for productivity. The classic examples—Britain in the nineteenth century and the USA in the twentieth century—provide confirmation of the suggested economic causation and the possible transmission mechanisms. Indeed, during their periods of dominance in the world, both Britain and the USA were engines of growth, in so far as they provided the rest of the world not only with markets for exports and resources for investment, but also with finances for development and technologies for productivity. And, despite the diminished dominance, the US economy continues to be an engine of growth for the world. At this juncture, China is not quite an engine of growth in every dimension. Economic growth in China provides a stimulus to economic growth elsewhere, in large part as a market for exports. So far, India and Brazil cannot be characterized as engines of growth in any dimension, perhaps not even as markets for exports. But, along with China, India and Brazil have some future potential in terms of markets for exports, resources for investment, and technologies for productivity. South Africa is the obvious outlier in this picture, although it could provide some impetus to the growth process in Africa if linkages develop appropriately. In this context, it is worth noting that the four CIBS economies could, in times to come, provide a significant impetus to the growth process in their respective regions. What is more, even if these CIBS economies cannot be a substitute for the United States, as an engine of growth for the world economy, they could be an important complement to the older engine in driving global growth.

Causation and mechanisms

The economic causation outlined above is necessary but not sufficient. The overall effects of economic growth in lead economies on economic growth elsewhere depend on: (i) whether such growth is complementary or competitive; (ii) whether the direct effects are reinforced or counteracted by the indirect effects; and (iii) whether, on balance, the impact is positive or negative.[10]

In principle, economic growth in lead economies might be complementary or competitive to economic growth elsewhere. It might be complementary in so far as it increases the demand for exports, but it might be competitive in so

---

[10] For a detailed discussion, see Kaplinsky 2006. The literature on this subject is limited. However, the implications and consequences of rapid growth in China and India, for the developing world, are analysed in Kaplinsky and Messner 2008.

far as it develops alternative sources of supply. It might be complementary if it provides resources for investment or finances for development, but it might be competitive if it pre-empts such resources for investment or finances for development. It might be complementary if it provides technologies to others, but it might be competitive if it stifles the development of technologies elsewhere. This distinction between the complementary and the competitive aspects is widely recognized. However, the distinction between direct effects and indirect effects is less clear because the latter sometimes are difficult to discern, let alone measure. In situations where direct effects are complementary, indirect effects could be reinforcing if complementary, but counteracting if competitive. Some examples might be illustrative. The direct effects might be complementary if the lead economies—say, CIBS—provide cheap wage goods to other developing countries, but the indirect effects might be competitive if competition from firms in lead economies squeezes out local firms in other developing countries. The direct effects might be complementary if firms from these lead economies invest in other developing countries, but the indirect effects might be competitive if firms from industrialized countries relocate production and invest in CIBS rather than in other developing countries. The direct effects might be complementary if these lead economies provide cheaper inputs for manufactured exports from other developing countries, but the indirect effects might be competitive if competition from the lead economies squeezes out manufactured exports from other developing countries in the markets of industrialized countries. In principle, then, the impact of economic growth in lead economies on economic growth elsewhere, in different spheres, could be positive or negative, or a combination of both. Therefore, on balance, such impact could be either positive or negative. The outcomes could differ across space and change over time, so generalizations are difficult.[11]

The main mechanisms of interaction through which outcomes would be shaped are international trade, investment, and finance. These are considered later in the chapter. In this context, however, it is worth noting that domestic developments within such large countries could also have international consequences. For instance, macroeconomic policies in China, India, and Brazil, once these countries become lead economies, might exercise an important influence on economic growth elsewhere. If such policies are countercyclical, which has been the case for the USA, these would be supportive of economic growth elsewhere. However, if these policies are pro-cyclical, which is common in developing countries, these could be disruptive for economic growth

---

[11] There is a clear need for more systematic research on the subject, where information and understanding are both limited.

elsewhere. Similarly, exchange rates and interest rates in lead economies could exercise a significant influence, either positive or negative, on economic growth elsewhere in the world. For example, an undervalued exchange rate in China, which has persisted for quite some time, constrains the prospects for labour-intensive manufactured exports from other developing countries, thereby limiting the potential demand stimulus to economic growth that could be provided by exports. Similarly, the combination of a high interest rate and a strong exchange rate, which has been the case for some time in both India and Brazil (albeit for different reasons), pre-empts possible foreign capital inflows, thereby limiting the potential external finance necessary to support economic growth in other developing countries.

POSSIBLE IMPACT OF RAPID GROWTH IN CIBS

Rapid economic growth in China and India, if it is sustained at the projected rates, is bound to exercise considerable influence on prospects for the world economy, the industrialized countries, and the developing countries. This impact could be either positive or negative.

World economy

The consequences for the world economy could be positive if, as the old engine of growth slows down, CIBS emerge as new engines of growth that drive the process. Ultimately, it is possible that the new engines replace the old engines of growth. This is, at best, a scenario for the future. The preceding discussion suggests that rapid growth in China supports but does not yet lead growth in the world economy. India and Brazil have the potential to provide similar support but this has not materialized so far. South Africa does not even exhibit such potential. It is clear that for some time to come the US economy would continue to be the engine of growth for the world economy. But this dominance is bound to diminish as rapid growth in the large emerging economies of the developing world slowly, yet surely, changes the balance of economic power in the world.

The impact of rapid economic growth in CIBS on the world economy could also be negative in the form of consequences for the environment and the labour market. Much of the literature tends to focus on the environmental consequences of rapid economic growth in China and India. The energy needs of these two mega-economies are enormous. This is not surprising, as levels of consumption per capita are low and income elasticities of demand are high. In absolute terms, China's demand for oil is catching up rapidly with that of Europe and the USA, while China's CO_2 emissions are now only exceeded by the USA. India lags behind China, but the catch-up process has commenced. Energy consumption in Brazil and South Africa is also likely to grow, even if not as rapidly as in China and India. It would mean too much of a digression to enter into a discussion of this complex issue here.[12]

In the context of the world economy, the other issue that has received attention is the consequences for the labour market. The focus, once again, is on China and India. It has been argued by Richard Freeman that entry into the world economy by China, India, and the erstwhile socialist countries of Europe has had a dramatic impact on the size of the global workforce. He argues that, if nothing had changed, the world labour force would have increased from almost 1 billion people in 1980 to about 1.5 billion people in 2000—attributable, in large part, to population growth. In fact, however, he concludes that the world labour force in 2000 was double the size, at 3 billion, attributable largely to the economic integration of China, India, and the transition economies with the world.[13] Freeman believes that this transformation is good for workers in low-income countries and bad for workers in high-income countries. The conclusion drawn is not protectionist. It is much more nuanced. Freeman suggests that government intervention, in the national and international contexts, would be conducive to a more harmonious integration of China and India (to which could be added Brazil and South Africa) into the world economy. In pursuit of this objective, he suggests that it would be important to follow the good examples of integration, such as the integration of Western Europe and Japan into the world economy after the Second World War, rather than the bad examples of integration, such as the integration of the southern part of the USA into the USA after the Civil War or the integration of East Germany into Germany after unification. This proposition is clearly sensible. Even so, it is important to recognize two essential limitations of the Freeman hypothesis:[14] (i) it seeks to focus far too much on the supply side in terms of labour market consequences in the world economy, while it neglects the demand side in so far as rapid economic growth in China and India, as well as Brazil, could also provide an impetus to growth in the world economy; (ii) it underestimates the strength and dynamism of the US economy, embedded in history that provides it with a competitive edge even in the early twenty-first century.

---

[12] For some evidence and discussion on this issue, see Rowthorn 2006 and Kaplinsky 2006.

[13] For a more detailed discussion on this proposition, see Freeman 2005.

[14] For a critical, yet nuanced, evaluation of the Freeman hypothesis, see Singh 2007.

Industrialized countries

The impact of rapid economic growth in CIBS on the industrialized countries could be either positive or negative.

There are three reasons why the impact might be negative. First, rapid economic growth in CIBS might worsen the terms of trade for industrialized countries. The burgeoning demand from CIBS could drive up the prices of primary commodities in the world market. At the same time, rising wages in CIBS could drive up prices of labour-intensive manufactured goods in the world market. Both could turn the terms of trade against industrialized countries. Rowthorn (2006), who examines this issue in some depth, argues that terms of trade for industrialized countries might worsen over time but that the consequences would be easy to absorb because the process would be spread over a long period.[15] What is more, its impact in terms of loss of real income in the industrialized world would be modest.

Second, for the industrialized countries, CIBS could emerge as new destinations that could become a source of competition for investment. This might happen if firms from the industrialized countries, whether the USA or Europe, relocate production in CIBS. Even if they do not, it would strengthen capital and weaken labour in terms of bargaining power, thereby exercising some outward pressure on wages. Rowthorn, who also examines this issue in depth, concludes that it is a limited phenomenon so far and is not likely to happen on a larger scale for quite some time to come.[16]

Third, the economic rise of CIBS might lead to a downward pressure on employment levels and real wages in the industrialized countries. It needs to be said that this concern is somewhat exaggerated. It is important to recognize that the stagnation in real wages and the high levels of unemployment in the industrialized countries are attributable to the nature of technical progress, which is replacing several unskilled workers with a few skilled workers, and the impact of macroeconomic policies, which have sought to maintain price stability at the expense of full employment. The source of these problems lies within the industrialized countries and not in their trade with developing

---

[15] It is argued that such a loss could be quite severe if all of it came at the same time, but if it were spread over many years it would have only a marginal impact. For instance, if the USA experienced deterioration in its terms of trade that lowered real income by the equivalent of 5 per cent of GDP over a period of twenty-five years, per capita income would grow by 1.6 per cent per annum instead of its present trend rate of 1.8 per cent per annum (Rowthorn 2006: 9).

[16] For a discussion, see ibid. It must also be recognized that the high mobility of capital combined with the low mobility of labour in the contemporary world economy have already strengthened capital and weakened labour, so that any observed downward pressure on wages cannot be attributed to trade with CIBS alone.

countries.[17] And even if the expansion of such trade in manufactured goods with CIBS could exert some downward pressure on employment levels or real wages in industrialized countries, such pressures are bound to diminish with the ageing of industrial societies.[18] There are two other reasons, stressed by Rowthorn (2006) and Singh (2007), which confirm that such concerns about employment and wages are probably exaggerated. There is the Krugman proposition that 'economic history offers no examples of a country that experienced long-term productivity growth without a roughly equal rise in real wages'.[19] Thus, in the long run, productivity increase in China and India would also be followed, after a time, by a commensurate increase in real wages. Also, a coordination of macroeconomic polities, reinforced by the logic of international collective action, could be an important means of minimizing the social costs for workers in the industrialized countries during the transition period in which CIBS integrate into the world economy.

It is just as important to recognize that rapid economic growth in CIBS could have a positive impact on the industrialized countries.[20] First, starting from low levels of income per capita juxtaposed with high-income elasticities of demand, higher incomes associated with rapid growth would create expanding markets for exports from industrialized countries. Second, these emerging economies could be a source of cheap manufactured goods that could help reduce inflationary pressures in industrialized countries, thereby enabling them to maintain higher levels of output and employment than would otherwise be possible. Third, these emerging economies could be a source of new technologies in the future that could help extend production possibility frontiers and consumer possibility frontiers in the industrialized economies.

Developing countries

During the first quarter of the twenty-first century, economic growth in CIBS could have a positive impact on developing countries if it improves terms of trade, provides appropriate technologies, and creates new sources of finance for development, whether investment or aid.

---

[17] This argument is developed, at length, in Nayyar 1996.

[18] For a discussion, and some evidence, see Nayyar 2002a.

[19] Krugman 1994. This argument is developed further, in the China–India context, by Rowthorn 2006 and Singh 2007.

[20] The underlying factors mentioned in this paragraph are also emphasized by Singh 2007 and Rowthorn 2006, with reference to China and India.

It is clear that, for some time to come, the positive impact on developing countries would be transmitted through an improvement in their terms of trade.[21] Rapid economic growth in China and India is bound to boost the demand for primary commodities exported by developing countries. The reasons are simple enough. Both China and India have large populations. However, that is not all. In both countries, levels of consumption per capita in most primary commodities are low, while income elasticities of demand for most primary commodities are high. This burgeoning demand will almost certainly raise prices of primary commodities in world markets and thereby improve the terms of trade for developing countries. It would benefit Brazil and South Africa, as exporters of primary commodities, while the revival of growth in Brazil and South Africa, when it happens, would reinforce this process. What is more, China already is, while India and Brazil are likely to become, sources of manufactured goods in the world market. Such manufactures—particularly wage goods, but also capital goods from China, India, and Brazil—are likely to be cheaper than competing goods from industrialized countries. At the same time, Brazil and South Africa could provide cheaper natural resource-based manufactures. This would also improve the terms of trade for developing countries.

The positive impact of CIBS on developing countries through the other potential channels of transmission is not as clear. We do not yet have either the evidence or the experience. In principle, it is possible that CIBS would develop technologies that are more appropriate for the factor endowments and the economic needs of developing countries. But it is too early to come to a judgement on this matter. Similarly, CIBS are potential sources of finance for development. Their foreign aid programmes, particularly in Africa, constitute a modest beginning.[22] However, so far, their contribution in terms of foreign direct investment is limited.

The emergence of CIBS in the world economy could also have a negative impact on developing countries if these economies provide developing countries with competition in markets for exports or as destinations for investment.

At this juncture, China is clearly the largest supplier of labour-intensive manufactured goods in the world market. Similarly, India is also a significant supplier, though not as large as China. Brazil and South Africa are important suppliers of natural resource-based manufactures. China, India, and Brazil are emerging suppliers of capital goods. There can be little doubt that manufactured exports from CIBS span almost the entire range of manufactured

---

[21] This proposition is stressed by Kaplinsky 2006, Rowthorn 2006, and Singh 2007.
[22] For a discussion on China's trade with, and aid to, Africa, see Toye 2008.

exports in which other developing countries could have a potential comparative advantage. Hence, it is plausible to argue—though impossible to prove—that, on balance, CIBS possibly have a negative impact on manufactured exports from other developing countries that have to compete with these four economies for export markets in industrialized countries.[23] This can change if and when China and India vacate their space in the international trade matrix, in much the same way as latecomers to industrialization in Asia such as Japan, Korea, Hong Kong, Taiwan, and Singapore vacated their space in the market for simple labour-intensive manufactures for countries that followed in their footsteps. It is not likely, at least in the medium term, because both China and India have large reservoirs of surplus labour at low wages not only in the rural hinterlands, but also in the urban informal sectors. Brazil and South Africa might not have such large reservoirs of surplus labour but, given their abundance in primary commodities and natural resources, it is not likely that they would vacate their space in the market for processed products or resource-based manufactures for other developing countries that have similar natural endowments.

The evidence presented later in the chapter shows that CIBS absorb a significant proportion of inward foreign direct investment in developing countries, in terms of both stocks and flows. Given that China, India, and Brazil are now among the most attractive destinations for transnational firms seeking to locate production in the developing world, it is once again plausible to suggest that perhaps foreign direct investment in China, India, and Brazil might be at the expense of developing countries. South Africa might not have the same attraction as a destination, but it might draw foreign direct investment that could have gone to developing countries in Africa. At the same time, the share of CIBS in outward foreign direct investment in the world economy, as also from developing countries, is modest in both stocks and flows, so that firms from these four countries do not compensate with foreign direct investment in other developing countries.

The implicit barriers to change in the traditional division of labour and specialization in production are a less discernible but more significant negative impact of the four economies, particularly China, on developing countries. For example, China and India might pre-empt opportunities for other developing countries to industrialize through exports of labour-intensive manufactures, which is attributable to their surplus labour and low wages and which might continue for some time to come. Further, Brazil and South

---

[23] Kaplinsky and Morris (2008) show that China's emergence as a large exporter of manufactured goods in the world economy poses severe problems for export-oriented growth in sub-Saharan Africa, particularly in textiles and clothing.

Africa might pre-empt opportunities for other developing countries to industrialize through agro-based or resource-intensive manufactures, which is attributable to their abundance in primary commodities and natural resources. But this is no more than a plausible hypothesis about possible future developments and one that cannot be tested.

The problem has, however, surfaced in one dimension. China's present division of labour with the developing world, reflected in the composition of trade flows, is not different from the old North–South pattern of trade, in so far as Chinese imports from the developing world are largely primary commodities, while Chinese exports to the developing world are largely manufactured goods.[24] China's trade with countries in South-East Asia is the exception to this rule. But Chinese trade with, and investment in, Africa conforms even more closely to this caricature of a neocolonial pattern. It should be recognized that such traditional patterns of trade can neither transform the structure of production in developing countries, nor make for a new international division of labour. Indeed, such trade can only perpetuate the dependence of developing countries on exports of primary commodities without creating opportunities to increase value-added before export or entering into manufacturing activities characterized by economies of scale. Such path-dependent specialization can only curb the possibilities of structural transformation in developing countries. Trade with China can sustain growth and support industrialization in developing countries only if there is a successful transition from a complementary to a competitive pattern of trade, so that inter-sectoral trade is gradually replaced by intra-sectoral or intra-industry trade and specialization.

CHANNELS OF ENGAGEMENT AND TRANSMISSION

The preceding discussion is largely in terms of macroeconomic aggregates. It is also necessary to consider the forms of engagement with the world economy, through which the impact of rapid economic growth in CIBS, whether

---

[24] An unpublished study by Rhys Jenkins and Chris Edwards on China's trade with eighteen developing countries (six in Asia, six in Africa, and six in Latin America), cited at United Nations 2006b: 22, shows that countries that had significant trade with China were exporting mostly agricultural or extractive primary commodities. A study on China's economic interaction with Latin America and the Caribbean also confirms the traditional pattern of trade, importing mostly primary commodities and exporting mostly manufactured goods (Inter-American Development Bank 2005). Another study on the impact of China's trade with, and foreign direct investment in, Latin America and the Caribbean shows that there are winners and losers that can be identified: primary-commodity-producing sectors and countries are the winners while sectors and countries producing or exporting manufactured goods are the losers (Jenkins, Peters, and Moreira 2008).

positive or negative, is transmitted elsewhere. The obvious, and most important, channels of transmission are international trade, international investment, international finance, and international migration.

International trade

International trade is, perhaps, the most important form of engagement with the world economy, not only for CIBS, but also for developing countries. Available evidence provides confirmation. Exports and imports of goods and services as a proportion of GDP rose from 44 per cent to 69 per cent in China, from 28 per cent to 45 per cent in India, from 23 per cent to 29 per cent in Brazil, from 53 per cent to 56 per cent in South Africa, and from 56 per cent to 67 per cent in developing countries.[25] Table 2.4 presents evidence on trade in goods, for CIBS, with the developing countries, the industrialized countries, and the world as a whole in 2000 and 2005. It shows the relative importance of CIBS, as markets for exports and sources of imports for the world. During this brief period, the CIBS share in world trade almost doubled, from 5.7 per cent in 2000 to about 9.8 per cent in 2005. Their share in the trade of developing countries increased from 19 per cent to 27 per cent and, in the trade of industrialized countries, increased from 6 per cent to 10 per cent.[26] The emerging significance is clear. In 2005, CIBS, taken together, accounted for about one-tenth of merchandise trade in the world, more than one-quarter of the merchandise trade of developing countries, and one-tenth of the merchandise trade of industrialized countries. It is worth noting that these aggregate proportions could be somewhat deceptive because, in 2005, China accounted for as much as 72 per cent, India accounted for 12 per cent, Brazil accounted for 10 per cent, and South Africa accounted for only 6 per cent of CIBS trade with the world. The respective shares of these countries in CIBS trade with developing countries and industrialized countries were about the same.[27]

[25] These figures, obtained from data reported in World Bank 2007, relate to exports *and* imports of goods *and* services as a proportion of GDP. Even so, it needs to be said that for large countries such as China and India these trade:GDP ratios are high and might not be sustainable in the long term. Merchandise trade flows, presented in Table 2.4 and discussed in this paragraph, are perhaps the more appropriate indicator.

[26] The shares of CIBS in the trade of developing countries, industrialized countries, and the world, reported in this paragraph, are calculated from the data in Table 2.4 and relate to total trade: that is, the sum total of exports and imports.

[27] The share of South Africa was somewhat higher in trade with industrialized countries and somewhat lower in trade with developing countries.

Table 2.4. *Trade flows: China, India, Brazil, and South Africa, 2000 and 2005 (US$ billion)*

	Total exports		Total imports	
	2000	2005	2000	2005
China	249	762	225	660
India	42	100	52	139
Brazil	55	118	59	78
South Africa	30	52	30	62
Total above	377	1,031	365	939
World	6,444	10,441	6,642	10,712
(CIBS as percentage of)	(5.8)	(9.9)	(5.5)	(8.8)
	Exports to developing countries		Imports from developing countries	
China	102	317	104	330
India	17	52	17	45
Brazil	21	56	24	38
South Africa	8	15	9	22
Total above	148	440	154	434
Developing countries	803	1,614	791	1,664
(CIBS as percentage of)	(18.4)	(27.3)	(19.4)	(26.1)
	Exports to industrialized countries		Imports from industrialized countries	
China	144	421	106	254
India	23	44	21	46
Brazil	31	54	37	41
South Africa	14	31	20	38
Total above	212	550	184	380
Industrialized countries	3,161	4,645	3,151	4,553
(CIBS as percentage of)	(6.7)	(11.9)	(5.8)	(8.3)

Notes: The figures in this table are on merchandise trade, exports and imports, in US$ billion at current prices.

Source: UNCTAD, *UNCTAD Handbook of Statistics Online.*

International investment

The picture of international investment is different. In the global context, the relative importance of CIBS is mixed. Table 2.5 sets out evidence on foreign direct investment, inward and outward, in CIBS, compared with developing countries, industrialized countries, and the world. The figures on stocks are for 2000 and 2005, while the figures on flows are annual averages for the period 2001–5. In the early 2000s, CIBS accounted for 20 per cent to 25 per cent of the inward stock of foreign direct investment in developing countries

Table 2.5. *Foreign direct investment: stocks and flows (US$ billion), 2000 and 2005*

	Stocks				Flows (average per annum)	
	Inward		Outward		Inward	Outward
	2000	2005	2000	2005	2001–5	2001–5
China	193	318	28	46	57	4
India	18	45	2	10	6	2
Brazil	103	201	52	72	16	3
South Africa	43	69	32	39	3	0
Total above	357	634	114	166	82	8
Developing countries	1,697	2,655	856	1,268	225	80
(CIBS as percentage of)	(21.1)	(23.9)	(13.3)	(13.1)	(36.6)	(10.3)
Developed countries	4,035	7,219	5,593	9,278	476	602
World	5,803	10,130	6,471	10,672	727	691
(CIBS as percentage of)	(6.2)	(6.3)	(1.8)	(1.6)	(11.3)	(1.2)

Source: *UNCTAD*, Foreign Direct Investment Database.

and about 6 per cent of that in the world. During the period 2001–5, CIBS accounted for about 37 per cent of inward flows of foreign direct investment in developing countries and about 11 per cent of those in the world. In the early 2000s, CIBS accounted for about 13 per cent of the outward stock of foreign direct investment from developing countries and less than 2 per cent of that in the world. During the period 2001–5, CIBS accounted for 10 per cent of the outward flows of foreign direct investment from developing countries and about 1 per cent of those from the world. These aggregate proportions could also be deceptive but the distribution of the stock of foreign direct investment, whether inward or outward, among CIBS was not as unequal as it was in trade and China was not as dominant. In 2005, China accounted for 50 per cent of the inward stock but only 27 per cent of the outward stock, India accounted for just 7 per cent of the inward stock and 6 per cent of the outward stock, Brazil accounted 32 per cent of the inward stock and 43 per cent of the outward stock, while South Africa accounted for 11 per cent of the inward stock and 24 per cent of the outward stock.[28] It is possible to draw three inferences from this evidence. First, foreign direct

---

[28] The distribution of flows among the CIBS was different. During the period 2001–5, China accounted for 70 per cent of the inflows and 45 per cent of the outflows, Brazil accounted for 20 per cent of the inflows and 33 per cent of the outflows, while India accounted for 7 per cent of the inflows and 22 per cent of the outflows. The residual share of South Africa was only 3 per cent in inflows and negligible in outflows. It would seem that the relative importance of China in inflows and outflows of FDI from CIBS registered an increase during the early 2000s.

investment in, and from, CIBS is small as a proportion of both stocks and flows in the world. Second, for CIBS, inward foreign direct investment is much more significant than outward foreign direct investment in terms of both stocks and flows. Third, it would seem that CIBS are more competition for, rather than a source of, foreign direct investment for developing countries.[29]

International finance

International finance is, perhaps, the most limited form of engagement for CIBS with the world economy, at least so far, but this could change. In principle, these four countries could be potential sources of finance for development through current account surpluses, foreign exchange reserves, and foreign aid flows.

The current account surplus in the balance of payments is significant for China but this is not the case for India, Brazil, and South Africa. In China, the current account surplus, as a proportion of GDP, increased from 2.3 per cent during 1996–2000 to 3.5 per cent during 2001–5.[30] In India, there was a modest current account surplus during 2001–5, the equivalent of 0.9 per cent of GDP, while there was a current account deficit during 1996–2000, the equivalent of 1.1 per cent of GDP. In Brazil, the current account deficit decreased from 4 per cent of GDP during 1996–2000 to 0.4 per cent of GDP during 2001–5. In South Africa, the current account deficit, as a proportion of GDP, increased from 1 per cent during 1996–2000 to 1.4 per cent during 2001–5. These figures are quinquennial averages that might conceal fluctuations over time. Figure 2.3 outlines the trends in the current account balances for these countries, as a percentage of GDP, during the period 1996–2005. It shows that, during 2001–5, the current account balance improved rapidly in China and Brazil, while it worsened slowly in India and South Africa. These trends are easily explained in a wider macroeconomic context (Figure 2.4). Throughout the period 2001–5, as a proportion of GDP,

---

[29] In this context, it is worth noting that the sectoral composition and geographical distribution of outward FDI from India provides two sharp contrasts with that from developing countries: three-fifths of international investment from India is in manufacturing activities while this proportion is about one-eighth for developing countries; almost three-quarters of international investment from India is in industrialized countries, while this proportion is less than one-fifth for developing countries. The proportions for China are similar to those for developing countries as a group. In fact, FDI from China is probably even more concentrated in primary commodities and developing countries. For a discussion, see Nayyar 2008a.

[30] The data on the current account balance, as a percentage of GDP, for China, India, Brazil, and South Africa cited in this paragraph are obtained from World Bank 2007.

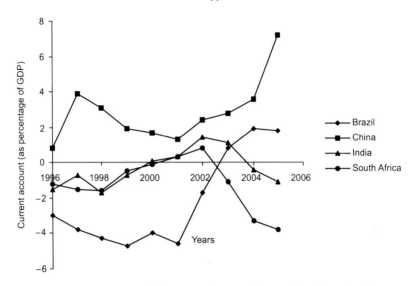

Figure 2.3. *Current account balance in China, India, Brazil, and South Africa*
Source: World Bank 2007.

gross domestic savings exceeded gross capital formation in China and Brazil. This was also the case in South Africa for three of the five years, which is puzzling on the surface but is probably attributable to low levels of investment rather than high levels of saving. In India, however, gross capital formation exceeded gross domestic savings.[31] This evidence suggests that China is a potential source of international finance for developing countries but that India, Brazil, and South Africa are not, at least not yet.

In the sphere of foreign exchange reserves, however, the similarities are greater than the differences. Table 2.6 outlines the trends in foreign exchange reserves from 1996 to 2005 for CIBS, developing countries, and the world. It shows that both China and India accumulated international reserves at a rapid rate. In Brazil, international reserves went down and then recovered. In South Africa, international reserves increased slowly but remained at modest levels. Between 1996 and 2005, the share of CIBS in the total foreign exchange

---

[31] During the period 2001–5 in China, gross domestic saving was 43.4 per cent of GDP and gross capital formation was 40.4 per cent of GDP; in India gross domestic saving was 26.7 per cent of GDP and gross capital formation was 28.4 per cent of GDP; in Brazil gross domestic saving was 23.3 per cent of GDP and gross capital formation was 20.5 per cent of GDP, whereas in South Africa gross domestic saving was 19 per cent of GDP and gross capital formation was 16.8 per cent of GDP. These averages for the period are calculated from data reported in World Bank 2007.

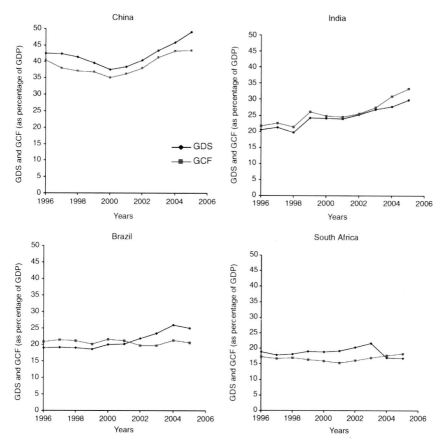

Figure 2.4. *Gross domestic savings (GDS) and gross capital formation (GCF) in China, India, Brazil, and South Africa, 1996–2005*

Source: World Bank 2007.

reserves of developing countries rose from 22 per cent to 35 per cent, while their share of foreign exchange reserves in the world as a whole more than doubled from 11.1 per cent to 24 per cent. Once again, it is important to note that these aggregates are deceptive because, in 2005, China accounted for 80 per cent of the international reserves held by the four countries taken together, whereas India accounted for 13 per cent, Brazil just 5 per cent, and South Africa a mere 2 per cent. The substantial importance of China, India, and Brazil in foreign exchange reserves held by central banks, however, does not quite translate into a potential source of finance for developing countries. This is so for two reasons. First, an overwhelming proportion of these foreign exchange reserves are held in the form of fiduciary deposits or government

Table 2.6. *Foreign exchange reserves: China, India, Brazil, and South Africa, 1996–2005 (Special Drawing Rights (SDRs) billion)*

Years	China	India	Brazil	South Africa	Total CIBS	Developing countries	CIBS as percentage of	World	CIBS as percentage of
1996	75	14	41	1	131	601	21.8	1,178	11.1
1997	106	19	38	4	166	691	24.1	1,297	12.8
1998	106	20	30	3	160	706	22.7	1,282	12.5
1999	115	24	25	5	170	786	21.6	1,405	12.1
2000	130	29	25	5	189	902	20.9	1,586	11.9
2001	172	37	28	5	242	1,022	23.7	1,741	13.9
2002	215	50	28	5	297	1,127	26.4	1,890	15.7
2003	275	67	33	5	380	1,306	29.1	2,155	17.6
2004	396	82	34	9	521	1,588	32.8	2,521	20.7
2005	575	93	37	13	719	2,035	35.3	3,000	24.0

Note: The data relate to international reserves held by the central banks of countries or country-groups at the end of the calendar year.

Source: IMF, *International Financial Statistics Online Database.*

bonds in industrialized countries, so that actual placements are not put to any strategic use, let alone provide a potential source of finance for development. Second, even these massive foreign exchange reserves are marginal in relation to transactions in international finance, given that daily transactions in foreign exchange in world markets are perhaps as large as the foreign exchange reserves held by all the central banks in the world.[32]

The possibilities are much greater in the sphere of foreign aid and development assistance. CIBS are emerging as donors, with a significant presence in Africa. The thrust of China's aid programmes is development finance, whereas the focus of India's aid programmes is technical assistance. Evidence on foreign aid flows from CIBS to developing countries is not readily available. It is clear, however, that foreign aid from these four countries is relatively small, as compared with foreign aid provided by the industrialized countries.[33] Yet, it

[32] In April 1997, for example, the average turnover in foreign exchange markets in the world was the equivalent of US$1,490 billion per day, while at the end of 1997 the combined foreign exchange reserves of all the central banks in the world totalled US$1,550 billion (Nayyar 2006).

[33] During the period 2001–5, net official development assistance (ODA) disbursements from Development Assistance Committee (DAC) countries were US$73,200 million per annum, while net ODA disbursements from non-DAC donors were a mere US$575 million per annum. For the annual statistics, see <http://stats.oecd.org/Index.aspx>. It is worth noting that non-DAC donors include Saudi Arabia, Korea, Turkey, Kuwait, United Arab Emirates, Czech Republic, Hungary, and Poland, among others, but net ODA disbursements from China, India, Brazil, and South Africa are not even reported in these OECD statistics on foreign aid.

is possible that the multiplier effects of aid from CIBS, as also from other emerging donors such as Korea, could be significant for two reasons. For one, technical assistance might alleviate infrastructural constraints in developing countries. For another, emerging donors could be a catalyst for aid flows from the industrialized countries in much the same way as foreign aid from the socialist countries was a catalyst in the cold war era.

International migration

International migration is, possibly, a significant form of engagement with the world economy, particularly for India and, to some extent, China, but much less so for Brazil and almost negligible for South Africa. In the contemporary world economy, it is possible to distinguish between four categories of cross-border movements of people. The traditional category is emigrants who move to a country and settle there permanently. The new categories are guest workers, illegal migrants, and professionals. Guest workers are people who move to a country on a temporary basis for a specified purpose and a limited duration. Illegal migrants are people who enter a country without a visa, take up employment on a tourist visa, or simply stay after their visa has expired. Professionals are people with high levels of education, experience, and qualifications, whose skills are in demand everywhere and who can move from country to country, temporarily or permanently. Both China and India have always been, and continue to be, important countries of origin for international migration. Globalization has, however, increased the mobility of labour in the new categories.[34] India and China—and possibly Brazil—are also countries of origin for such cross-border movements of people.

Remittances are, perhaps, the most important source of development finance associated with international migration.[35] Indeed, for India, remittances are a substantial source of external finance.[36] This is not so for China, Brazil, and South Africa. During the period 1996–2005, remittance inflows were the equivalent of 2.7 per cent of GDP in India, but only 0.15 per cent of GDP in China, 0.26 per cent of GDP in Brazil, and 0.08 per cent of GDP in South Africa.[37] In this context, it is important to note that India, China, and

---

[34] The changing nature of international migration is analysed, at some length, in Nayyar 2002a.

[35] See Nayyar 2008d and Solimano 2005.

[36] For an analysis of the macroeconomic significance of remittances in India, see Nayyar 1994.

[37] These percentages have been calculated from data on remittances obtained from the IMF balance of payments statistics online database and from data on GDP in World Bank 2007.

Brazil export labour to, rather than import labour from, the outside world. Consequently, remittances from India, China, and Brazil cannot simply enter the picture as a source of development finance. The engagement of India and China with the world, through international migration, is attributable in the past to the diaspora. In the present, the engagement of India, China, and Brazil with the world economy, through cross-border movements of people, is attributable to globalization.

The diaspora has historical origins. Following the abolition of slavery in the British Empire, starting around the mid-1830s and for a period of fifty years, about 50 million people left India and China to work as indentured labour in mines, plantations, and construction in the Americas, the Caribbean, South Africa, South-East Asia, and other distant lands.[38] This was probably close to 10 per cent of the total population of India and China circa 1880. The migration from India and China continued, in somewhat different forms, during the first half of the twentieth century, particularly in the period between the two world wars. There is, consequently, a significant presence of the diaspora from China and India across the world, not only in the industrialized countries, but also in the developing countries. This is associated with entrepreneurial capitalisms, Chinese and Indian, in developing countries as well as the industrialized world, where the migration stream has aged.

The second half of the twentieth century also witnessed significant waves of international migration from India, comprising permanent emigration to the industrialized countries and temporary migration to the oil-exporting countries in the Middle East.[39] The international migration from China, however, was limited during this period. Of course, such migration, particularly to the industrialized countries, is now constrained by immigration laws and consular practices. But the gathering momentum of globalization during the past two decades has led to a significant increase in the new categories of cross-border movements of people. In this sphere, the engagement of India with the world economy is much more than that of China, Brazil, or South Africa. The advent of globalization—which has also made it easier to move people across borders—is associated with managerial capitalisms, especially with professionals from India and, to some extent, Brazil, who can migrate permanently, live abroad temporarily, or stay at home and travel frequently for business. These people are almost as mobile across borders as capital.

[38] See Lewis 1977 and Tinker 1974. See also Nayyar 2002a.
[39] For a discussion of, and evidence on, international migration from India, see Nayyar 1994.

THE GLOBAL CONTEXT

It is necessary to recognize that the significance of CIBS in the world would be shaped not only in the sphere of economics but also in the realm of politics. Their emerging significance in the world economy is attributable, in part, to their share in world population and world income and also, in part, to their engagement with the world through international trade, investment, and finance. The early 2000s are perhaps a turning-point. Even so, in the economic sphere, their potential importance in the future far exceeds their actual importance at present. In the realm of politics, however, their importance is more discernible at the present juncture, which is attributable partly to their size and partly to their rise. It is plausible to argue that this represents the beginnings of a profound change in the balance of economic and political power in the world. History does not repeat itself; it would, however, be wise to learn from history. The early twentieth century was a turning-point. It was the beginning of the end of Britain's dominance in the world. And it was the beginning of the rise of the USA to dominance in the world. The catch-up and the transformation spanned half a century. The early twenty-first century perhaps represents a similar turning-point. It could be the beginning of the end of the dominant status of the USA in the world. The emergence of countries outside North America and Western Europe, particularly the powerhouse economies in Asia, which began with the East Asian success stories and is now manifest in the rise of China and India, represents a striking transformation. In addition, there are emerging economies in other continents of the developing world, among which Brazil and South Africa deserve mention. Of course, in the decades to come, the continued rise of these countries is not predictable and is by no means certain. This catch-up and transformation might also span a half century, or longer. Yet, the beginnings of a shift in the balance of power are discernible.

This is going to shape the international politics of nation states in the future, not only through bilateralism, but also through plurilateralism. CIBS are each engaged in a bilateralism that is both intra-regional and inter-regional. There are intra-regional initiatives led by China and India in Asia, by Brazil in Latin America, and by South Africa in Africa. There are also some inter-regional initiatives on the part of these countries, such as China taking a lead in forging APEC and India seeking a partnership with ASEAN. CIBS are also beginning to engage in a plurilateralism. There are two striking examples. At one level, India, Brazil, and South Africa have constituted a plurilateral group, the G3 (or IBSA), attempting to develop a strategic alliance that would foster partnership between them, promote cooperation with developing countries, and articulate a collective voice in international politics. At another level, CIBS, together with Mexico, constitute the Outreach 5, who have been invited to the G8 Summit in recent years. There is a hint of discontent about their status as observers peripheral to deliberations and decisions, and the Outreach 5 are now seeking a place at the high table with the G8.

From the perspective of the developing world, CIBS, together, might be able to exercise significant influence, in the global context, through multilateralism, whether through institutions or rules. The United Nations, the World Bank, the International Monetary Fund (IMF), and the World Trade Organization (WTO) are among the most important multilateral institutions.[40]

Of CIBS, only China is a permanent member of the United Nations Security Council with a right to veto. China is also a member of the P5. However, India, Brazil, and South Africa are engaged in knocking at the door, seeking permanent membership of the Security Council, with or without a veto. There can be little doubt that, if and when there is an increase in the number of permanent members of the Security Council in the United Nations, these three countries would have the strongest claim to permanent membership.

In the Bretton Woods institutions, the World Bank and the IMF, CIBS are permanent members of the Executive Boards. The industrialized countries might be the principal shareholders, but the developing countries are the principal stakeholders. Given the democratic deficit in these institutions, which is embedded in unequal voting rights, CIBS, together, could influence decisions or even reshape rules. So far, however, there is only limited, if any, coordination among CIBS for this purpose.[41] They have neither articulated a collective voice nor exercised collective influence.

The situation in the WTO is different. India and Brazil have been long-standing advocates of developing countries in the WTO. China has a low profile, possibly because of its recent accession. South Africa is not quite part of the strategic alliance among developing countries. However, India and Brazil, along with USA and the European Union, are now members of the Quad, which is the principal institutional mechanism for resolving differences and finding solutions.

[40] For a detailed discussion on the possibilities of reform and change in these multilateral institutions, in the wider context of global governance, see Nayyar 2002b.

[41] There is, perhaps, a modest beginning in the G20, where India, Brazil, and South Africa, with some participation from China, have made an attempt to coordinate their stance on reform and change in the IMF. But this is no more than a beginning. It has not influenced, let alone shaped, outcomes.

In conclusion, it would seem that CIBS have a considerable potential for articulating a collective voice in the world of multilateralism. Coordination and cooperation among them carries a significant potential for exercising influence on multilateral institutions, which could reshape rules and create policy space for countries that are latecomers to development. Such coordination and cooperation, which is in the realm of possibility, has not yet surfaced. There could be two reasons for the near absence of coordination and cooperation so far. In the early stages of change, these countries might not have recognized their potential for exercising collective influence. Also, their relationship with each other might be characterized more by rivalry, economic or political, and less by unity. It is obviously difficult to predict how reality might unfold in the future. Even so, it is important to recognize that once these countries become major players there is a danger that they might opt for the pursuit of national interest rather than the spirit of solidarity among developing countries or the logic of collective action.

REFERENCES

Freeman, R. B. (2005) 'What Really Ails Europe and America: The Doubling of the Global Workforce', *Globalist*, 3 June.

IMF, *International Financial Statistics Online Database.* <http://imf.org/external/data. htm>.

Inter-American Development Bank (2005) *The Emergence of China: Opportunities and Challenges for Latin America and the Caribbean* (Washington, DC: IADB).

Jenkins, R., E. D. Peters, and M. M. Moreira (2008) 'The Impact of China on Latin America and the Caribbean', *World Development*, 36: 235–53.

Kaplinsky, R. (ed.) (2006) 'Asian Drivers: Opportunities and Threats', *IDS Bulletin*, 37.

—— and D. Messner (2008) 'The Impact of the Asian Drivers on the Developing World', *World Development*, 36: 197–209.

—— and M. Morris (2008) 'Do the Asian Drivers Undermine Export-oriented Industrialization in SSA?', *World Development*, 36: 254–73.

Krugman, P. (1994) 'Competitiveness: A Dangerous Obsession', *Foreign Affairs*, 73: 28–44.

Lewis, W. A. (1977) *The Evolution of the International Economic Order* (Princeton, NJ: Princeton University Press).

Maddison, A. (2003) *The World Economy: Historical Statistics* (Paris: OECD).

Nayyar, D. (1994) *Migration, Remittances and Capital Flows: The Indian Experience* (Delhi: Oxford University Press).

Nayyar, D. (1996) 'Free Trade: Why, When and for Whom?', *Banca Nazionale del Lavoro Quarterly Review*, 49 (198): 333–50.

—— (2002a) 'Cross-border Movements of People', in D. Nayyar (ed.), *Governing Globalization: Issues and Institutions* (Oxford: Oxford University Press for UNU-WIDER).

—— (2002b) 'The Existing System and the Missing Institutions', in D. Nayyar (ed.), *Governing Globalization: Issues and Institutions* (Oxford: Oxford University Press for UNU-WIDER).

—— (2006) 'Globalization, History and Development: A Tale of Two Centuries', *Cambridge Journal of Economics*, 30: 137–59.

—— (2008a) 'The Internationalization of Firms from India: Investment, Mergers and Acquisitions', *Oxford Development Studies*, 36: 111–31.

—— (2008b) 'The Rise of China and India: Implications for Developing Countries', in P. Artesis and J. Eatwell (eds), *Issues in Economic Development and Globalization* (Basingstoke: Palgrave Macmillan).

—— (2008c) 'Learning to Unlearn from Development', *Oxford Development Studies*, 36.

—— (2008d) 'International Migration and Economic Development', in J. Stiglitz and N. Serra (eds), *The Washington Consensus Reconsidered: Towards a New Global Governance* (Oxford: Oxford University Press).

O'Neill, J., S. Lawson, D. Wilson, et al. (eds) (2004) *Growth and Development: The Path to 2050* (London: Goldman Sachs).

Rowthorn, R. (2006) 'The Renaissance of China and India: Implications for the Advanced Economies', UNCTAD Discussion Paper 182 (Geneva: UNCTAD).

Singh, A. (2007) 'Globalization, Industrial Revolutions in India and China and Labour Markets in Advanced Countries: Implications for National and International Economic Policy', ILO Working Paper 81 (Geneva: Policy Integration Department, ILO).

Solimano, A. (2005) 'Remittances by Emigrants: Issues and Evidence', in A. B. Atkinson (ed.), *New Sources of Development Finance* (Oxford: Oxford University Press for UNU-WIDER).

Tinker, H. (1974) *A New System of Slavery: The Export of Indian Labour Overseas, 1830–1920* (Oxford: Oxford University Press).

Toye, J. (2008) 'China's Impact on Sub-Saharan African Development: Trade, Aid and Politics', in P. Artesis and J. Eatwell (eds), *Issues in Economic Development and Globalization* (Basingstoke: Palgrave Macmillan).

UNCTAD, Foreign Direct Investment Database. <http://www.unctad.org/Templates/Page.asp?intItemID=1923>.

—— *UNCTAD Handbook of Statistics Online*. <http://www.unctad.org/Templates/Page.asp?intItemID=1890>.

United Nations (2006a) *Diverging Growth and Development, World Economic and Social Survey 2006* (New York: United Nations).

—— (2006b) National Accounts Main Aggregates Database (New York: UN-DESA Department of Economic and Social Affairs). <http://unstats.un.org/unsd/snaama/Introduction.asp>.

—— (2006c) *Demographic Yearbook* (New York: UN-DESA. Department of Economic and Social Affairs. <http://unstats.un.org/unsd/demographic/products/dyb/dyb2.htm>.

Wilson, D., and R. Purushothaman (2004) 'Dreaming with BRICS: The Path to 2050', in J. O'Neill, et al. (eds), *Growth and Development: The Path to 2050* (London: Goldman Sachs): chap. 2.

World Bank (2007) *World Development Indicators 2007* (Washington, DC: World Bank).

3

Southern Engines of Global Growth: Very Long Cycles or Short Spurts?

Meghnad Desai

INTRODUCTION

The emergence of a small number of economies from the 'South' or the 'Third World' as important players in the global economy has attracted much attention. All the four economies being discussed here—China, India, Brazil, and South Africa (CIBS)—were thought to be hopeless 'basket cases' (Desai 2005) during the second half of the last century, though for different reasons. India and China were plagued by famines and economic policies that, while radical from a nationalist perspective, were driving their economies into stagnation (India) or excessive political and economic volatility (China). South Africa had the seemingly insoluble problem of apartheid, and even its economy was highly state owned and corporatist but in favour of the privileged white minority. Brazil had chalked up impressive growth rates in the period 1951–80, albeit under authoritarian regimes, and yet it has not sustained its growth spurt in the following twenty years. There has been some revival in growth in the twenty-first century.

Since the 1990s, their story has changed and we are contemplating their rise in the world GDP ranks (purchasing power parity (PPP) still, but soon actual dollars). Growth rates have been spectacular in China now for some twenty-five years; in India, since the reform process of 1991, the economy has achieved a growth rate of GDP that, on average, is double the average of the thirty years between 1950 and 1980, and has reached three times that average since the mid-2000s. South Africa and Brazil have not had an equally rapid acceleration. They are already middle-income countries and they are noticed more for their potential than actual performance in recent years. Brazil's size makes it a likely candidate as an 'engine' and South Africa's leading position in Africa makes it a country worthy of inclusion in this exclusive club.

SOME BASICS ABOUT CIBS

The four economies, even though they share their status as 'new miracle economies' or 'already emerged economies', are very different in their nature, their histories, and their factor endowments. Two are Southern-hemisphere countries and two are Northern.

In broad macro-terms of area and population, China comes top on both counts, with 9.6 million square kilometres (m km^2) and a population of 1.3 billion. Brazil is the next largest in terms of area, with 8.5 m km^2 and a population of 184 million. India is the third largest, with 3.7 m km^2 and a population of 1.1 billion, while South Africa has an area of 1.2 m km^2 and a population of 47 million. China has 136 people per km^2, Brazil 22, India 297, and South Africa 39. Thus, there is a sharp contrast in the ratio of people–land between the two economies in the Northern hemisphere and the two in the South. There are other contrasts as well.

The contrast in initial endowments means that the two pairs of economies have to follow different strategies. Growth theories have typically used a two-factor production function, with capital and labour. But it might be that, if we take a three-factor approach, with land added to the two standard inputs, one might be able to think out a better growth strategy. Thus, for example, in economies that are land-rich but people-scarce, the real wage tends to be high. They face a labour shortage, which is paradoxical in what we think of as Third World economies. But our ideas are shaped by the surplus labour Asian economies and not the land-rich/people-scarce economies of Africa and South America. Given such labour constraint, in order to induce people to take up waged work, you have to equip them with sufficient human and non-human capital to match their productivity to their real wage.

This was the experience of the US economy in the eighteenth and nineteenth centuries. There, the high real wage of 'free' Americans was diluted by slaves, whose lower implicit real wage made labour-intensive agriculture, such as growing cotton, profitable. But, in the slave-free states, the growth pattern was capital intensive. Later again, in the second half of the nineteenth century, migration from Europe softened the real-wage constraint but, even then, large amounts of capital were required to employ the newcomers.

Brazil and South Africa face the real-wage constraint, albeit that it is modified by some institutional barriers. In South Africa, during the nineteenth century, the policy adopted to attract rural labour into mines was a head tax that had to be paid in money. This compelled at least one member of the household to work away from the farm. But this was resisted until the policy became more drastic. In the early colonial period, in Spanish South America, similar inducements had to be provided to make the 'Indians' work for the market economy. In Brazil, it was the importing of slaves that kept the local economy relatively free of the labour constraint. At the time of its independence in the early nineteenth century, 30 per cent of Brazil's population were slaves.

In the twentieth century, apartheid kept the real wages of black South Africans artificially below the wages of white South Africans. Now, with the new situation, the black real wage has implicitly gone up. South Africa witnesses the simultaneous situation of unemployment among the black South Africans, especially in urban areas, and complaints that there is immigration of labour from surrounding African nations, whose people are undercutting the South African blacks. The need in such a situation is to enhance the human capital of the black workforce and adopt capital-intensive activities that also require high human capital. Brazil has a similar problem with urban unemployment and underemployment. While agriculture and the resource extraction industries provide the mainstay of export earnings, there is still extensive wastage of human capital: puzzling in an economy that faces a labour constraint. But what this implies is that many manufacturing activities that are feasible in land-poor/people-abundant economies—low-tech textiles, and so on—are not economically viable for the land-rich countries. They need to upgrade their labour force, equip it with capital, and seek feasible medium-tech or high-tech manufacturing activities. They could also import labour from labour-surplus economies.

The situation of the Northern-hemisphere economies is altogether different and much more amenable to the standard analysis. They have abundant cheap labour and lack capital. In this respect, China has managed to transfer large parts of its rural population to urban areas, thus keeping the effective price of labour low. Capital is generated by the high domestic savings rate plus foreign direct investment (FDI). This has resulted in rapid growth fuelled by exports of manufacture, especially in low tech goods. China's land reforms also helped raise labour productivity on the farms and made the transfer of surplus feasible.

India has not experienced successful land reform to the same extent as China. Productivity in agriculture, both per person and per acre, remains low. India has also passed labour laws that inhibit hiring and firing in the organized sector (that is, firms employing more than 100 workers). This has meant that Indian manufacturing is a medium- to high-tech niche activity but does not generate large-scale employment. India has, in effect, made its abundant cheap labour expensive by institutional rigidities. Thus, employment in informal urban-sector activities and, lately, in information technology (IT) activities (typically, small firms) has grown. The bulk of the population is still in rural under-employment and represents a potential force for extra growth, if only reform of the labour laws could unleash it.

The two Northern economies are very old and, indeed, two of the oldest continuous urban civilizations—bywords for populous and prosperous countries until the middle of the eighteenth century. Their share of global GDP (given that imperfection in such figures is unavoidable) matched their share of the world population in 1700. They declined during the nineteenth and much of the twentieth centuries and, by the 1960s, were thought to be 'basket cases'. If anything, the inequalities in their wealth are lower today than they were, say, one or two centuries ago. Recently, income and wealth inequality in China is reported to have gone up; however, relative to the Southern-hemisphere economies, these inequalities are modest (especially since land ownership is not particularly unequal).

The Southern-hemisphere economies are 'younger' in centuries, relative to the Northern-hemisphere economies. Brazil and South Africa had very small populations before 1500 CE and, especially, a very large resources:population ratio, however one values the resources. The local populations in both countries were overwhelmed by settlers from Europe—Portugal (Brazil) and the Netherlands and, later, the British (South Africa)—and added to by African slaves (Brazil more so than South Africa) or indentured labour (South Africa). South Africa's experience of apartheid was unique in the modern age and has only been overcome since 1994.

Both were seen as areas of mineral resources where the main problem was to generate sufficient labour supply. South Africa was also largely rural, with small concentrations around mining towns or ports and very late (that is, twentieth-century) development of urbanization. South Africa was never a 'poor' or 'underdeveloped' country and, even today, is the richest in sub-Saharan Africa. However, it has an immensely unequal distribution of income, wealth (land, but also other assets), as well as human-development scores. Brazil had a higher level of urbanization relative to South Africa, even by the late eighteenth century. Rio, Salvador, and São Paulo were thriving towns and the bulk of the population was concentrated around the eastern coast. Agriculture was carried out in large landholdings and mining activities were focused around small concentrations of the population. Brazil has always had an unequal distribution of wealth (especially land) and also income. These inequalities are mapped by race or ethnic origins, though there are also inequalities within each ethnic group.

Thus, the one major difference between the two pairs of economies is that, in the very long run, in an epochal sense, the Northern-hemisphere economies are resuming their rightful place in the global ranks. In 1500, they were the two richest economies—though, again, in total income terms and with a great deal of inequality—and, indeed, continued to be so until 1700. They then entered a two-centuries-long decline as a result of the impact of the rise of the West and Imperial conquest (India) or Imperial domination (China). The nineteenth century was better for China than India but in the first half of the twentieth century both stagnated, China to a greater degree than India. In 1975, they were level pegging in terms of their relative position of income and population shares in the global economy. It is during the last thirty-five years that China has outstripped India. Again, in the last five years, there has been a growth spurt in India and it is narrowing the distance in terms of growth rates relative to China (Desai 2005; Nayyar 2007).

Are India and China experiencing 'an epochal wave'? If so, will they 'catch up' and regain their relative ranking in the global economy? And, if so, when? Of course, there are no 'cycles', since we can barely observe one wave over three or four centuries. Even Kondratieff cycles with fifty-year periods are sufficiently difficult to verify, and there is scepticism about Kuznets cycles of twenty-five years. But, whether a cycle or not, the speculation will not go away. So, I would like to pursue that here.

For the Southern-hemisphere economies, this is not an issue. They were not high in the global league in any event. (The only Southern American economy that was high in the global ranking is Argentina. Colin Clark, in his pioneering work *The Conditions of Economic Progress*, ranked Argentina as one of the top five economies. Unlikely as it seems today, in 1913 Argentina's per capita income was just under half that of the USA and even in 1950 only about 35 per cent. By 1989, it was under a quarter and, of course, has worsened since.) Their share of world income kept pace with their share of world population, which, in any case, did not amount to more than around 2 per cent each. They are already upper-middle-income countries, while China is lower-middle-income and India is low-income. Yet, it is useful to carry the two Southern economies as comparators for the Northern pair.

GROWTH DYNAMICS IN A MADDISONIAN
PERSPECTIVE

In very broad (almost Maddisonian) terms, if the Iberian exploration in the 1490s inaugurated a Global Economy (or World System), then for the first half of around the next 250 years, it was the Iberian countries—Spain and

Portugal—who were dominant powers. They had a lead in naval warfare technology, having light manoeuvrable ships that could carry guns for long journeys. Their interest was in surplus extraction and transfer rather than transforming the economies' production possibilities. Thus, it was the mineral exports, especially gold and silver, that were the main activities pursued. Agriculture developed to feed the imported slave population plus the original inhabitants, who had been deprived of their means of livelihood. South Africa had only a slight encounter with this phase of the World System. The Portuguese reached Angola in the fifteenth century but, for 100 years, were satisfied with only coastal contact. Later, in the sixteenth century, they traded slaves for European goods, guns, and trinkets with interior tribal leaders. The Dutch began to colonize the Cape region in the early seventeenth century and pushed the Portuguese away. Their interest at this juncture was in farming the somewhat unrewarding but ample land available.

During this first phase, 1500–1750, India and China were sizeable trading economies. There was extensive maritime trade across the Indian Ocean and the South China Sea. The western limits of maritime trade were the Red Sea and the Gulf. Portuguese naval expeditions went around the Cape of Good Hope and opened a new trading route to Asia, thus removing the barrier due to the gap between the Red Sea and Mediterranean, which later became the Suez Canal. They came in search of spices but they—and, later, the British, Dutch, Danes, and French—joined the Portuguese to take part in the newly expanded trade. Besides spices, they also traded silk and cotton textiles as well as food grains both intra-Asia and to Europe. This phase was 'trade without dominion', as far as Asia was concerned. There was an export surplus that Asia enjoyed with Europe and this was financed by the treasure from South America. The treasure came either directly from Iberia to Asia or via Western Europe (with which the Iberian Peninsula also had a trade deficit).

The next phase belongs to the North Western European countries that displaced the Iberian countries in Asia and North America. The Netherlands and Britain—who led in terms of governance reform, financial revolution, and, later in the eighteenth century for Britain, industrial revolution—occupied India and Indonesia (the Netherlands East Indies, as it was then called). The French lost out in India but went on to colonize Indo-China (as it was called, until recently). It was in this phase, 1750–1950, that China and India lost their leads. In this phase, the industrial revolution came as a major shock, displacing the advantage that Asia had in textiles. This phase had trade with dominion and the pattern of trade changed, with textiles becoming an import rather than an export item for Asia. The inflow of treasure to finance India's trade surplus was replaced by an Indian revenue surplus, and a triangular trade was set up exchanging Indian opium (a government monopoly) for Chinese tea; the proceeds of sale from the tea were sent to London as treasure.

In this second phase of globalization, the pattern of trade, capital, and labour flows became restricted to individual metropolis-periphery channels—British, French, Dutch, and so on, rather than fully global, as before. The direction of capital flows was via London, mainly for North America and the white British Empire, as well as much of South America and Asia. Labour flows were within the imperial domains, and trade was not free but encumbered by tacit or explicit 'imperial preference'. The fortunes of India were tied to the dynamics of the British economy. China was tied more to Britain than any other imperial country, but its twentieth-century history was plagued by war with Japan and the breakdown of unified rule from the centre. The stagnation in the twentieth century that both China and India experienced was considerably due to the slowing down of the British economy after the mid-1870s.

Brazil was under Portuguese domination, even after its decline as a European power. Even after independence in the early nineteenth century, it had Portuguese kings until it became a republic in the 1880s. After 1820, the British settled South Africa as a colony in the Cape and Natal, while the Dutch (Boers) moved into the Orange Free State and Transvaal. After the Boer War, at the turn of the century, the Union of South Africa was born in 1910 and became a republic in 1961. Both continued to be exporters of precious metals and minerals and, to a lesser extent, agricultural exporters. Labour shortages continued to plague them, and immigration (either voluntary or as indentured or slave labour) continued throughout the nineteenth century.

Thus, we have two economies that are long-settled, with a low resources: people ratio and two economies with a very high ratio. China and India are relatively labour-rich, and Brazil and South Africa are land-rich. But, much more than the difference in factor endowments is their history. For India and China, the major drive in the last sixty years has been restoring the dignity of the nation in the international sphere and preserving the territorial integrity of the nation state. These political goals dominate the economic goals of rising per capita income and the elimination of poverty. India and China, unlike Brazil and South Africa, see themselves as potential global players displaced from their rightful place by two centuries of western domination. They are, thus, much more liable to spend money on armaments and be willing to go to war, either internally or externally, to preserve what they believe is their rightful territorial domain. In addition, India has an internal dynamic of inclusion to give equality in social status to groups that have been downtrodden for centuries, which is a major objective of its political and economic policies.

INDIA AND CHINA AS GROWTH ENGINES

Much of the growth in China and India has been input driven. Labour productivity has risen mainly by transferring labour from low-productivity to high-productivity sectors. Yet, growth in total factor productivity (TFP) has been modest. There have been no remarkable innovations coming out of either country—which, by their sheer size, have had a large impact on trade and investment flows (though China is registering many more patents than India and is one of the leading countries in patents ranking). They have taken advantage of the climate for freer trade, reformed their trade regimes to take advantage of market access to developed countries, and taken over the manufacture and exports of 'mature' industrial products. There are some differences between the two countries. China has spread its industrial growth across the spectrum from low- to medium-tech sectors and also into high-tech at a minimal level, while India has focused on medium-tech, skill-intensive industrial growth. China has relied on under-consumption, high savings, plus a large FDI contribution and export growth; India has relied on growth in domestic consumption, low FDI, and moderate export growth. In this respect, a crude aggregative calculation would reveal that China achieves around 10 per cent to 12 per cent GDP growth rate from around 50 per cent of GDP invested (45 per cent domestic savings plus 5 per cent FDI), while India achieves between 7 per cent and 9 per cent growth from 30 per cent to 35 per cent investment (mostly domestic savings with a small 1 per cent to 2 per cent FDI). China is, thus, less capital efficient than India. This might be due partly to the composition of China's sectoral growth, with considerable investment in infrastructure, as well as its ageing population compared to India's. India has underinvested in infrastructure. However, the rate of return on equity is also higher in India than in China. Despite these caveats, the capital-intensive nature of the Chinese growth pattern is worrying, as is its material intensity.

The growth in China's population is slowing and its population has aged faster than India's. China's gender imbalance is worse than India's, though it is bad in both countries. India falls behind China in infrastructure, in primary and secondary education, and in health but has, however, had a relative lead on China in higher education and the ability to use English. Despite many episodes of sub-national revolts across India—Kashmir, Punjab, Assam, and Nagaland—India has not experienced a period of excessive political volatility such as that of China during the Cultural Revolution. The opacity of the Communist Party decision-making process makes doing business in China a costly process, though its dominance delivers quick results. In India, the decision-making process is open, slow, and reversible under populist pressure (for example, the instances of special export zones and the problems faced by the West Bengal government with regard to acquiring land for industrial development for Tata's small *Nano* car): hence, any investment, once committed, can often prove worthless since concessions won with difficulty (and a large bribe) can be lost.

In all current discussions, it is taken for granted that this process will continue with the inexorable logic of compound interest rate growth. This might well be so, but I wish to spend the rest of this chapter on pointing out what could go wrong with such simple scenarios. The 'snags' are external and internal.

EXTERNAL 'SNAGS'

At present, there seems to be a symbiosis between Western capital outflows and the Asian need for investment. In return, manufacturing exports from Asia keep Western inflation low. Western countries have had to restructure their economies away from low-tech, mature manufacturing products towards high-tech R&D-intensive products and services. This has led to a massive churning of the labour force, with the losers being low-skilled and semi-skilled male manual manufacturing workers in the developed countries. This process can only continue if the Asian countries buy the goods and services the West has to sell: the debate on China's exchange rate policy shows that there are limits to this process. China under-consumes and accumulates its export surplus. The USA over-consumes and runs a capital outflow to finance its excess consumption. Since China does not recycle its accumulated surplus back into global demand, there is a perception that China is not playing fair. This is the nub of the debate on the exchange rate. As yet, the numbers are small in relation to global flows but, following the 2008 presidential elections in the USA, this 'snag' could present itself as a possible disrupter of smooth growth. China's sovereign wealth fund has begun to recycle some of the accumulated reserves and this will ease the burden a little. This is greatly needed, especially in light of the deep financial crisis of late 2007 and early 2008. (The financial crisis has deepened much further than when I wrote this. However, this is not the place to discuss the major consequences the crisis will have on the world economy as well as the 'engines of growth'.)

On the part of the four emerging nations, WTO negotiations loom large as an example of the lack of symmetry in international trade negotiations. The agricultural subsidies given by the USA and the EU, and their insistence on the Singapore conditions, have held up the resolution of the Doha Round. This is another 'snag' that could hinder smooth developments.

There are geopolitical considerations that also hover in the background. China is seen as the only nation state today that can challenge American supremacy in the near future. On the one hand, in arrangements such as the Shanghai process, Russia and China club together, which worries the USA. The USA–India nuclear agreement is a countermove to the Shanghai process by the USA. India and China have an unsettled border dispute, though they have agreed to negotiate peacefully. Japan's attitude is ambivalent about the rise of China, and any possible reunification of the two parts of Korea will also influence Chinese perceptions of national security. For China, the Taiwan issue remains unresolved.

India is in a neighbourhood that has many failed, or potentially failing, states. Sri Lanka has had a civil war raging for twenty-five years, a war that has claimed the life of one Indian Prime Minister. Pakistan and India have had four wars and now, with both countries having nuclear weapons, one can only hope that future relations will be peaceable. The terrorist attack in Mumbai on 26 November 2008 has further soured relations between the two countries (but, again, this is not the place to discuss its implications). Pakistan itself is under pressure from Al Qaeda and the Taleban militants on its Afghan border. Its transition to democracy is a fraught process, as the recent assassination of Benazir Bhutto has shown. Myanmar, on India's eastern border, is still a repressive regime with an uncertain future, and Nepal has just experienced revolution, albeit with India's tacit approval.

INTERNAL 'SNAGS'

India faces the tricky problems of inclusion with its dalits and backward castes, as well as its large Muslim minority. These are struggles for equality in social status as much as economic betterment. There is a large and growing army of Maoists—the Naxalites, as they are called—that exploit tribal and other marginal groups' discontent with exclusion of the economic processes that could benefit them. One-sixth of India's districts have a substantial Naxalite presence. While this is not a long-term threat, it is a substantial short- and medium-term problem. India has also had sub-nationalist movements over the last sixty years—Kashmir, Punjab, Nagaland, and Assam—which have had to be dealt with ruthlessly, and some of which, such as Nagaland and Kashmir, are not as yet resolved.

For China, the lack of the rule of law is a problem. Internal unrest has taken many forms, mainly in rural areas where people have found they have lost their property without proper compensation. This unrest is spreading to urban areas as well. There is religious dissent in the form of the Falun Gong and Christian groups, who are demanding greater religious tolerance. Again, it is unlikely that these threats will cause a serious rupture to the regime; however, they will grow and not just go away. China might need to relax its under-consumptionist stance and allow greater consumption freedoms to its population, much as India has done to divert some of the unrest.

For the other two countries, there are no external snags as such. Their problems are internal, such as the problems of equality of status for groups within their populations, and the overwhelming problem of inequalities of wealth and lifetime opportunities. In a sense, the problem of inclusion that India is tackling through its democratic process is also the problem facing the two countries in the Southern hemisphere. If Brazil could upgrade the education of its poor people, it could harness the additional human capital for a growth spurt. Similarly, for South Africa, eliminating the economic and social distances between the black majority and the white minority will be a growth-enhancing policy.

CONCLUSION

The Southern Engines of global growth are a reality. They herald a new shape to the twenty-first-century global economy. But one should not take their sustained growth for granted. Each country needs, consciously, to pursue policies that will overcome some of the internal and external snags mentioned above. One thing is certain: the half millennium inaugurated by the 'discoveries' of Christopher Columbus and Vasco da Gama has now ended. A new millennium will see a new global economy with a smaller disproportionality between population shares and income shares.

REFERENCES

Clark, C. (1957) *The Conditions of Economic Progress* (London: Macmillan).
Desai, M. (2005) 'India and China: An Essay in Comparative Political Economy', in W. Tseng and D. Cowan (eds), *India's and China's Recent Experience with Reform and Growth* (Washington, DC and New York: IMF/Palgrave Macmillan).
Nayyar, D. (2007) 'China, India, Brazil and South Africa: Engines of Growth?' Paper presented at the UNU-WIDER Conference on Southern Engines of Global Growth.

Part II

Development Approaches
and Growth Paths

4

China's Economic Growth: Trajectories and Evolving Institutions

Jun Zhang[1]

INTRODUCTION

Even though China has been able to continue a record growth rate of 9.3 per cent in its total annual output since the early 1990s, the results of faster growth in the past decade have turned out to be quite different from those of the 1980s. Economic growth in the 1980s was able to bring 13.5 million people out of poverty every year and create huge job opportunities for rural immigrants. As a consequence of this income surge, growth was sustained by acceleration of domestic consumption spending. In the 1980s, as a result of consumption-led growth, consumption accounted for over 70 per cent of China's total GDP. Typically, China experienced frequent occurrences of trade deficit rather than surplus during this phase of growth.

China's growth since the mid-1990s, however, has been unexpectedly accompanied by increasing imbalances of payment, mostly through the huge influx of foreign direct investments (FDIs) and an accelerated pile-up of trade surplus. In 1985, the value of Chinese exports was less than 10 per cent of its GDP. In 2006, however, the export : GDP ratio had increased to nearly 40 per cent. Large amount of surplus in the balance of payments and

[1] The research on which this chapter is based was co-sponsored by both the School of Economics at Fudan University through a national grant named '985 project', which contains a sub-project on regional economic growth and decentralization in China, and by Shanghai Education Committee through the funding for constructing the key disciplines in sciences #B101. I am grateful to Dr Guanghua Wan and the referees for providing insightful comments on the earlier version of this chapter. I also extend appreciation to all the participants at the UNU-WIDER Conference on Southern Engines of Global Growth: China, India, Brazil, and South Africa, held 7–8 Sept. 2007 in Helsinki. Dr Yong Fu provided research assistance and data processing; his contribution is highly appreciated. Errors remaining are, of course, mine.

accumulation of foreign exchange reserves of over US$2 trillion have exerted growing pressure on its fixed exchange rate regime and have continuously increased the trade tension with the USA and EU.

Domestically, since the mid-1990s, the growth of capital investments has accelerated, so that the investment : GDP ratio rose from less than 20 per cent in the early 1980s to over 45 per cent in 2005. After the mid-1990s, the trend towards regional convergence observed in the 1980s began to reverse, leading to regional divergence. The investment-led growth helped to enlarge the gap between the rich and poor provinces and resulted in rising regional imbalance. Job creation has been declining since the mid-1990s. The trickle-down effect of economic growth has not occurred.

Why are the results of economic growth since the mid-1990s so different from the preceding decade? What are the causes behind the change in growth trajectory? With regard to successful transition and growth, China has been regarded as a noteworthy case in the world of centrally planned economies, but much of the success in its performance is based on the experience of dissolved institutions, the emergence of the non-state sector, and the improved efficiency of existing sectors in the 1980s. The role of the changes in institutions governing decentralization and growth associated with political centralization following the 1989 political crisis has not received adequate notice, even though it has not been totally neglected. A growing interest has been directed at the outcomes of investment-led growth in China recently, but the discussion has been only limited, so far, to the causes of change in the growth trajectory of the mid-1990s.

In this chapter, we argue that the change in the trajectory of growth since the mid-1990s is the outcome of the disruptive changes in political and intergovernmental fiscal institutions in the post-1989 era. Attention will be paid particularly to the role of political and fiscal recentralization that followed the political crisis in 1989. Political centralization and a tax-sharing system, responsible for the prevailing regional competition, produce the dynamics that have underlain and propelled the process of investment-led growth since the mid-1990s.

This chapter is organized as follows: in the next section, the trajectory of growth is discussed in the context of growth accounting for China, where emphasis is placed on the changing pattern in the growth of total factor productivity. An explanation is then offered for the change in growth trajectory, followed by some empirical evidence based on the results of various recent studies. The chapter closes with a series of conclusions.

THE TRAJECTORY OF GROWTH AND ITS CHANGE
IN THE POST-1989 ERA

There have been numerous studies that examine the sources of economic growth in post-reform China since the mid-1980s. The sources of data and methodologies might differ, but one finding is commonly shared by these studies; that is, the growth rate of total factor productivity (TFP) in China has declined since the mid-1990s.

For example, in a re-estimation of TFP growth for the Chinese economy, Zhang and Shi (2002) find that the growth of TFP began to decelerate after 1992. This finding is a confirmation of some earlier results of growth decomposition for industrial enterprises in China (for example, Jefferson, Rawski, and Zheng 1996). These results have been replicated by many other studies. Table 4.1 includes some of the results estimated in these studies, showing a quite similar pattern in the change in the growth rate of TFP.

Kuijs and Wang (2005), for example, recently updated the results of growth accounting. In their account, assuming the output elasticity of labour being 0.5, they find that compared with 1978–93 the contribution of capital accumulation to GDP growth increased in 1993–2004, as the capital : output ratio rose from an estimated 2.2 in 1994 to an estimated 2.8 in 2004, reflecting the rapid investment growth in the last decade, while TFP growth slowed down. When they updated the revised GDP data for 1993–2005, they found little deviation in their results. On the basis of new data, for example, the contribution of capital accumulation was 60 per cent rather than 62 per cent, while TFP growth would be 3 per cent, instead of 2.7 per cent.

Table 4.1. *Growth of total factor productivity (TFP) and its decline in China: various studies*

Source	Period	TFP growth percentage
Zhang and Shi 2002	1977–88	4.1
	1989–98	2.1
	1992–8	3.6
Zheng and Hu 2004	1978–95	4.64
	1995–2001	2.28
OEDC 2005	1979–96	4.0
	1997–2002	3.2
Kuijs and Wang 2005	1978–93	3.7
	1993–2004	2.7
Jefferson, Rawski,	1984–8	3.68 (4.52)
and Zheng 1996	1988–92	1.58 (2.98)

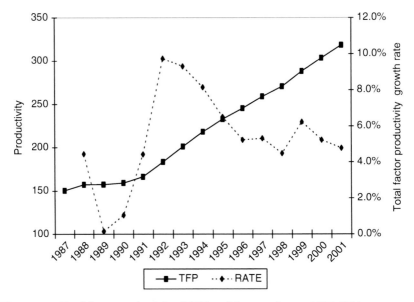

Figure 4.1. *Total factor productivity (TFP) and its growth rate, 1987–2001*

Source: Zhang, Wan, and Jin 2007.

Based on a recent compilation of China's provincial capital stock series (Zhang, Wu, and Zhang 2007), Zhang, Wan, and Jin (2007) also find that the aggregated growth rate of provincial TFPs for 1987–2001 presents a similar pattern of change in the growth trajectory, as shown in Figure 4.1.[2]

The concern here is why TFP growth has begun to slow down since the 1990s, but GDP has not. China still maintained an output growth rate of over 9 per cent in the 1990s. From a growth theory perspective, if the growth of TFP does decline, then capital accumulation (as measured by the capital: labour ratio) should have contributed a far larger share to output growth.

In order to find evidence to support this assertion, let us assume that something happened in the early 1990s that caused capital intensity to accelerate and TFP growth to slow down. If this were true, then capital intensity might have had a non-linear relationship with TFP growth for the whole post-reform period. If we assume the following quadratic equation between the growth of TFP and the change in capital intensity, then we should

[2] The data set developed by the China Center for Economic Studies at Fudan University covers twenty-nine Chinese provinces and municipalities for the period 1987–2001. The data of real capital stock series are based on Zhang, Wu, and Zhang 2007.

Table 4.2. *Estimates of quadratic equation*

	A_0	A_1	A_2
Coefficients	1.141	0.984	−0.0722
Standard error	1.281	0.229	0.025
T-value	0.891	4.297	−2.86
X^*	6.814		
Y^*	4.494		

Note: Quadratic equation for regression is $g(TFP) = \alpha_0 + \alpha_1 g(\frac{K}{L}) + \alpha_2 [(\frac{K}{L})]^2$.

expect the sign of a_2 to be negative, when it is fitted statistically by the data of Chinese economy:

$$g(TEP) = a_0 + a_1 g(K/L) + a_2 [g(K/L)]^2 \qquad (4.1)$$

Table 4.2 reports the estimates of regression for Equation 4.1. The data used to estimate the parameters come from the China Center for Economic Studies (CCES) at Fudan University. The fitted values of parameters are statistically significant, and all the signs of parameters are as we expected. Table 4.2 also reports the critical value (X^*) of g(K/L), where $X^* = -a_1/(2a_2)$, and the maximum value of g(TFP) is Y^*.

From the perspective of standard growth accounting, the capital : output ratio can also be decomposed into the following two parts:

$$g(K/Y) = ag(K/L) - g(TEP) \qquad (4.2)$$

Inserting Equation 4.1 into Equation 4.2, we have

$$g(K/Y) = -a_0 + (a - a_1)g(K/L) - a_2 [g(K/L)]^2 \qquad (4.3)$$

Because a_2 has a negative sign, acceleration of capital intensity will, therefore, cause the capital : output ratio to rise. In order for g(K/L) to drive g(K/Y) up in Equation 4.3, we let the first derivative of g(K/Y) with regard to g(K/L) be greater than 0, then we obtain:

$$g(K/L) > (a_1 - a)/(2|a_2|) \qquad (4.4)$$

Using the estimated values of parameters, a_1 and a_2, and assuming the output elasticity of labour, a, is 1/2,[3] then we estimate that the critical value of g(K/L),

---

[3] Most studies on growth accounting for post-reform China assume a lower output elasticity of labour, as the share of labour in the country's national income ranges from 0.4 to 0.5.

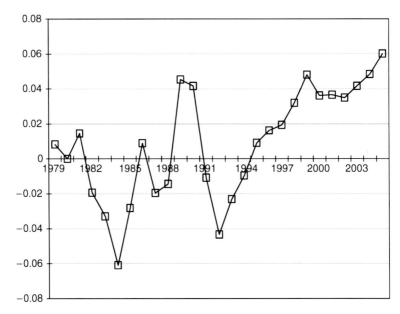

Figure 4.2. *Percentage change of capital : output ratio in China*

Source: Author's computation.

which is the minimum value for the change in the capital : labour ratio, to trigger a rise in the capital : output ratio. The annual percentage change in China's capital : output ratio during 1979–2004, which is based on our estimations, is depicted in Figure 4.2. It shows that China's capital : output ratio has unexpectedly accelerated since the mid-1990s.

Given the assumptions of standard growth accounting, (K/Y) is also the product of the output elasticity of capital, a, multiplied by the incremental capital : output ratio (ICOR). Therefore, the rising capital : output ratio can be translated into rising ICOR, indicating deteriorating efficiency of aggregate investments over time. The evolution of China's incremental capital : output ratio is presented in Figure 4.3, which is largely drawn from Zhang 2003b. It shows that the ICOR experienced a stable, slight decline in the 1980s, but has increased dramatically since the mid-1990s.

Figure 4.3 also indicates that the investment : GDP ratio has accelerated dramatically since the mid-1990s. Indeed, total annual investments in fixed assets rose from about 20 per cent in the early 1980s to over 47 per cent by 2003. Similarly, gross fixed capital formation as a percentage of GDP increased from around 25 per cent in the 1980s to over 45 per cent by 2005. China's investment : GDP ratios are far higher than those of Hong Kong

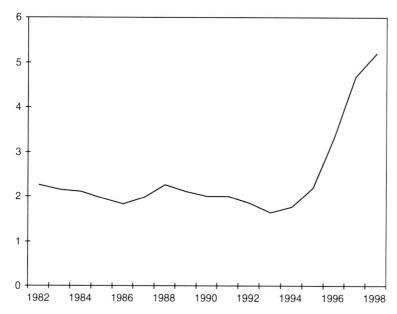

Figure 4.3. *China's incremental capital : output ratio (five-year moving average)*
Source: Zhang 2003b.

and Taiwan, where investment rates for 1966–98 were just 25.4 per cent and 23.7 per cent, respectively (Toh and Ng 2002). They are also higher than those of Singapore and South Korea (from the 1970s to the 1980s). For example, the average ratio of investment to GDP in Singapore was 35.4 per cent for 1966–98, which was the highest among the four little tigers in East Asia (Zhang 2003a).

EXPLANATION

Both Table 4.1 and Figure 4.3 show that the trajectory of growth was much more typical during the 1980s than in the post-1992 era. Why is the trajectory of growth between these two periods so different? Why has it changed since the mid-1990s?

In this chapter, we look at the evolving roles of China's political and fiscal institutions in explaining the variation in the growth trajectory. Emphasis is given to the critical impact of the political crisis in 1989 on the change in political and fiscal institutions that have induced the regional competition of local governments.

During the initial phase of economic liberalization in the 1980s, shortly after the end of the Cultural Revolution (1966–76), the ultimate objective of the Chinese reformers was to achieve the partial decontrol of the planned economy and to improve the *allocative efficiency* of existing resources by reassigning and diffusing property rights, creating incentives and autonomy for farmers, enterprises, and local governments. One important step to decentralizing fiscal accountability and delegating decision-making powers to local governments was the introduction of the revenue-sharing system between central and local governments.

While these institutional reforms had enhanced efficiency, which had led to rapid output growth, economic liberalization and fiscal decentralization were eroding the ideological legitimacy of the party/government, and were creating the potential for political crisis.

Why would China's fiscal decentralization and micro-institutional reforms in the 1980s have an eroding effect on the legitimacy of the party/government, and produce potential for political crisis? There are several reasons.

The top-down economic decentralization through the reassignment and diffusion of property rights to local and non-state sectors has created high-powered incentives and autonomy for economic agents and local governments, but has increasingly challenged ideological orthodoxy and brought in a growing awareness of, or desire for, political pluralism and political reforms.[4]

Fiscal decentralization, largely via various revenue-sharing schemes, has led to a considerable decline in the central government's share of total national fiscal revenues and in aggregate GDP, as evidenced in Figure 4.4. This fiscal situation empowered local governments, and is widely believed to have jeopardized the authority and fiscal capacity of central party leadership.

Fiscal decentralization and institutional reforms in the 1980s, characterized by sectoral redistribution without losers, led to frequent incidents of macro-economic imbalance during that decade and at the same time, because of fiscal decentralization, the government's ability to control and maintain macro-stability was highly eroded.[5]

A political crisis was eventually ignited by the students' protests in Tiananmen Square in June of 1989. Although it was not the first political crisis during the economic reform process in the 1980s,[6] it definitely produced a

---

[4] In China, this awareness was officially condemned and criticized as capitalist liberalization and spiritual contamination.

[5] Brandt and Zhu 2000, as well as Feltenstein and Iwata 2005, argue that fiscal decentralization and the diminished ability of central government in the 1980s explain the periods of hyperinflation in China.

[6] Another major crisis occurred in 1986 after the death of the former party secretary Hu Yaobang.

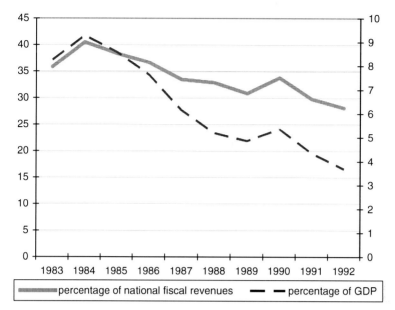

Figure 4.4. *Deteriorating fiscal status of central government in China, 1983–92*
Source: National Bureau of Statistics var. years.

profound effect on the trajectory of economic reforms and growth in China. This political crisis was followed by a disruptive drop in GDP growth, together with an international embargo and isolation from the west for three years. The important lessons that can be highlighted to Chinese reformers from the political crisis in 1989 are threefold:[7] (i) economic decentralization and micro-liberalization cannot guarantee macroeconomic stability, rather, it will erode the central capability of political control; (ii) without macro-balance and political stability, China cannot maintain rapid economic growth; and (iii) without faster economic growth, it is hard to maintain the legitimacy of the party leadership in China.

Shortly after the crisis and economic retrenchment between 1989 and 1991, the reformers, especially the senior leader Deng Xiaoping, decided to rebuild and reinforce leadership legitimacy by putting the economy back onto a fast growth track. At the same time, they sought to bring back political stability by initiating new reform programmes in political and fiscal institutions.[8]

---

[7] A more detailed exposition of these lessons was included in the collected works of Deng Xiaoping.

[8] Deng Xiaoping gave a series of speeches in the early spring of 1992 on an inspection tour of south China's provinces.

Indeed, the goals of the various reforms could hardly be effective without making the incentives compatible between the central and local governments. In line with such objectives, the authorities proposed some fundamental changes in both fiscal and political institutions.

Although Chinese local officials are generally appointed by central government, it does not imply that they are weak and are always subject to central control. In fact, one of the results of fiscal decentralization in the 1980s was that the incentives facing both central and local governments were not compatible, and local governments increasingly enjoyed bargaining power with the central government. Under revenue-sharing schemes in the 1980s, it became quite common that local governments (especially in rich regions) often shielded local state-owned enterprises from taxation to avoid sharing revenues with central government (Wong and Bird 2008). Such incentive incompatibility could be generally evidenced by the existence and increasing proportion of fiscal revenues that were not recorded as budgetary funds (namely, the 'extra-budgetary funds').

Radical reforms in the intergovernmental fiscal system, implemented in 1994, consolidated the fiscal revenues and rebuilt the central–local fiscal relationship by (1) recentralizing the fiscal revenues to the central government without changing the expenditure responsibility for both local and central governments; (2) separation of central office of tax administration from local ones; (3) replacing the revenue-sharing scheme with production-based VAT sharing scheme; (4) raising the share of central governmental transfer and tax rebates in local fiscal incomes; (5) eliminating local governments' extra-budgetary revenues and converting them within budgetary revenues.

The most salient feature of the fiscal consolidation reform in 1994 is that although central government began to acquire more controls over fiscal revenues it does not mean local governments lost fiscal autonomy. After fiscal reform, local governments were still responsible for about 70 per cent of total fiscal expenditure. In fact, the 1994 fiscal reforms represent a shift from bargaining mechanism to incentive mechanism. Since then, local governments have become more incentivized, because after the 1994 fiscal reforms central government began enjoying more fiscal revenues by making transfers to local governments and having more power to reward and punish local governments. Therefore, we could still interpret the Chinese fiscal system as the one that is better characterized by regional decentralization. But the incentive structure facing local governments under the Chinese intergovernmental fiscal system should be very different from the general case of fiscal federalism. Otherwise we could not understand why such fiscal arrangement after 1994 could have incentivized the local governments to 'race to the top'.

It is true that local fiscal autonomy was successfully preserved, in addition to achieving a substantial improvement in the fiscal status and capacity of central government.[9]

Accompanying such fiscal recentralization was the tighter control of the party over provincial leaders and the re-establishment of patronage politics. Such control schemes include a change in governance structure, the introduction of the cadres system within both the party and the government hierarchy for monitoring purposes, and a performance-based promotion scheme for the party (Li and Lian 1999). Local officials, especially the provincial party secretaries and governors, were to be strictly appointed, rotated, and promoted in order to guarantee their loyalty to central government and to overcome the informational asymmetry between the different tiers of governments (Huang 2002; Zhang and Gao 2008).[10]

One of the outcomes of this political recentralization was the creation of *political championship* governing local governments.[11] There are several reasons why political championship works so well in China: the country has an authoritarian political system that enables central government to set the rules of the game and the standards of measurement, and to decide who will be promoted. Second, China has a history of an 'M-form' organizational hierarchy within which the performance of each agent is highly comparable to that of the others,[12] and this makes it much easier to implement the championship game. Lastly, even although there has been a growing non-state sector since the 1980s, most financial resources, land, other factors of production, and economic policies are still controlled and allocated by local governments. Therefore, political institutions governing incentive mechanisms have a profound influence on local economic performance.

Through the above-mentioned institutional reforms, by the mid-1990s, decentralized authoritarianism was reconstructed, and local government

[9] The central government has agreed to recycle a portion of tax revenues to local governments as an equalization transfer in order to bridge the gap in their expenditure. None the less, the variation across provinces is still huge.

[10] The official proclamation was issued in March 1990. Using a panel consisting of twenty-eight Chinese provinces, Li and Zhou (2005) find a positive relationship between the relative economic performance of local officials and their probability of being promoted. Based on a data set consisting of 302 provincial leaders and twenty-nine provinces for 1978–2004, Zhang and Gao (2008) find that term limitations and rotation of local officials are inductive to local economic growth.

[11] Championship as an incentive mechanism is studied in economics literature. See Lazear 1995 for a theoretical discussion.

[12] See Xu and Qian 1993 for a more detailed account of the evolution of the Chinese hierarchical system based on the distinction of 'M-form' versus 'U-form'.

officials got politically motivated to 'put growth first', if they wished to safe-guard their political careers and potential for promotion to higher positions.

In an account of why regional decentralization works better in China than in Russia, Blanchard and Shleifer conceptualized the framework of 'fiscal federalism, Chinese style' based on the experiences of these two countries. In particular, they concluded that:

it has been neglected in the recent discussions of China praising the decentralization benefits of federalism. As best we can tell, the economic benefits of decentralization obtained from federalism rely crucially on some form of political centralization. Without such centralization, the incentives to pursue regionalist policies are too high, and cannot be eliminated solely through clever economic and fiscal arrangement. (Blanchard and Shleifer 2001: 178)

Economic growth since the mid-1990s therefore rests on very different institutional foundations. Faster growth has been triggered within the frame-work of a more centralized political hierarchy. The incentive mechanism of the local governments is built largely on their tax autonomy and the motiva-tion of political championship they face. Since the mid-1990s, economic growth has become increasingly highly regionally driven, investment led, fragmented, and uneven across provinces and regions.

STATISTICAL EVIDENCES

In what follows, we provide some empirical evidence based on recent studies of China's regional decentralization, competition, and growth. If the changes in political and fiscal institutions in the aftermath of the 1989 political crisis have helped to steer local governments toward investment-led (or export-led) growth, it is important to seek out such empirical evidence.

The evidence for which we are looking can be summarized as follows. If the explanation above is plausible—namely, that investment-led growth was the outcome of political championship and the fiscal autonomy that characterized the incentive mechanism of regional governments—we should expect to find that: (i) the fiscal autonomy of local governments should be enhanced rather than diminished by the tax-sharing system which replaced the revenue-sharing mechanism in 1994; (ii) within performance-based political control, as well as the tax-sharing system and the resulting regional competition, local govern-ments are expected to favour capital construction and investment-led growth, and considered less likely to support the provision of equity-enhancing public goods; and/or (iii) fiscal decentralization and the accompanying regional competition from 1994 onwards should have a significantly positive effect on local economic growth in general.

FISCAL AUTONOMY

The robustness of the link between local expenditure and revenues should indicate whether local governments are fiscally motivated to be committed to local growth. A simple way to capture the change in the fiscal autonomy enjoyed by governments is to examine the correlation between fiscal expenditure and revenues at the local level (for example, Jin, Qian, and Weingast 2005; Zhang 2005; Zhuravskaya 2000).

In Table 4.3, using panel data provided by CCES at Fudan University, we present the estimated coefficients of budgetary expenditure regressed on budgetary revenues. The dataset used in this chapter consists of twenty-nine provinces covering the period 1980–2004. In order to control for time trend and the effect of various amounts of fiscal spending, all the regressions in the upper half of Table 4.3 are run with a year dummy and population size because total fiscal spending is positively related to the local population.

The lower half of Table 4.3 reports the results of a first difference regression, which captures the dynamic effect of fiscal autonomy over time. Both results are similar. The coefficient of budgetary revenues increased from 0.8539 in the 1980s to 0.9518 in 1994–2004. In the first difference regression, the coefficient of budgetary revenues increased substantially from 0.4337 in the first period to 0.8201 during the second. The larger the coefficients, the greater the budgetary autonomy and the greater the motivation of local governments becomes.

The results in Table 4.3 are consistent with those of Zhang (2005) who, based on data from 1,860 Chinese counties for 1993 and 2000, also finds that political centralization and the tax-sharing system introduced in 1994 substantially improved local motivation in triggering growth.

REGIONAL COMPETITION AND BUDGETARY SPENDING BIAS

The assumption developed in this chapter is that political championship, together with the tax autonomy that has been in place since 1994, encourages regional competition between local governments towards achieving better economic performance. The most prevalent competitive measure is attracting

Table 4.3. *Estimated fiscal autonomy of provincial governments in post-reform China*

Dependent variable: in-budget fiscal expenditure	1970–9		1980–92		1994–2004	
In-budget fiscal revenue	0.1689***	0.1597***	0.8529***	0.7818***	1.0884***	0.9518***
	(−0.0183)	(−0.0219)	(−0.0306)	(−0.0233)	(−0.0254)	(0.0339)
Population		0.0046***	0.0101***	0.0032***		0.2034***
		(−0.0013)	(−0.0031)	(−0.0009)		(−0.0346)
R^2	0.7543	0.921	0.9679	0.9314	0.9514	0.9789
Hausmann	3.0	13.01		Negative	1.03	30.54
Pr>	0.2227	0.0046			0.5975	0.000
Note	RE	FE	FE	RE	RE	FE
First difference						
In-budget fiscal revenue	0.1586***		0.5218***	0.4337***	0.9416***	0.8201***
	(−0.0237)		(−0.0363)	(−0.0405)	(−0.0449)	(−0.0592)
R^2	0.1545		0.5042	0.5419	0.7313	0.8258
Hausmann	2.0		Negative		Negative	
Pr>	0.9515					
Note	RE	FE	RE	FE	RE	FE
Groups	28		28		29	
Observations	180	280	364	364	319	319

*** Statistical significance at the 1 per cent level.

an influx of FDIs through preferential tax treatment and improvement of local infrastructure (Zhang, et al. 2007). Since FDIs are export generating, trade processing usually therefore becomes the engine of local economic growth.

If local governments are committed to such regional competition, then they are most likely to spend more budgetary revenue on productive investments and capital construction. To capture the effect of regional competition on the expenditure structure of the local governments, Fu and Zhang (2007) regress both capital construction and non-direct productive expenditure as percentage of total budgetary expenditure (RPCAP and RPCUL), respectively, on the following explanatory variables: fiscal decentralization (FD); regional competition (COMPE); intersection of FD and COMPE; real per capita GDP; and other control variables such as basic education (PRIMARY, JUNIOR, and so on), net rate of migration (NETMIG), and relative size of the state-owned sector (SOU).

A measure of real tax differentiation is used in Fu and Zhang (2007) as a proxy for regional competition (COMPE). This tax variation constitutes the average tax rates divided by the tax rate charged to FDIs in each province. Fiscal decentralization is measured by provincial level overhead fiscal expenditure relative to national overhead fiscal expenditure. The panel data used for the regression are again obtained from CCES, covering twenty-nine provinces for the period 1986–2004. The year 1994, as mentioned, is the effective year of the tax-sharing system.

Their results of fixed effect regression for 1994–2004 are summarized as follows (note that we omit the constant and insignificant variable:[13]

$$
\begin{aligned}
RPCAP = &-0.1291PERGDP + 0.0411PERGDP^2 + 0.0123FD + 0.0050FD * COMPE \\
&\quad (-0.0356)\ (-0.013)\ (-0.0033)\ (0.002) \\
&- 0.0117COMPE + 0.0701SOU + 0.0125T + 0.0382DUMEXP \\
&\quad (-0.0059)\ (-0.0334)\ (-0.0013)\ (-0.00530) \\
&- 0.0151DUM96 - 0.0088DUM02 - 0.0151DUM03 + 0.2905PRIMARY \\
&\quad (-0.0037)\ (-0.0037)\ (-0.0043)\ (-0.116) \\
&- 0.5367JUNIOR - 1.2054UNINCUN \\
&\quad (-0.2112)\ (-0.3409)
\end{aligned}
$$

$$
\begin{aligned}
RPCUL = &\ 0.1050PERGDP - 0.0325PERGDP^2 - 0.0038FD - 0.0069FD * COMPE \\
&\quad (-0.0293)\ (-0.0108)\ (-0.0017)\ (-0.0013) \\
&+ 0.0239COMPE - 0.07521SOU - 0.0136T - 0.0091DUMEXP \\
&\quad (-0.0042)\ (-0.0238)\ (-0.001)\ (-0.0034) \\
&+ 0.0139DUM02 + 0.0102DUM03 + 0.8201JUNIOR + 0.4593UNINCUN \\
&\quad (-0.0027)\ (-0.0028)\ (-0.1681)\ (-0.2414) \\
&- 0.0002NETMIG \\
&\quad (-0.0001)
\end{aligned}
$$

---

[13] The figures in parenthesis shown under the regressed equation are standard errors.

The results of the regression support our hypothesis that regional competition tends to motivate local governments to target more spending on capital investments. In their study, Fu and Zhang (2007) also report the results of regressions covering various regions and periods and, according to their findings, the year 1994 (when the tax-sharing system was implemented) does make a difference: the spending bias is considerably more significant in both the eastern and western provinces of China.[14]

FISCAL DECENTRALIZATION AND GROWTH: BEFORE AND AFTER 1994

In a recent paper, using an improved dataset and measurements, Zhang and Gong (2005) examine the effects of fiscal decentralization on economic growth in China. The dataset covers twenty-eight provinces and the period 1986–2002. The authors adopt three different measures of fiscal decentralization in their estimation of equations for the robustness test. To capture the effects of the changes in fiscal and political institutions in 1994, they break down the entire period into both phases: 1986–92 and 1994–2002, respectively.

They note in their regression that the 1994 intergovernmental fiscal reform considerably changed the relationship between fiscal decentralization and economic growth, which had been significantly negative in the pre-reform era but has become significantly positive in the nine-year period since then. The coefficient of fiscal decentralization is no longer significantly negative for the entire sample 1986–2002.

This result is partially consistent with that of Zhang and Zou (1998), who also observe a negative correlation between fiscal decentralization and growth in China for the period 1978–92.[15] They also find that the significantly positive relationship between fiscal decentralization and growth exists in localities with a higher per capita GDP (as measured by the cut-off point of RMB 7,000), but not in provinces with much lower overhead income.

[14] For more details of their results, see Fu and Zhang 2007.
[15] The only exceptions are Lin and Liu (2000), who, using provincial data covering 1970–93, find a positive relation between fiscal decentralization and economic growth in China. For more detailed survey of such literature on China's fiscal decentralization and growth, see Zhang 2007.

IMPLICATIONS FOR REGIONAL DISPARITY

One of the most important outcomes of the change in the economic growth trajectory since the mid-1990s is that economic growth is regionally more decentralized and increasingly led by capital investments. While the politicized incentives geared to local governments account for this regional commitment to growth, this neither generally guarantees nor brings about the convergence of the regional GDP growth. Rather, it is, by its nature, a mechanism of endogenous growth.

Indeed, the intergovernmental tax-sharing system introduced in 1994 encouraged local governments to dedicate efforts to pro-growth policies but, because initial positions between regions differed substantially, it increased regional disparity. For example, great differences in economic structure and revenue bases exist, causing the implicit tax rate and fiscal burden to vary significantly across jurisdictions. This difference in initial position and endowment can translate into rising regional difference. According to Zhang (2005), who uses a county-level panel for 1,860 Chinese counties for 1993 and 2000, the Gini coefficient of per capita productive public expenditure rose from 68.28 in 1993 to 73.34 in 2000, an increase of 7.4 per cent; and the Gini coefficient of the share of productive investment in total public expenditure grew from 33.04 in 1993 to 41.61 in 2000, an increase of about 26 per cent.

In a recent study on the variation in regional infrastructure in China, Zhang, et al. (2007) find that, after the mid-1990s, the distribution of increments in physical infrastructure began to indicate a bias more towards the east and coastal provinces, which are relatively rich and enjoy better geo-political endowments. And as these provinces have better infrastructure they are also more successful in attracting FDI, thus generating much faster growth. As a result, these rich provinces are in a better position to rely on their own financing to improve infrastructure for added inflows of FDI. The western provinces, however, lag behind and mainly rely on central transfers for the construction of infrastructure. Regional variation in the level and growth of infrastructure across provinces largely explains the rising regional disparity apparent since the mid-1990s.

CONCLUSION

This chapter investigates the institutional reasons underlying the change in the trajectory of economic growth in post-reform China, and argues that the growth trajectory is the outcome of changes in political and inter-governmental fiscal institutions following the 1989 political crisis. By any standards, these institutional modifications were successful, because they induced faster growth and achieved political stability. Without them, China might not have been able to maintain the political stability of the last twenty years or so since 1989.

However, the nexus between growth and political stability is never linear. In this chapter, we explored the pattern of growth since the mid-1990s, and find that triggering economic growth under a decentralized authoritarian system is costly. This system enabled local governments to favour and compete for investment-led growth. However, it also generated negative spillovers from rapid growth, including rising disparity across incomes and regions, environmental degradation, frequent macro-disturbance, external imbalance of payments, financial fragility, and prevalent corruption.

The resolution of these issues, and the transition to inclusive growth, necessitate open access to further institutional reforms at both economic and political levels. Issues such as building good governance, sound financial and fiscal systems, effective identification and protection for civil and private property rights (including land)—issues that have progressed slowly and with delay during the past decades—cannot be ignored in the reform agenda of the future.

REFERENCES

Blanchard, O., and A. Shleifer (2001) 'Federalism With and Without Political Centralization: China versus Russia', NBER Working Paper 7616 (Cambridge, Mass.: NBER).

Brandt, L., and X. Zhu (2000) 'Redistribution in a Decentralized Economy: Growth and Inflation in China under Reform', *Journal of Political Economy*, 108: 422–39.

Feltenstein, A., and S. Iwata (2005) 'Decentralization and Macroeconomic Performance in China', *Journal of Development Economics*, 76: 481–501.

Fu, Y., and Y. Zhang (2007) 'Chinese Style Decentralization and Government Spending Bias: The Cost of Growth' (Shanghai: China Center for Economic Studies, Fudan University). Manuscript.

Huang, Y. (2002) 'Managing Chinese Bureaucrats: An Institutional Economics Perspective', *Political Studies*, 50: 61–79.

Jefferson, G., T. Rawski, and Y. Zheng (1996) 'Chinese Industrial Productivity: Trends, Measurement and Recent Development', *Journal of Comparative Economics*, 23: 146–80.

Jin, H., Y. Qian, and B. Weingast (2005) 'Regional Decentralization and Fiscal Incentives: Federalism, Chinese Style', *Journal of Public Economics*, 89: 1719–42.

Kuijs, L., and Y. Wang (2005) 'China's Pattern of Growth: Moving to Sustainability and Reducing Inequality', *China and the World Economy* (Jan.).

Lazear, E. (1995) *Personnel Economics* (Cambridge, Mass.: MIT Press).

Li, S., and P. Lian (1999) 'Decentralization and Coordination: China's Credible Commitment to Preserve the Market under Authoritarianism', *China Economic Review*, 10: 161–90.

Li, H., and L.-A. Zhou (2005) 'Political Turnover and Economic Performance: The Incentive Role of Personnel Control in China', *Journal of Public Economics*, 89: 1743–62.

Lin, J. Y., and Z. Liu (2000) 'Fiscal Decentralization and Economic Growth in China', *Economic Development and Cultural Change*, 49: 1–21.

National Bureau of Statistics (NBS) (var. years) *Statistical Yearbook in China* (Beijing: China Statistical Press).

OECD (2005) *OECD Economic Surveys: China*, 12 (Paris: OECD).

Toh, M., and W. Ng (2002) 'Efficiency of Investment in Asian Economies: Has Singapore Over-Invested?', *Journal of Asian Economics*, 13: 52–71.

Wong, C., and W. Bird (2008) 'China's Fiscal System: A Work in Progress', in L. Brandt and T. Rawski (eds), *China's Great Economic Transformation* (Cambridge: Cambridge University Press).

Xu, C., E. Maskin, and Y. Qian (2000) 'Incentives, Information, and Organizational Form', *Review of Economic Studies*, 67: 359–78.

——and Y. Qian (1993) 'Why China's Economic Reforms Differ: The M-Form Hierarchy and Entry/Expansion of the Non-State Sector', *Economics of Transition*, 1: 135–70.

Zhang, J. (2003a) 'Investment, Investment Efficiency and Economic Growth in China', *Journal of Asian Economics*, 14: 731–43.

—— (2003b) *Industrial Reform and Economic Growth in China* (Shanghai: Shanghai People's Press).

—— (2007) 'Decentralization and Growth: China Context', *China Economic Quarterly*, 10: 21–52.

—— and Y. Gao (2008) 'Term Limits and Rotation of Chinese Governors: Do They Matter to Economic Growth?', *Journal of the Asia Pacific Economy*, 13: 274–97.

—— —— Y. Fu, and H. Zhang (2007) 'Why China Enjoys Better Infrastructure?', *Economic Research Journal*, 3: 3–19.

—— and S. Shi (2002) 'Trajectory of Growth in Total Factor Productivity Growth in China (1952–1998)', *World Economic Papers*, 1 (Feb.).

—— G. Wan, and Y. Jin (2007) 'The Financial Deepening-Productivity Nexus in China: 1987–2001', *Journal of Chinese Economic and Business Studies*, 5: 37–49.

—— G. Wu, and J. Zhang (2007) 'Compilation of Provincial Capital Stock Series in China Using Perpetual Inventory Method'. Working Paper 001/07 (Shanghai: China Center for Economic Studies, Fudan University).

Zhang, T., and H.-F. Zou (1998) 'Fiscal Decentralization, Public Spending, and Economic Growth in China', *Journal of Public Economics*, 67: 221–40.

Zhang, Y., and L. Gong (2005) 'Tax Sharing System, Fiscal Decentralization and Economic Growth', *China Economic Quarterly*, 5: 75–108.

Zhang

Zhang, X. (2005) 'Fiscal Decentralization and Political Centralization in China: Implications for Regional Inequality', DSDG Discussion Paper 21 (Washington, DC: IFPRI).

Zheng, J., and A. Hu (2004) 'An Empirical Analysis of Provincial Productivity in China (1979–2001)'. Working Paper in Economics (SwoPEc) 127 (Gothenburg: Gothenburg University).

Zhuravskaya, E. (2000) 'Incentives to Provide Local Public Goods: Fiscal Federalism, Russian Style', *Journal of Public Economics*, 76: 337–68.

5

Global Growth and Distribution: Are China and India Reshaping the World?

Maurizio Bussolo,
Rafael E. De Hoyos, Denis Medvedev,
and Dominique van der Mensbrugghe[1]

INTRODUCTION

In 1980, China and India accounted for 2 per cent of global output, and the remaining low- and middle-income countries made up 16 per cent of world GDP. By 2005, the contribution of China and India had nearly quadrupled to 7 per cent of global production, while the share of other developing countries declined to 15 per cent. The growing importance of developing economies can thus be largely explained by the economic expansion of China and India. In the future, the increasing level of China and India's integration with the global economy, combined with sustained high growth, is likely further to cement their position as an important engine of global development.

This chapter explores the potential consequences of sustained economic expansion in China and India by considering the effects the two emerging giants are likely to have on global trade, structure of production, and the distribution of income. While growth rates in China and India are likely to decelerate in the future, their growth path will still outperform growth outcomes of most other countries. Not only are these developments likely to drive convergence of per capita incomes at the global level; they are also a key force behind the expected entry of millions of Chinese and Indian consumers into the global middle class. Growing demand for goods is likely to boost trade in manufactured products, but also to raise demand for highly skilled workers. This implies that the rules of the global marketplace will be increasingly determined by the preferences of citizens of China and India, and

---

[1] The authors are grateful to Hans Timmer for helpful contributions, comments, and suggestions.

pressures for policies favouring global integration are therefore likely to increase in the future.

An outstanding growth performance of relatively poor and highly populated countries such as China and India signifies a reduction in the number of poor around the world and a decline in global income disparities. Nevertheless, as is shown by Chaudhuri and Ravallion (2006), fast growth in China and India is characterized by high rates of urbanization and growing demand for skills, both of which resulted in deteriorations in the distribution of income within these countries. These apparently opposing distributional effects highlight the importance of analysing global disparities, taking into account income differences not only between nation states, but also within them. The definition of global income distribution used in this study captures income differences between all the citizens in the world; we may think of the resulting global inequality as showing the income differences that would prevail if the world were seen as a single country. The concept of global income distribution becomes increasingly relevant as people's perception regarding their relative position in society is no longer based solely on a national yardstick, but is influenced by the increased awareness of living standards of people around the world (Milanovic 2006). On the other hand, within-country distributional changes should not be disregarded, since economic policy is still decided and implemented at the national level.

The empirical results of this chapter are produced with LINKAGE, the World Bank's global general equilibrium model, and the newly developed global income distribution dynamics (GIDD) tool. GIDD is a framework for *ex ante* analyses of the distribution and poverty effects of changes in macro-economic policy and/or trends in global markets. It complements a global computable general equilibrium (CGE) analysis with global micro-simulations based on standardized household surveys. The tool pools most of the currently available household surveys covering 1.2 million households in sixty-three developing countries; household information from developed countries comes from the Luxemburg Income Study dataset. These microdata are complemented with more aggregate information for countries where no surveys are available; the final dataset covers 91 per cent of the world's population (see Table 5.4 for details).

The chapter is organized as follows. The next section sketches the methodology, assumptions, and data behind the GIDD and is followed by a section presenting the macroeconomic results of the baseline scenario, showing the importance of China and India for global growth and trade. The chapter continues with an assessment of the importance of growth in China and India for the changes in global income distribution and the emergence of a global middle class. The final section offers concluding remarks.

METHODOLOGY

The empirical analysis in this chapter relies on two tools developed at the Development Economic Prospects Group of the World Bank: the LINKAGE global CGE model and the GIDD, which combines a consistent set of price and volume changes from the CGE model with expected changes in demographic structure to create a hypothetical distribution of income in 2030. We begin with a brief description of the LINKAGE model and then proceed to introduce the GIDD framework and its ability to map macroeconomic outcomes to disaggregated household survey data.

LINKAGE: A GLOBAL DYNAMIC MULTI-SECTORAL MODEL

The 'forward looking' sections in this chapter have been produced with the World Bank's LINKAGE model. At its core, LINKAGE is essentially a neoclassical growth model, with aggregate growth predicated on assumptions regarding the growth of the labour force, savings/investment decisions (and, therefore, capital accumulation), and productivity. Unlike more simple growth models, however, LINKAGE has considerably more structure (see van der Mensbrugghe 2005, for a detailed description). First, it is multi-sectoral. This allows for more complex productivity dynamics, including differentiating productivity growth between agriculture, manufacturing, and services, and picking up the changing structure of demand (and, therefore, output) as growth in incomes leads to a relative shift into manufactures and services. Second, it is linked multi-regionally, allowing for the influence of openness—via trade and finance—on domestic variables such as output and wages. Third, the LINKAGE model has a more diverse set of productive factors, including land and natural resources (in the fossil fuel sectors), and labour is split between unskilled and skilled categories.

The LINKAGE model has a 2001 base year and relies on the Global Trade Analysis Project (GTAP) 6.1 database[2] to calibrate initial parameters. A scenario is developed by solving for a new equilibrium in each subsequent year up until 2030. The growth in the labour force is driven by demographics—essentially given by the growth of the working age population.

---

[2] See <https://www.gtap.agecon.purdue.edu/default.asp> for details.

Differentiated growth of skilled versus unskilled workers is partly driven by demographics and partly driven by changes in education rates. As education levels rise (in the younger populations), they eventually increase relative growth of skilled workers once they enter the labour force (and older un- skilled workers retire). Savings decisions are partly driven by demographics— rising as youth dependency ratios fall and falling as elderly dependency ratios rise. Investment rates are driven by changes in growth rates (the accelerator mechanism) and differential rates of return to capital. Net foreign savings is the difference between domestic savings and investment.

Productivity is derived by a combination of factors, but is also partially judgemental. First, agricultural productivity is assumed to be factor-neutral and exogenous, and is set to estimates from empirical studies. Productivity in manufacturing and services is labour augmenting, and a constant wedge is imposed between productivity growth in the two broad sectors with the assumption that productivity growth is higher in manufacturing than in services. Finally, the model assumes that energy efficiency improves autono- mously by 1 per cent per year in all regions and that international trade costs also decline by 1 per cent per year.

GIDD: LINKING MACROECONOMIC OUTCOMES TO MICRO-SURVEY DATA

The GIDD framework is based on micro-simulation methodologies devel- oped in the recent literature, including Bourguignon and Pereira da Silva 2003; Bussolo, Lay, and van der Mensbrugghe 2006; Chen and Ravallion 2003; Ferreira and Leite 2003; and Ferreira and Leite 2004. The starting-point is the global income distribution in 2000, assembled using data from household surveys for eighty-four countries and data on income groups (usually vintiles) for the remaining countries; the final sample covers 91 per cent of the world population (see Table 5.4 and http://www.worldbank.org/prospects/gidd for a detailed list).[3] The hypothetical 2030 distribution is then obtained by apply- ing three main exogenous changes to the initial distribution: (i) demographic changes, including ageing and shifts in the skill composition of the popula- tion; (ii) shifts in the sectoral composition of employment; and (iii) economic growth, including changes in relative wages across skills and sectors.

---

[3] Throughout the chapter, when we talk about global distribution, we are referring to the GIDD's sample covering 91 per cent of the world population.

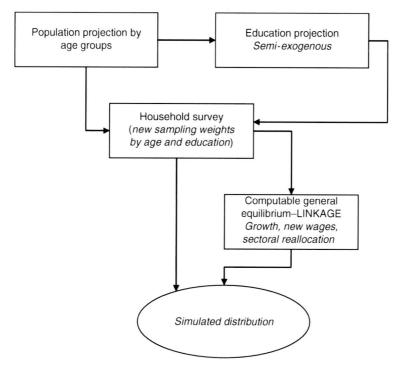

Figure 5.1. *Global income distribution dynamics (GIDD) methodological framework*

The empirical framework is depicted in Figure 5.1. Our simulations will include the expected changes in the shares of population by groups formed by age and education characteristics (top boxes of Figure 5.1). The future changes in population shares by age (upper left part of Figure 5.1) are taken as exogenous from the population projections provided by the World Bank's Development Data Groups. Therefore, we assume that fertility decisions and mortality rates are determined outside the model. The change in shares of the population by education groups incorporates the expected demographic changes (linking arrow from top left box to top right box in Figure 5.1). Next, new sets of population shares by age and education subgroups are computed, and household sampling weights are rescaled according to the demographic and educational changes above (larger box in the middle of Figure 5.1). In a second step, the demographic changes will impact overall labour supply by age and skill groups. These changes are incorporated into the CGE model to simulate overall economic growth, growth in relative incomes by education groups, and sector reallocation of labour (link between the middle and bottom rectangles). Finally, the results of the CGE are passed on to the reweighted household survey (bottom link in Figure 5.1).

In reality, these changes take place simultaneously; however, in the GIDD's simplified framework, they are accommodated in a sequential fashion. In the first step, total population in each country is expanded until it reaches the World Bank's projections for 2030. The structure of the population is also changed; for example, as fertility rates decrease and life expectancy increases, older age cohorts will become larger in many countries. To accommodate these changes in the survey data, larger weights have been assigned to older people than those assigned to younger individuals.[4] In the next step, workers move from traditional agricultural sectors to more dynamic industrial and service sectors, and new incomes are estimated for these movers. Finally, consistent with an overall growth rate of real income per capita, changes in labour remuneration by skill level and sector are applied to each worker in the sample depending on their education and sector of employment. The number of workers changing sector of occupation and the growth differential in labour remuneration, which are used to 'shock' the micro data, are consistent with the results of the CGE model described in the previous section. (Note that the outcomes of the CGE model are also influenced by the same demographic changes described above.)

The sequential changes described above reshape national income distribution under a set of strong assumptions. In particular, income inequality within population subgroups (formed by age, skills, and sector of employment) is assumed to be constant over the period. Moreover, data limitations affect estimates of the initial inequality and its evolution. Although consumption expenditure is a more reliable welfare measure than income, and its distribution is normally more equal than the distribution of income, consumption data are not available for all countries' surveys. To achieve a global picture, the present study had to include countries for which only income data were available. Finally, measurement errors implicit in purchasing power parity (PPP) exchange rates, which have been used to convert local currency units, also affect comparability across countries.

The resulting income distribution should thus not be seen as a *forecast* of what the future distribution might look like; instead, it should be interpreted

---

[4] In fact, weights are not changed for each single individual but for whole households. Therefore, in the example in the text, households whose heads are older are assigned larger weights than households with younger heads. For a complete technical description of this reweighting procedure, which in addition to the age structure also involves education attainments, see Bussolo, De Hoyos, and Medvedev 2007.

as the result of an exercise that captures the *ceteris paribus* distributional effect of demographic, sectoral, and economic changes.

THE WORLD ECONOMY IN 2030

Developing countries will grow faster owing to favourable demographic and productivity trends

Under the baseline scenario of this chapter, global GDP grows at an average annual rate of 2.9 per cent between 2005 and 2030.[5] Measured at constant 2001 prices, the global economy would reach US$75 trillion in 2030 up from US$35 trillion in 2005, an overall increase of some 2.1 times (Figure 5.2). The developing country GDP would jump from US$8 trillion to US$24.3 trillion, increasing its global share of output from 23 per cent to 33 per cent.[6]

The accelerated growth path of many developing countries is a consequence, in the authors' judgement, of the combination of improved initial

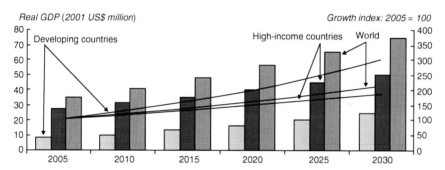

Figure 5.2. *Developing countries will account for a larger portion of world output in the coming decade*

Notes: Bars are measured on the left axis; lines are measured on the right axis.

Source: World Bank simulations using the LINKAGE model.

---

[5] This represents a modest acceleration of what was observed between 1980 and 2005. For high-income countries, projected growth rates decrease slightly from 2.0 to 1.9, but a more significant acceleration is attributed to developing countries from 2.4 to 3.1.
[6] Evaluated at 2001 market exchange rates and constant prices. The rapidly emerging economies would normally be associated with rising real exchange rates, so their weight in the global economy will actually be measurably higher in value terms than in constant price volume terms.

conditions, better policies, demographic trends, and the still wide gap in productivity—relative to high-income countries. The influence of these factors on growth is already visible in the recent performance. If one decomposes the last twenty-five years in two periods—1980–2000 and 2000–5—average growth in developing countries jumped from 3.2 per cent per year in the first period to 5 per cent per year in the second. Over time, China and India played a major role in the quickening pace of growth in the developing world: the contribution of the two giants to growth of low- and middle-income countries has increased from 45 per cent in the first period to 50 per cent in the second (Figure 5.3). The baseline scenario envisions a slight slowing of this recent performance: over the next twenty-four years, China and India are likely to account for 18 per cent of growth in global output and 46 per cent of growth in real output of today's low- and high-middle income countries.

Given their importance in explaining the projected growth rates, demographic and productivity future trends deserve some further consideration. Assumptions about technological changes and the ensuing productivity growth are subject to a wide range of possibilities. There is no agreement on how to interpret recent productivity growth, let alone how to anticipate future patterns. The macro assumptions on productivity built into the fore-

Share of developing countries in real global output (percentage)

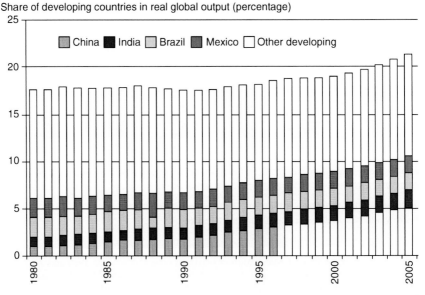

Figure 5.3. *Share of developing countries to global output has increased, with China and India playing a major role*

Source: World Bank simulation using the LINKAGE model.

cast are largely consistent with the estimates of total factor productivity (TFP) growth from the literature (see, for example, Bosworth and Collins 2003). The world saw a period of very rapid TFP growth in the 1960s, followed by a decade of stagnation coinciding with the energy crisis of the 1970s, recovery to an estimated rate of 0.8 percentage points per year in the 1980s and 1990s, and an acceleration in the 2000s. There have been large variations across regions. The central scenario assumes a long-term rate of TFP growth in the range 1.0 to 1.4 for the high-income countries, somewhat on the high end of the Bosworth and Collins estimates. The range for developing countries is somewhat wider— between 0.7 and 2.9 toward 2015 and declining slowly thereafter as the positive impacts of rural-to-urban migration fade.

TFP improvements are modelled as labour-augmenting productivity (Harrod-neutral technical change), which is skill neutral but sector biased. Consistent with the existing literature, productivity in agriculture expands at an average annual rate of 2.5 per cent in all countries. Improvements in labour productivity take place at a much faster pace in manufacturing, where China and India register annual increases of 15 per cent for manufacturing sectors (for comparison, US manufacturing productivity grows at 2.5 per cent per year over the same period).

Two significant demographic changes are occurring at the moment: (i) virtually all of the increase in global population will be in developing countries; and (ii) the population in today's high-income countries and some developing countries, such as China and Russia, will become significantly older. Changing demographics weigh heavily on the results influencing the growth of employment, demand trends, and changes in savings and investment behaviour (and even productivity). The world will add 1.5 billion persons to its population between 2005 and 2030, growing from (about) 6.5 billion to 8 billion. Roughly 12 per cent will be living in high-income countries, down sharply from the 18 per cent in 1980 and 14.5 per cent in 2005 (see Figure 5.4). Due to the differential in fertility rates, all but 40 million of this growth in population will occur in developing countries. While this represents a substantial increase in the number of persons, with concomitant effects on already scarce resources, it also represents a slowing of the world population growth that added 2 billion persons between 1980 and 2005.

The largest contribution to the nearly 1.5 billion population increase in developing regions can be attributed to India, representing 320 million additional persons, and to sub-Saharan Africa (excluding Nigeria and South Africa), with a similar increment of 320 million—each contributing 20 per cent to the global increase. Despite China's one-child policy and overall ageing population, the momentum of the current population will generate 170 million additional Chinese by 2030, another 11 per cent of the global increase.

Population (billion)

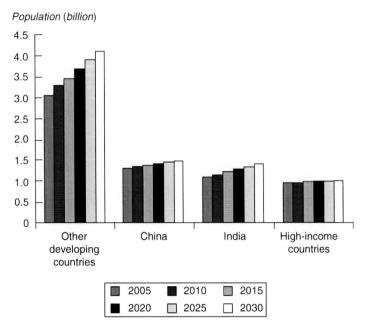

Figure 5.4. *World population growth will be concentrated in developing countries in the coming decades*

Sources: UN Population Division; World Bank Development Data Groups; World Bank calculations.

This disparity in population trends is also reflected in divergent paths for labour force and employment across developing and developed countries. Developed countries' employment growth, though positive until 2010 at about 1.2 million new jobs per year, becomes negative thereafter, with an average loss of about 700,000 jobs between 2010 and 2015, jumping to an annual average loss of over 3.2 million jobs between 2025 and 2030.[7] Labour force growth is still rapid in developing countries, though on a declining trend throughout the period.

For developing countries, ageing populations (as defined by the number of elderly per 100 workers) will rise only slowly from current levels until about 2020, but will start accelerating modestly afterwards to reach a level of nearly nineteen per 100 starting from twelve per 100 in 2005. This is still well below the developed-country average of thirty today, and differs widely across regions. China will see a sharper rise in its elderly dependency rate, moving from twelve per 100 currently to twenty-five per 100 by 2030. This could be

[7] This latter number represents a decline of about 1 per cent per year.

contrasted with India, which has a level similar to China's at eleven per 100, but rising to only sixteen per 100 by 2030.[8]

Per capita incomes will begin to converge across countries

Under the growth scenario just described, and using PPP exchange rates,[9] the speed of convergence between developing- and developed-country incomes would be noticeable, but perhaps not major. At today's income in PPP terms, the average developing-country resident receives about 16 per cent of the average income of high-income countries—US$4,800 versus US$29,700 (Figure 5.5). This ratio would rise to 23 per cent in twenty-five years' time, representing an average developing-country income of US$12,200 versus US $54,000 for high-income countries.

There is great variance across countries. Chinese incomes would rise from 19 per cent of the average high-income level to 48 per cent (in PPP terms), a significant narrowing of the gap, and would achieve an average income close to the lower range of today's poorest high-income countries. Per capita incomes in India are likely to rise much more slowly—from 11 per cent in 2005 to 17 per cent in 2030—due to faster population growth and more measured expansion in real GDP. There would be a further falling behind in sub-Saharan Africa with its modest per capita growth below the high-income average, and Latin America would see little if any convergence on average. As the previous twenty-five years have shown, there is plenty of scope for surprises and countries doing significantly better, even compared with countries with similar initial conditions.

---

[8] For developed economies, the standard economic impacts of slowing population growth and ageing suggest that aggregate savings will decline, all else being equal, as ageing populations tend to dis-save or consume out of existing assets. This would tend to decrease the amount of savings available for developed countries. The evidence for this dis-saving is, however, mixed. Ageing populations can have other consequences. Productivity growth could be higher in economies with rapid increases in the number of youth joining the labour force. They can also be associated with changes in consumer behaviour with less demand for food and educational services and a greater demand for leisure and health services Bryant 2004; Helliwell 2004; McKibbin 2005; Tyers and Shi 2005. There could also be fiscal implications, as promises to earlier generations in terms of social welfare benefits prove hard to finance with a lower tax base. This eventually could involve a combination of lower benefits and delay of retirement age, or other forms of higher labour force participation rates by the elderly.

[9] Using the market dollar exchange rate of an economy provides a biased estimate of individual well-being because prices differ substantially across economies—particularly for non-traded goods such as personal and housing services. For this reason, it is more appropriate to use the PPP exchange rates, which take into account these differences in prices.

Index: high-income countries = 100

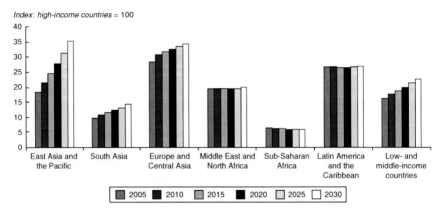

Figure 5.5. *In some developing regions, per capita incomes will begin to converge with those in high-income countries*

Note: Ratio of purchasing power parity (PPP)-adjusted per capita incomes relative to high-income average. PPPs fixed at base year (2001) level.

Source: World Bank simulations using the LINKAGE model.

The rather modest level of convergence overall, nevertheless, obscures the fact that market opportunities for both developed and developing countries will increase dramatically as the sheer size of the population of developing countries ensures the growth of a very significant middle and upper class likely to rival the purchasing power of today's high-income consumer.[10] Thus, notwithstanding the challenge that poverty will continue to hold on the global community, the wider spread of wealth globally will also provide greater means to deal more substantively with poverty and other global concerns such as the environment and health.

ACCELERATED GROWTH AND CHANGES IN PRODUCTION AND TRADE STRUCTURE: CONSEQUENCES FOR FACTOR PRICES

The previous sections have shown that, under baseline conditions, growth in China and India will account for a large share of global output. Similarly, as both of the giants are already major participants in the global trade arena, the continued expansion of Chinese and Indian economies is likely to have

[10] See below for a more detailed discussion of the expanding middle class.

far-reaching consequences for world trade. This section highlights four main developments: increasing orientation of the giants' economies towards services, growing demand for skilled workers, further improvements in competitiveness of manufactured goods, and rising imports of agricultural products from high-income countries.

As average incomes of developing countries converge to OECD levels, demand for services in the developing world is likely to increase faster than in high-income countries because services tend to have higher income elasticities than agricultural and manufactured products. Some of this catch-up will be moderated by growing demand for health and public services by the ageing OECD populations but, overall, faster growth in low- and high-middle-income countries—and particularly China and India—is likely to translate into a more pronounced shift of production towards service activities (Figure 5.6).

In order to accommodate this growing share of services in total output, the contribution of other sectors to aggregate production will decrease. For developing countries, the expansion is likely to come at the cost of agricultural output: China's agricultural output share is likely to decrease by more than one-half, while India's agricultural production share could decline by one-third. This is driven by sustained large increases in manufacturing productivity in both countries, which underpin their leading growth performance. The

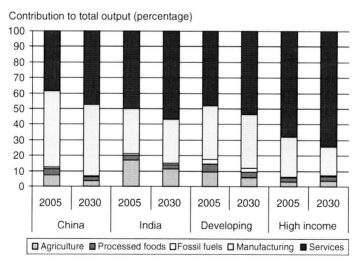

Figure 5.6. *Shift into services is more pronounced in China and India*

Source: World Bank simulation using the LINKAGE model.

fast pace of productivity growth in manufacturing sectors allows their share of total output to remain roughly constant between 2005 and 2030, despite the demand-driven pulling of resources into the service sectors. For the high-income countries, the converse is likely to be true. Because productivity in manufacturing among OECD countries grows more slowly, the share of manufacturing in total output declines from 26 per cent in 2005 to 19 per cent in 2030.

The changing sectoral structure of Chinese and Indian economies is likely to have profound effects on factor returns. Because services tend to be more skill intensive than other sectors, increasing demand for services is likely to exert upward pressure on skilled wages. In 2005, 79 per cent (China) and 91 per cent (India) of the total skilled wage bill was paid to service sector workers, and these shares could rise further by 2030. Demand for skilled workers over the coming decades is likely to be particularly acute in China, where slower population growth will add to the relative scarcity of white-collar employees. Improvements in education service provision, combined with the fact that younger cohorts tend to be better educated than their older colleagues, are likely to lessen some of the pressures in the labour market. None the less, our baseline scenario envisions an increasing relative scarcity of skilled workers in China and India (as well as most of the developing world) and, as a result, the skill premium is expected to rise (Figure 5.7). This widening of wage gaps could lead to increasing inequality within fast-growing economies, although such pressures could be counteracted by a host of effects,

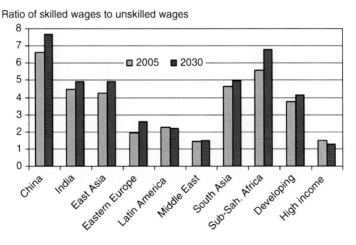

Figure 5.7. *Skill premiums are likely to rise across the developing world*
Source: World Bank simulation using the LINKAGE model.

including falling rural–urban wage differentials, decrease in the gender wage gap, or changing returns to other worker characteristics.

Productivity growth, changing sectoral structure, and widening skill premiums lead to important changes in the international competitiveness of developing countries. Low- and middle-income nations solidify their comparative advantage in exports of manufactured goods, which rise from 79 per cent to 88 per cent of total merchandise exports between 2005 and 2030 (Figure 5.8). The trend is even more pronounced in China and India, which benefit from a TFP growth significantly above the developing country average. In our scenario, 97 per cent of Chinese and 98 per cent of Indian merchandise exports are likely to originate from manufacturing sectors. As high-income countries lose competitiveness in the manufacturing sector due to their lower productivity, the share of manufacturing products in their total exports is likely to decline significantly.

The result that agricultural products become a more important component of high-income countries' exports might seem counter-intuitive at first glance. There are two main reasons for this development. First, our baseline does not include any significant removal of domestic support in agriculture, which allows high-income farm producers to sell a significant portion of their output on the world markets. Second, as developing countries, led by China and India, gain competitiveness in the manufacturing sector, the relative price

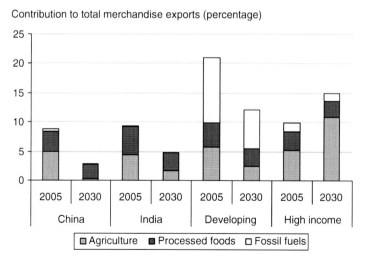

Figure 5.8. *Developing-country exports will be increasingly concentrated in manufactured goods*

Source: World Bank simulation using the LINKAGE model.

Table 5.1. *World trade shares (percentage)*

	Agriculture		Processed foods		Fossil fuels		Manufacturing		Services		Total	
	2005	2030	2005	2030	2005	2030	2005	2030	2005	2030	2005	2030
Export shares												
China	10	1	11	17	1	0	11	21	1	0	9	16
India	1	0	1	2	0	0	1	3	1	0	1	2
East Asia (excluding China)	4	2	8	12	6	7	6	10	2	0	6	8
Eastern Europe	4	1	6	9	13	14	6	8	4	1	6	7
Latin America	15	10	12	14	11	13	6	8	3	0	6	7
Middle East	1	1	2	1	39	38	3	6	3	1	4	5
South Asia (excluding India)	1	1	1	1	0	0	1	1	0	0	0	1
Sub-Saharan-African	3	2	3	3	9	12	1	2	1	0	1	2
Developing	38	19	43	60	79	84	34	60	15	2	33	48
High income	62	81	57	40	21	16	66	40	85	98	67	52
Import shares												
China	24	45	1	1	4	12	8	8	5	14	7	11
India	1	1	1	1	4	6	1	1	1	2	1	1
East Asia (excluding China)	4	4	6	6	3	4	4	6	5	8	4	6
Eastern Europe	8	11	8	7	9	12	6	6	5	8	6	7
Latin America	7	8	6	5	3	3	6	7	6	9	6	7
Middle East	6	6	5	7	1	1	4	4	5	8	4	5
South Asia (excluding India)	1	0	1	1	0	0	0	1	1	1	0	1
Sub-Saharan-African	2	2	2	2	1	1	1	1	2	4	2	2
Developing	53	77	30	31	26	39	30	35	30	54	31	40
High income	47	23	70	69	74	61	70	65	70	46	69	60

Source: World Bank simulation using the LINKAGE model.

of agricultural products imported from high-income countries declines. This is illustrated in Table 5.1, which shows global market shares for China and India, as well as the standard set of World Bank defined regions. While the global market shares in exports of manufactured goods in China double and in India triple, their significance as exporters in world agricultural markets diminishes even more dramatically. Furthermore, while India's share of global food imports does not change appreciably, by 2030 China could account for a large share of total imports of agriculture and processed food. It is important to note that the numbers in Table 5.1 are not forecasts, and are predicated on a number of assumptions, including the same rate of productivity improvement in farm products across high-income and developing countries. If, on the other hand, China's productivity growth in agriculture is able to follow the path of its manufacturing productivity more closely, the relative price of imported agriculture would rise and limit the country's willingness to purchase agricultural products from abroad.[11]

The last two columns of Table 5.1 show that the exports of low- and high-middle-income countries could account for one-half of total global exports by 2030, up from one-third in 2005. This expansion is driven to a large extent by the growth in trade originating in China and other Asian countries, with the former already the world's second leading exporter in 2005 behind high-income European countries. This growing importance of developing countries is also reflected in changes in the direction of trade, which is also likely to undergo significant shifts over the next twenty-five years. Figures 5.9 and 5.10 show that the faster pace of growth in developing countries translates into their rise as destinations for Chinese and Indian exports. At the same time, China and India buy many more of their manufacturing imports from developing countries, while agricultural imports are increasingly sourced from high-income countries (consistent with the analysis above). Much of the growing trade dependence between developing countries is due to trade in intermediate goods—today, 63 per cent of China's imports are classified as intermediate goods, with roughly half of them coming in the form of parts and components. With the increasing orientation of developing countries towards manufacturing sectors, these linkages are likely to become even stronger in 2030.

SLOWER GROWTH IN CHINA AND INDIA: CONSEQUENCES FOR THE GLOBAL ECONOMY

The previous sections have argued that the pace of growth in China and India over the next twenty-five years is likely to outpace the growth in the rest of the developing world significantly, driven to a large extent by rapid improvements in productivity. How would our outlook on the global economy change if, instead, productivity in the two giants grew at a rate equal to the developing-country average? In this section, we present an illustrative simulation where the 2015–30 TFP growth rate in China and India is set to the average TFP growth in low- and middle-income countries excluding the two giants,

---

[11] An additional factor influencing the results is the relative land scarcity in China. Since the 1980s, about 0.7 per cent of arable farmland has been converted to non-agricultural use annually—including for roads, factories, and residential and business construction.

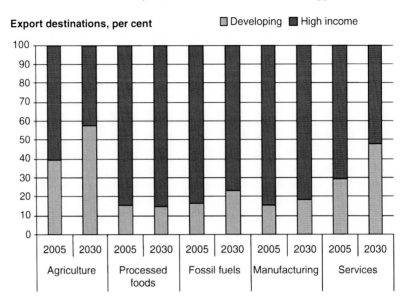

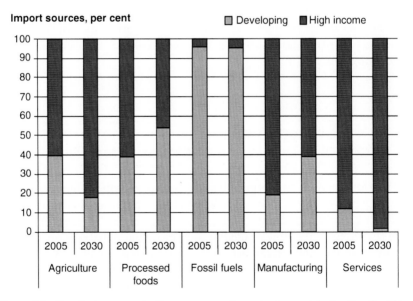

Figure 5.9. *Developing countries become a more important export destination for China*

Source: World Bank simulation using the LINKAGE model.

Export destinations, per cent

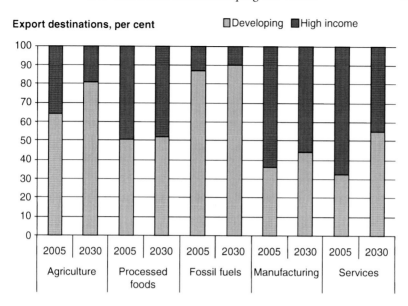

Import sources, per cent

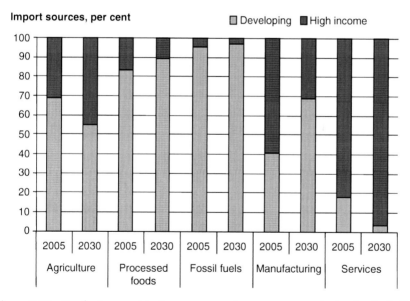

Figure 5.10. *Developing countries become a more important export destination for India*
Source: World Bank simulation using the LINKAGE model.

roughly 1 per cent per year.[12] In addition, foreign saving is kept at baseline levels to sterilize the effects of international capital mobility and to focus the analysis on the spillover effects through international trade.

In this simulation, China's 2005–30 real GDP growth declines from 5.8 per cent to 5.2 per cent, while that of India is reduced from 4.9 per cent to 4.4 per cent. World GDP growth over the same period declines by 0.06 per cent per year; this effect is mostly driven by a reduced contribution of the giants to global output (direct effects). The indirect effects—spillovers to other countries through changing trade patterns and world prices—have only minor impacts on real GDP. The main reason for this result is that the growth process is determined by accumulation of labour and capital, and TFP improvements. Slower growth in China and India does not have an impact on labour force growth or capital accumulation in other countries, and affects TFP only marginally through reduced openness.[13] However, effects on consumption are more pronounced (Figure 5.11). In 2030, global consumption is 1 per cent lower relative to the baseline, although most of the decline is accounted for by the large losses in China and India. If the two giants are removed from the global aggregate, consumption losses are reduced to 0.2 per cent. In relative terms, consumption in developing countries (excluding China and India) and high-income countries declines by the same amount (0.2 per cent), but the aggregate losses are much more pronounced in high-income countries, where consumption in 2030 is lower by US$66 billion.

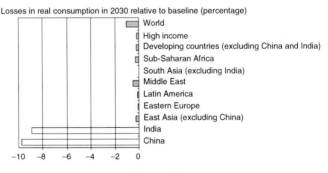

Losses in real consumption in 2030 relative to baseline (percentage)

World
High income
Developing countries (excluding China and India)
Sub-Saharan Africa
South Asia (excluding India)
Middle East
Latin America
Eastern Europe
East Asia (excluding China)
India
China

Figure 5.11. *Global consumption declines and high-income countries lose more*

Source: World Bank simulation using the LINKAGE model.

---

[12] The TFP growth rate of all low- and middle-income countries including China and India over the same period in the baseline is 1.5 per cent per year.

[13] The model incorporates a feedback mechanism from increases in the exports-to-GDP ratio to total factor productivity. Slower growth in China and India leads to lower volumes of global trade, which reduces the positive productivity spillovers from openness.

There are two factors responsible for the fall in global consumption outside China and India: on the one hand, consumers in the rest of the world must now pay higher prices for Chinese and Indian products (which are produced using less efficient technologies) and, on the other hand, producers in these countries receive lower prices for the products they sell to China and India due to reduced global demand.

GLOBAL INCOME DISTRIBUTION: CHINA, INDIA, AND THE MIDDLE CLASS

As briefly described in the methodology section, the demographic shifts and economic changes simulated with the CGE model are used to 'shock' individual household incomes and a new counterfactual global income distribution for 2030 is estimated.[14] By comparing the simulated and the initial global income distributions, one can infer the importance of China and India in explaining some of the key changes in global distribution as the reduction of global inequality and the emergence of a global middle class.

Global income inequality

If the world were a single country, it would be one of the worst distributed,[15] with a Gini coefficient of 0.68 (see Table 5.2), well above the world's simple average of 0.39 and the population-weighted average of 0.35. The fact that global inequality is higher than the inequality level within most countries is explained by disparities in average incomes *between* countries. This is also clear from the results of two different population decomposition[16] exercises:

---

[14] It is worth noticing that the results of our model are not a forecast of future income distribution: the GIDD creates, within a global CGE-micro-simulation framework, a hypothetical income distribution accommodating assumptions regarding the future rate of population growth, human capital accumulation, sectoral allocation, and GDP growth; see Bussolo, De Hoyos, and Medvedev 2007.

[15] Only Haiti, with a Gini coefficient of 0.71, showed more inequality than the world as a whole in 2000.

[16] A simple way of evaluating the importance of differences in average incomes between countries versus differences in incomes within countries is to undertake inequality decomposition by population subgroups. A subgroup decomposition exercise separates or partitions the population—in this case, the world population—into mutually exclusive groups and assesses how much inequality is accounted for by difference in incomes between groups versus within these groups (Mookherjee and Shorrocks 1982). The importance of a particular characteristic

Table 5.2. *Subgroup decomposition of global income inequality*

Year	Global inequality Gini	Global inequality Theil	Subgroups Countries		Subgroups China–India versus RoW	
2000	0.68	0.93	Between	0.69	Between	0.17
				(0.75)		(0.18)
			Within	0.23	Within	0.76
				(0.25)		(0.82)
2030	0.63	0.77	Between	0.54	Between	0.03
				(0.70)		(0.04)
			Within	0.23	Within	0.74
				(0.30)		(0.96)

Notes: Decomposition results are based on the Theil index (generalized entropy index with aversion parameter equal to 1) decomposition. Proportion of total income inequality between brackets.

Source: Authors' calculations using the global income distribution dynamics (GIDD) model.

(i) defining the subgroups as countries; and (ii) defining two subgroups, China and India, versus the rest of the world. The results show that a measure of international inequality based on countries' average incomes, completely ignoring within-country differences in incomes, would capture three-quarters of total global inequality in 2000. In other words, eliminating all within-country income differences would bring global income inequality down by 25 per cent. In a second exercise, the world's population is partitioned in two subgroups, one containing the populations of China and India and the other the citizens from the rest of the world. This decomposition shows that, in 2000, comparing average incomes of the Chinese and Indian group with average income in the rest of the world (RoW) would be enough to capture 18 per cent of total income inequality (Table 5.2).

The importance of China and India becomes more significant when considering changes between the 2000 and 2030 global distributions. By 2030, the Gini for global income distribution is five points lower than its level in 2000. According to the decomposition results, the reduction in inequality between 2000 and 2030 is entirely accounted for by a reduction in disparities in average incomes across countries. Since reductions in average incomes differentials are weighted by population, *a rapid growth of poor countries like China and India can have a great impact on global inequality.*

As a matter of fact, the decomposition results for China and India versus RoW shows that 14 out of a total of 16 points reduction in the Theil index

determining the partition rule will be captured by the proportion of inequality that can be accounted for by differences in average incomes between groups (Cowell and Jenkins 1995).

between 2000 and 2030 are explained by a reduction in inequality in average incomes between the Chinese and Indian group versus RoW (compare the result of 0.17 Theil points explained by China and India in 2000 with the 0.03 points for 2030). In other words, average incomes in China and India are closer to the world's average in 2030 than they were in 2000.

The emergence of the global middle class

In 2030, according to our baseline, 16.1 per cent of the world population will belong to what can be called a 'global middle class', up from 7.6 per cent in 2000. That is, in 2030, more than 1 billion people in developing countries will buy cars, engage in international tourism, demand world-class products, and require international standards for higher education. Compare that with only 250 million people in developing countries who had access to these kinds of living standards in 2000. This large middle class will create rapidly growing markets for international products and services—and become a new force in domestic politics.

The *global middle class* is defined here as in Milanovic and Yitzhaki 2002. The authors propose disaggregating the world population into three categories: the poor, the middle class, and the rich, where the middle class is defined by two absolute thresholds equal to the per capita incomes of Brazil and Italy.[17] By assigning an individual to the global middle class according to his or her income, Table 5.3 shows the evolution of this income group and contrasts it with the groups of the poor and the rich.[18] This table also shows that the great majority of the global middle-class entrants are citizens of developing countries; hence, tomorrow's global middle class will comprise, primarily, the citizens from today's poor countries. The total increase in the global middle class is explained by (i) population growth rates of cohorts within this class that are above the world average; and (ii) by higher economic growth rates in developing countries that pull their citizens out of *poverty* and into the global middle class. The population growth rates of households within the global middle class (as classified in 2000) was relatively low, with an average rate of 18 per cent over the entire period, as opposed to the world average of 32 per cent. Therefore, the great majority of the increase in the

[17] Italy's per capita income was used as the upper threshold because it was the country with the lowest income among the G7; Brazil's per capita income corresponded to the official poverty line used in rich countries such as the USA and Germany (about PPP $10 per capita per day).

[18] Notice that the definition of 'poor' used here is far from being comparable to the standard '$1 per day' definition.

Table 5.3. *The global middle class is growing and its composition is changing*

	Shares				Growth rates (percentage 2000–30)	
	2000		2030			
	Population	Income	Population	Income	Population	Income
Poor	82.0	28.7	63.0	17.0	2	29
Middle class, of which:	7.6	13.8	16.1	14.0	178	0
Developed-country nationals	3.5	6.8	1.2	1.0	−52	−2
Developing-country nationals	4.1	7.0	14.6	12.9	363	3
Rich	10.5	57.5	20.9	69.0	163	28
Total	100.0	100.0	100.0	100.0	32	109

Notes: Totals may not add up to 100 because of rounding up and down. The 'poor' are defined as individuals with an income below the average of Brazil; the middle class is defined as individuals with an income between the per capita incomes of Brazil and Italy; the rich are those individuals with incomes at or above the average income in Italy. Thresholds of Brazil and Italy are annual per capita incomes (2000 PPP) of US$3,914 and US$16,746.

Source: Authors' calculations using the global income distribution dynamics (GIDD) model.

global middle class is explained by high economic growth rates taking place in developing countries.

How much of the expected increase in the global middle class is attributable to the economic performance of China and India? Figure 5.12 divides the global middle class into citizens from China, India, and RoW. In 2000, Chinese nationals comprised only 13.5 per cent of the global middle class, and no Indians belonged to this group.[19] By 2030, citizens from China and India had a combined share of 44 per cent of the global middle class, with the great majority (38 per cent) being Chinese; in fact, half of the total 740 million new entrants into the global middle class will be Chinese nationals.

The importance of China and India in the global middle class will depend on their economic and population growth rates and the changes in their within-country income inequality. For instance, in China, 56 million people belonged to the global middle class in 2000, each of them earning more than 90 per cent of all Chinese citizens; that is, they belonged to the richest decile. By 2030, assuming income inequality in China remains constant, there will be 361 million Chinese in the global middle class, and their earnings will range

[19] It is quite likely that in reality some Indians are within the middle- and high-income ranges; nevertheless, by the way the Indian Household Survey data are being collected, *outliers* high-income citizens are not captured at all.

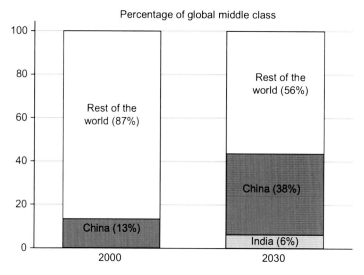

Figure 5.12. *Chinese and Indian weight in the global middle class*
Source: Authors' calculations.

from the sixth to the ninth decile of Chinese national income distribution. Chinese members of the global middle class will no longer be among the richest Chinese citizens but will probably be considered to be upper middle class in their country. On the other hand, if China manages to reduce income disparities, making middle-income cohorts fatter, they would contribute even further to the global middle class.

To inspect these effects in greater detail, in Figure 5.13 we fit a non-parametric kernel income density for China, India, and the world population in 2000 and 2030. Figure 5.13 consistently shows the proportion of world population to Chinese and Indian populations; hence, the Chinese and Indian densities can be interpreted as the probabilities of being within the different income ranges and being Chinese and Indian citizens, respectively. Figure 5.13 highlights several interesting features. In 2000, the mode of global income distribution (1993 PPP $114)—that is, the income value that more individuals in the world were receiving—was largely determined by the earnings level of a high proportion of Indian upper-middle-class citizens and members of the Chinese lower middle-class (overlapping of the Chinese and Indian income densities in Figure 5.13). Focusing on the country-specific distributions, we can see that, in 2000, incomes were less skewed in India compared with China (India's distribution had a larger density around the mean); in 2000, the Gini coefficient for India was equal to 0.29 compared with

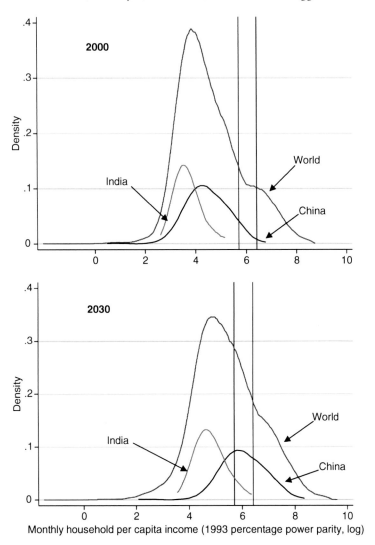

Figure 5.13. *China, India, and world income distribution, 2000 and 2030*

Source: Authors' calculation using the global income distribution dynamics (GIDD) model.

a value of 0.42 in China. In fact, due to the relatively unequal distribution in China, its richest citizens could be part of the global middle class in 2000. By year 2030, after several years of growth rates higher than the world average, China becomes the country that accounted for more global middle-class members—hence, reshaping global distribution.

Growth in China causes a decrease in the global density around the mode and an increase in the probability of being in income ranges above it. Although India will experience above-world-average growth rates in per capita incomes, the differential is not sufficiently large to make this country move significantly along the global distribution. Nevertheless, given that the thresholds defining the global middle class are absolute values, India's growth also results in an increase of numbers in the global middle class. India's entrance into the global middle class is also partly explained by an increase in India's income inequality, expanding the upper tail of its distribution further to the right along the global density.[20] This increase in income dispersion helps the richest 5 per cent of Indian citizens to enter the global middle class. Growth in China and India—and, to a lesser extent, changes in their within-country inequality—will have, as an effect, a tremendous increase in the global middle class, resulting in a substantial improvement in global income inequality.

THE CONSEQUENCES OF A GROWING GLOBAL MIDDLE CLASS

The ascent of hundreds of millions of Chinese, Indians, and nationals from other developing countries into the global middle class will produce a large group of people in the developing world who can afford, and will demand access to, the standards of living that were previously reserved mainly for the residents of high-income countries. This might have two major implications: the rise in demand for international goods and services, and the increase in pressures for policies that favour global integration.

Much of the effect of middle-class expansion on the world economy will be realized through a changing demand for goods. The fact that the middle class will be growing at a much faster rate than the overall population (Table 5.3) implies that multinational enterprises will be able to market their products to a much larger audience in 2030 than they do today. Furthermore, the rules of this new global marketplace will be increasingly determined by the tastes and preferences of the developing world, particularly the desires of consumers in China and, to a lesser extent, India. Therefore, while most of the world's purchasing power will continue to be concentrated in the OECD countries, the global economic influence of those countries will diminish considerably.

---

[20] India's inequality passes from a Gini of 0.29 in 2000 to 0.32 in 2030.

By 2030, marketing to the developing world will be a much more important strategy for multinationals than it is today.

The rise of the global middle class will also affect demand for services. For example, given the strong correlation between income and determinants of human capital accumulation such as health and levels of education, the growing middle class is likely to demand more and better health care and education. Therefore, the increased emphasis on health and education among the middle class will deepen the human capital stocks, thereby establishing the foundations for continued growth in the developing countries. However, the increasing demand for education and health is likely to put pressure on the budgets of developing-country governments and will require heightened attention to policy in the future.

Today, the median voter in most developing countries is unlikely to be a member of the global middle class; by 2030, the middle class members in developing countries will constitute a significant share of their home population, increasing the likelihood of finding the median voter among them. In China, for example, the median and mode earners will be members of the global middle class in 2030 (Figure 5.13). These changes are likely to have an impact on the domestic policy arena. Some evidence points to a correlation between rising incomes and a shift in demand towards more globalization supportive policies. Other policy goals—among them improved transparency, intensified anti-corruption efforts, and demand for a more open society and cleaner environment—are also likely to move to the forefront of the policy agenda with the expansion of the middle class.

CONCLUSIONS

This chapter analysed, in an *ex ante* fashion, the effects that economic expansion in China and India will have on global growth and global income distribution. The results under the baseline scenario show that, between 2005 and 2030, global GDP more than doubles, with China and India accounting for a significant share (18 per cent) of global expansion. In terms of income per capita, in 2005, the average Chinese person had an income one-fifth of the amount that the average citizen of a high-income country would earn and by 2030 this gap narrows to almost one-half. Due to faster population growth and more measured expansion in real GDP, per capita incomes in India are likely to rise much more slowly than in China, catching up from one-tenth of average incomes in rich countries in 2005 to less than one-sixth in 2030. This strong economic expansion of China and India also explains two key features of the evolution of global income distribution in the next twenty-five years: (i) a reduction of global inequality; and (ii) the emergence of a large 'global' middle class. According to our simulations, 4.3 of the 5 points reduction of the global Gini are due to the decline in income differences between Chinese and Indian citizens and the rest of the world. Besides, China, by itself, will account for almost half of the total increase in the global middle class (310 million out of the total 740 million new entrants).

These results highlight the fact that aggregate indicators of inequality in the global distribution of income depend heavily on changes between countries and much less on changes within countries. From a perspective of global inequality, this is certainly true in a situation where very populous and initially poor countries (China and India) are growing at a rate above that of rich countries. In an era of globalization, global inequality has become more policy relevant. Through easier international movement and communication, citizens in individual countries are more aware of the (economic) situation in other countries and this enhanced awareness is behind emerging political demands (for a more equal distribution of global income). Consider, for instance, the case of multilateral trade negotiations. As illustrated by the impasse in the Doha negotiations, the progress towards freer trade is currently stymied, and will take a major effort among the rich and poor countries together to realize even its limited progress. However, even though changes between countries explain much of the change in the aggregate index, a great deal is also happening within countries. These changes of income distribution at the national level are still crucial for domestic policy and the growth prospects of individual countries. Indeed, one of the main novelties of the GIDD framework consists of its modelling of within country income distribution. Although not explicitly analysed here, behind the aggregate (global) results reported in the main section of this chapter are changes in the distribution of income within all of the sixty-four countries for which individual data are available. In fact, increases of inequality within many countries contrast with the reported decrease of global inequality; however, a thorough analysis of these individual countries' trends is beyond the scope of this chapter and more information can be found in Bussolo, De Hoyos, and Medvedev 2007 and World Bank 2007.

Table 5.4. *Household surveys*

Region	Covered population	Actual population	
World	**5,513,123**	**6,076,509**	**90.73**
East Asia and Pacific	1,749,255	1,817,232	96.26
Eastern Europe and Central Asia	474,468	471,549	100.62
High-income countries	767,291	974,612	78.73
Latin America	503,418	515,069	97.74
Middle East and North Africa	192,128	276,447	69.50
South Asia	1,336,922	1,358,294	98.43
Sub-Saharan Africa	489,642	663,305	73.82

Economy	Covered population	Actual population	Coverage percentage	Data used
East Asia and Pacific	**1,749,255**	**1,817,232**	**96.26**	
China (rural)	866,670	866,670	47.69	Grouped
China (urban)	407,755	407,755	22.44	Grouped
Indonesia	209,173	206,000	11.34	Individual
Vietnam	78,670	78,500	4.32	Individual
Philippines	76,627	75,800	4.17	Grouped
Thailand	61,439	61,400	3.38	Individual
Malaysia	23,270	23,000	1.27	Grouped
Cambodia	12,744	12,700	0.70	Individual
Laos (People's Democratic Republic)	5,278	5,279	0.29	Grouped
Papua New Guinea	5,133	5,299	0.29	Grouped
Mongolia (urban)	1,576	1,576	0.09	Grouped
Mongolia (rural)	921	921	0.05	Grouped
Myanmar		47,700	2.62	Missing
Korea (Democratic Republic of)		21,900	1.21	Missing
Fiji		811	0.04	Missing
Timor-Leste		784	0.04	Missing
Solomon Islands		419	0.02	Missing
Vanuatu		191	0.01	Missing
Samoa		177	0.01	Missing
Micronesia (Federal States)		107	0.01	Missing
Tonga		100	0.01	Missing
Kiribati		91	0.00	Missing
Marshall Islands		53	0.00	Missing
Eastern Europe and Central Asia	**470,491**	**471,549**	**99.78**	
Russian Federation	146,560	146,000	30.96	Individual
Turkey	68,234	67,400	14.29	Individual
Ukraine	49,498	49,200	10.43	Grouped
Poland	38,649	38,500	8.16	Individual
Uzbekistan	24,652	24,700	5.24	Grouped
Romania	22,117	22,400	4.75	Individual

Kazakhstan	15,034	14,900	3.16	Individual
Serbia and Montenegro	10,639	8,137	1.73	Grouped
Czech Republic	10,275	10,300	2.18	Grouped
Hungary	10,226	10,200	2.16	Individual
Belarus	10,005	10,000	2.12	Grouped
Azerbaijan	8,048	8,049	1.71	Grouped
Bulgaria	7,999	8,060	1.71	Individual
Tajikistan	6,189	6,159	1.31	Individual
Slovak Republic	5,393	5,389	1.14	Grouped
Georgia	5,261	4,720	1.00	Grouped
Kyrgyz Republic	4,952	4,915	1.04	Individual
Turkmenistan	4,644	4,502	0.95	Grouped
Croatia	4,446	4,503	0.95	Grouped
Moldova	4,275	4,275	0.91	Individual
Lithuania	3,499	3,500	0.74	Individual
Armenia	3,082	3,082	0.65	Individual
Albania	3,062	3,062	0.65	Individual
Latvia	2,383	2,372	0.50	Grouped
Estonia	1,373	1,370	0.29	Individual
Bosnia and Herzegovina		3,847	0.82	Missing
Macedonia (Former Yugoslav Republic of)		2,010	0.43	Missing
High-income countries	**764,271**	**974,612**	**78.42**	
United States	282,223	282,000	28.93	Grouped
Germany	82,211	82,200	8.43	Grouped
France	58,895	58,900	6.04	Grouped
United Kingdom	58,798	59,700	6.13	Grouped
Italy	57,689	56,900	5.84	Grouped
Korea (Republic of)	47,008	47,000	4.82	Grouped
Spain	40,498	40,300	4.13	Grouped
Canada	30,771	30,800	3.16	Grouped
Netherlands	15,920	15,900	1.63	Grouped
Greece	10,905	10,900	1.12	Grouped
Belgium	10,254	10,300	1.06	Grouped
Portugal	10,129	10,200	1.05	Grouped
Sweden	8,875	8,869	0.91	Grouped
Austria	8,011	8,012	0.82	Grouped
Hong Kong (China)	6,669	6,665	0.68	Grouped
Israel	6,282	6,289	0.65	Grouped
Denmark	5,338	5,337	0.55	Grouped
Finland	5,177	5,176	0.53	Grouped
Norway	4,492	4,491	0.46	Grouped
Singapore	4,020	4,018	0.41	Grouped
New Zealand	3,864	3,858	0.40	Grouped
Ireland	3,815	3,805	0.39	Grouped
Slovenia	1,986	1,989	0.20	Grouped
Luxembourg	441	438	0.04	Grouped
Japan		127,000	13.03	Missing
Taiwan		22,200	2.28	Missing

(continued)

Table 5.4. Continued

Economy	Covered population	Actual population	Coverage percentage	Data used
Saudi Arabia		20,700	2.12	Missing
Australia		19,200	1.97	Missing
Switzerland		7,184	0.74	Missing
Puerto Rico		3,816	0.39	Missing
United Arab Emirates		3,247	0.33	Missing
Kuwait		2,190	0.22	Missing
Cyprus		694	0.07	Missing
Bahrain		672	0.07	Missing
Qatar		606	0.06	Missing
Macao (China)		444	0.05	Missing
Malta		390	0.04	Missing
Brunei Darussalam		333	0.03	Missing
Bahamas, The		301	0.03	Missing
Iceland		281	0.03	Missing
French Polynesia		236	0.02	Missing
New Caledonia		213	0.02	Missing
Netherlands Antilles		176	0.02	Missing
Guam		155	0.02	Missing
Channel Islands		147	0.02	Missing
Virgin Islands (US)		109	0.01	Missing
Antigua and Barbuda		76	0.01	Missing
Isle of Man		76	0.01	Missing
Bermuda		62	0.01	Missing
Greenland		56	0.01	Missing
Latin America	**503,418**	**515,069**	**97.74**	
Brazil	173,860	174,000	33.78	Individual
Mexico	100,088	98,000	19.03	Individual
Colombia	42,120	42,100	8.17	Individual
Argentina	36,897	36,900	7.16	Individual
Peru	25,953	26,000	5.05	Individual
Venezuela (Bolívarian Republic of)	24,418	24,300	4.72	Individual
Chile	15,412	15,400	2.99	Individual
Ecuador	12,306	12,300	2.39	Individual
Guatemala	11,166	11,200	2.17	Individual
Bolivia	8,318	8,317	1.61	Individual
Dominican Republic	8,265	8,265	1.60	Individual
Haiti	7,941	7,939	1.54	Individual
Honduras	6,423	6,424	1.25	Individual
El Salvador	6,281	6,280	1.22	Individual
Paraguay	5,468	5,346	1.04	Individual
Nicaragua	4,958	4,920	0.96	Individual
Costa Rica	3,928	3,929	0.76	Individual
Uruguay	3,343	3,342	0.65	Individual

Panama	2,949	2,950	0.57	Individual
Jamaica	2,585	2,589	0.50	Grouped
Guyana	744	744	0.14	Individual
Cuba		11,100	2.16	Missing
Trinidad and Tobago		1,285	0.25	Missing
Suriname		434	0.08	Missing
Barbados		266	0.05	Missing
Belize		250	0.05	Missing
St Lucia		156	0.03	Missing
St Vincent and the Grenadines		116	0.02	Missing
Grenada		101	0.02	Missing
Dominica		71	0.01	Missing
St Kitts and Nevis		44	0.01	Missing
Middle East and North Africa	**192,128**	**276,447**	**69.50**	
Egypt (Arab Republic of)	67,288	67,300	24.34	Individual
Iran (Islamic Republic of)	63,661	63,700	23.04	Grouped
Morocco	28,706	27,800	10.06	Grouped
Yemen (Republic of)	17,936	17,900	6.48	Individual
Tunisia	9,565	9,564	3.46	Grouped
Jordan	4,973	4,857	1.76	Individual
Algeria		30,500	11.03	Missing
Iraq		23,200	8.39	Missing
Syrian Arab Republic		16,800	6.08	Missing
Libya		5,306	1.92	Missing
Lebanon		3,398	1.23	Missing
West Bank and Gaza		2,966	1.07	Missing
Oman		2,442	0.88	Missing
Djibouti		715	0.26	Missing
South Asia	**1,336,922**	**1,358,294**	**98.43**	
India	1,021,082	1,020,000	75.09	Individual
Pakistan	142,650	138,000	10.16	Individual
Bangladesh	128,914	129,000	9.50	Individual
Nepal	24,430	24,400	1.80	Individual
Sri Lanka	19,847	19,400	1.43	Individual
Afghanistan		26,600	1.96	Missing
Bhutan		604	0.04	Missing
Maldives		290	0.02	Missing
Sub-Saharan Africa	**489,088**	**663,305**	**73.73**	
Nigeria	117,608	118,000	17.79	Individual
Ethiopia	68,527	64,300	9.69	Individual
South Africa	45,610	44,000	6.63	Individual
Tanzania	34,761	34,800	5.25	Individual
Kenya	30,094	30,700	4.63	Grouped
Uganda	24,309	24,300	3.66	Individual

(continued)

Table 5.4. Continued

Economy	Covered population	Actual population	Coverage percentage	Data used
Ghana	19,593	19,900	3.00	Grouped
Côte d'Ivoire	16,734	16,700	2.52	Individual
Madagascar	16,196	16,200	2.44	Individual
Cameroon	14,855	14,900	2.25	Individual
Zimbabwe	12,649	12,600	1.90	Grouped
Zambia	12,594	10,700	1.61	Individual
Niger	11,781	11,800	1.78	Individual
Burkina Faso	11,291	11,300	1.70	Individual
Senegal	10,342	10,300	1.55	Individual
Malawi	10,308	11,500	1.73	Grouped
Guinea	8,433	8,434	1.27	Individual
Rwanda	8,024	8,025	1.21	Individual
Burundi	6,488	6,486	0.98	Individual
Sierra Leone	4,509	4,509	0.68	Individual
Mauritania	2,643	2,645	0.40	Individual
Lesotho	1,743	1,788	0.27	Grouped
Congo (Democratic Republic of)		50,100	7.55	Missing
Sudan		32,900	4.96	Missing
Mozambique		17,900	2.70	Missing
Angola		13,800	2.08	Missing
Mali		11,600	1.75	Missing
Chad		8,216	1.24	Missing
Benin		7,197	1.09	Missing
Somalia		7,012	1.06	Missing
Togo		5,364	0.81	Missing
Central African Republic		3,777	0.57	Missing
Eritrea		3,557	0.54	Missing
Congo (Republic of)		3,438	0.52	Missing
Liberia		3,065	0.46	Missing
Namibia		1,894	0.29	Missing
Botswana		1,754	0.26	Missing
Guinea-Bissau		1,366	0.21	Missing
Gambia, The		1,316	0.20	Missing
Gabon		1,272	0.19	Missing
Mauritius		1,187	0.18	Missing
Swaziland		1,045	0.16	Missing
Comoros		540	0.08	Missing
Cape Verde		451	0.07	Missing
Equatorial Guinea		449	0.07	Missing
São Tomé and Principe		140	0.02	Missing
Seychelles		81	0.01	Missing

Table 5.5. *Structure of production, consumption, exports, and imports (percentage of total)*

	Agriculture		Processed foods		Fossil fuels		Manufacturing		Services	
	2005	2030	2005	2030	2005	2030	2005	2030	2005	2030
Production										
China	7	3	4	3	1	1	49	46	38	47
India	17	12	3	2	1	1	29	28	50	57
East Asia (excluding China)	9	6	5	4	3	2	42	43	41	44
Eastern Europe	10	7	6	5	4	3	33	31	46	54
Latin America	8	6	6	5	2	2	27	24	57	63
Middle East	8	5	3	2	12	9	19	23	58	61
South Asia (excluding India)	21	15	4	3	1	0	26	29	48	52
Sub-Saharan Africa	12	9	7	5	6	6	25	23	50	57
Developing	9	6	5	4	3	2	34	35	48	54
High-income	3	4	3	3	0	0	26	19	68	74
Exports										
China	5	0	3	2	0	0	88	97	4	0
India	4	2	4	3	0	0	76	92	16	3
East Asia	3	2	4	4	4	3	79	90	9	1
Eastern Europe	3	1	3	3	10	7	71	86	13	3
Latin America	12	8	6	5	7	6	64	80	11	1
Middle East	2	1	1	1	40	26	42	70	15	3
South Asia	7	6	3	3	1	1	77	88	12	2
Sub-Saharan Africa	8	6	5	4	24	22	54	67	10	1
Developing	5	2	4	3	10	6	71	87	10	2
High-income	4	7	2	2	1	1	68	57	24	33
Imports										
China	15	20	0	0	2	4	71	53	12	23
India	3	3	2	2	14	14	60	54	20	28
East Asia	4	3	4	2	3	2	70	70	20	23
Eastern Europe	6	8	4	2	6	5	67	62	17	21
Latin America	6	6	3	2	2	2	68	67	21	23
Middle East	7	7	4	4	1	1	65	61	23	28
South Asia	7	4	4	3	4	3	61	62	23	29
Sub-Saharan Africa	6	5	4	3	2	2	58	54	29	36
Developing	8	10	3	2	3	3	67	61	18	24
High-income	3	2	3	3	4	4	70	77	19	14
Private consumption										
China	28	17	13	9	0	0	23	18	36	55
India	33	22	7	6	0	0	13	13	46	58

(continued)

Table 5.5 Continued

	Agriculture		Processed foods		Fossil fuels		Manufacturing		Services	
	2005	2030	2005	2030	2005	2030	2005	2030	2005	2030
East Asia	17	13	12	10	0	0	20	18	51	59
Eastern Europe	15	11	12	9	1	1	19	17	53	62
Latin America	10	8	11	10	0	0	19	18	61	64
Middle East	16	13	9	8	0	0	17	17	58	63
South Asia	35	27	10	8	0	0	14	14	42	51
Sub-Saharan Africa	21	17	17	15	0	0	17	16	45	52
Developing	18	14	11	9	0	0	19	17	52	60
High-income	4	3	6	5	0	0	15	15	75	76

REFERENCES

Atkinson, A. B., and A. Brandolini (2004) 'Global World Inequality: Absolute, Relative or Intermediate'. Paper prepared for the 28th Conference of the International Association for Research in Income and Wealth, 22–8 Aug., Cork.

Bosworth, B. P., and S. M. Collins (2003) 'The Empirics of Growth: An Update', *Brookings Paper on Economic Activity*, 2: 113–206.

Bourguignon, F., and C. Morrison (2002) 'Inequality among World Citizens: 1890–1992', *American Economic Review*, 92: 727–44.

—— and L. Pereira da Silva (eds) (2003) *The Impact of Economic Policies on Poverty and Income Distribution: Evaluation Techniques and Tools* (New York: Oxford University Press for the World Bank).

Bussolo, M., R. E. De Hoyos, and D. Medvedev (2007) 'Demographic Change, Economic Growth, and Income Distribution: An Empirical Analysis Using ex-ante Microsimulations'. Background paper for 'Global Economic Prospects 2007: Confronting Challenges of the Coming Globalization' (Washington, DC: World Bank).

—— J. Lay, and D. van der Mensbrugghe (2006) 'Structural Change and Poverty Reduction in Brazil: The Impact of the Doha Round', World Bank Policy Research Working Paper 3833 (Washington, DC: World Bank).

Bryant, R. C. (2004) 'Cross-border Macroeconomic Implications of Demographic Change', Brookings Discussion Paper 166 (Washington, DC: Brookings Institution). <http://www.brookings.edu/papers/2004/09development_bryant.aspx>.

Chaudhuri, S., and M. Ravallion (2006) 'Partially Awakened Giants: Uneven Growth in China and India' (Washington, DC: World Bank). mimeo.

Chen, S., and M. Ravallion (2003) 'Household Welfare Impacts of China's Accession to the World Trade Organization', World Bank Policy Research Working Paper 3040 (Washington, DC: World Bank).

Cowell, F. A., and S. P. Jenkins (1995) 'How Much Inequality Can We Explain? A Methodology and an Application to the United States', *Economic Journal*, 105: 421–30.

David, P. A. (1990) 'The Dynamo and the Computer: An Historical Perspective on the Modern Productivity Paradox', *American Economic Review*, 80: 355–62.

Ferreira, F. H. G., and P. G. Leite (2003) 'Meeting the Millennium Development Goals in Brazil: Can Microsimulations Help?', *Economía*, 3: 235–79.

—— —— (2004) 'Educational Expansion and Income Distribution: A Microsimulation for Ceará', in A. Shorrocks and R. van der Hoeven (eds), *Growth, Inequality and Poverty* (Oxford: Oxford University Press for UNU-WIDER).

Gordon, R. J. (2000) 'Does the "New Economy" Measure Up to the Great Inventions of the Past?', *Journal of Economic Perspectives*, 14: 49–74.

Helliwell, J. F. (2004) 'Demographic Changes and International Factor Mobility', NBER Research Working Paper 10945 (Cambridge, Mass.: NBER).

McKibbin, W. J. (2005) 'The Global Macroeconomic Consequences of a Demographic Transition', Processed (Sydney: Centre for Applied Macroeconomic Analysis, Australian National University).

Milanovic, B. (2002) 'True World Income Distribution, 1988 and 1993: First Calculation Based on Household Surveys Alone', *Economic Journal*, 112: 51–92.

—— (2006) 'Global Income Inequality: What it is and Why it Matters', World Bank Working Paper Series 3865 (Washington, DC: World Bank).

—— and S. Yitzhaki (2002) 'Decomposing World Income Distribution: Does the World Have a Middle Class?', *Review of Income and Wealth*, 48: 155–78.

Mookherjee, D., and A. Shorrocks (1982) 'A Decomposition Analysis of the Trend in UK Income Inequality', *Economic Journal*, 92 (368): 886–902.

Quah, D. T. (1996) 'Twin Peaks: Growth and Convergence in Models of Distribution Dynamics', *Economic Journal*, 106 (437): 1045–55.

Tyers, R., and Q. Shi (2005) 'Global Demographic Change, Labour Force Growth and Economic Performance' (Canberra: Faculty of Economics and Commerce, Australian National University).

van der Mensbrugghe, D. (2005) 'The LINKAGE Model Technical Documentation' (Washington, DC: World Bank).

Winters, L. A., and S. Yusuf (2006) *Dancing with Giants: China, India and the Global Economy* (Washington, DC and Singapore: World Bank/Singapore Institute of Policy Studies).

World Bank (2007) *Global Economic Prospects 2007: Confronting Challenges of the Coming Globalization* (New York: Oxford University Press for the World Bank).

6

Vietnam Following in China's Footsteps: The Third Wave of Emerging Asian Economies

Jean-Raphael Chaponnière, Jean-Pierre Cling, and Bin Zhou

INTRODUCTION

Rapid industrialization is the major characteristic of East Asian economic development. It has been accelerated by export orientation and a specialization pattern that has evolved from simple products (for example, garments, shoes, toys, and so on) to more sophisticated products. Countries have been involved in a catch-up process in line with their comparative advantage. According to Okita (1985), the great diversity among the Asian nations in their stages of development and resource endowments 'works to facilitate the flying geese pattern of shared development as each is able to take advantage of its distinctiveness to develop with a supportive division of labour'.

The 'flight of wild geese' image has acquired different meanings over time. It was first used to describe the life-cycle of industries (Akamatsu 1962); it has been successively extended to the evolution of industrial structure, then to the shift of industries from one country to another. According to this latter meaning, as Japan and the other East Asian countries leave industries in which they have no comparative advantage, countries that industrialized later are able to move into these industries and join the 'flying-geese' formation. The textiles and clothing industry offers an example of the shift of industries in Asia, from Japan to Hong Kong/Korea, and then to Malaysia/the Philippines/Thailand and now to China/Vietnam, and so on.

This model was helpful to describe Asian development during recent decades, and the successive emergence of Japan, followed by the 'Dragons' (Hong Kong, Korea, Singapore, and Taiwan) and the 'Tigers' (Indonesia, Malaysia, Philippines, Thailand, and so on). Three major evolutions have made this transition process more difficult and might provoke a major disruption in the 'flight of wild geese'.

First, Asian development came to a halt in 1997 because of the Asian crisis, with a long-term impact in some countries. While Korea was able to grow out of the crisis very rapidly, Indonesia was the major victim and Thailand is still having difficulties moving from middle-income to high-income status.

Second, economic emergence has become more difficult as China has fully joined the 'flight' and has been rapidly moving up the value chain. Indeed, the pace of China's growth has accelerated since the Asian crisis, while that of other Asian emerging countries has slowed down compared with their pre-crisis performances.

Third, the new trade rules imposed by the WTO have been considered as an obstacle to the integration of new emerging countries in the world economy; according to Chang (2002), developed countries have 'kicked away the ladder' of economic development (Korea and the other dragons would not have been allowed to pursue the industrial policies that contributed to their success story). Moreover, the end of clothing quotas mostly benefited China and had a negative impact on other developing countries.

Following Eichengreen (2004), several studies (Lall and Albaladejo 2004; Eichengreen and Tong 2005; Humphrey and Schmitz 2006; Ravenhill 2006) have tried to assess the impact of China's economic growth on Asian middle-income emerging countries. They concluded that it was positive, as most of these countries were able to adjust to the Chinese threat. But, to our knowledge, the impact of China's economic emergence on its low-income neighbours has not been assessed yet, although it is most probably of a different nature. Studying this impact is all the more important, as it can present some answers concerning the possibility of new Asian countries emerging in the current international economic context.

In this chapter, in order to study Vietnam's potential for sustainable growth and international integration, we focus on international trade and the trade relationship between Vietnam and China. Our chapter draws on international foreign trade databases and uses traditional indicators of trade specialization and competition.

In the first section, we describe Vietnamese economic reform (especially trade policies) and its results in terms of economic growth and world integration. The subsequent section studies Vietnam's trade specialization and the bilateral relationship with China. This is followed by an assessment of the competition between Vietnam and China on world markets, and an analysis of the particular case of textiles and clothing, which, historically, was the initial basis of the industrialization process.

VIETNAM: THE LATEST ASIAN EMERGING ECONOMY

Vietnam is a neighbour of China, and Vietnam's capital Hanoi is less than 1,000 kilometres from Hong Kong and Guangzhou (Canton). Both countries share many cultural values (Confucianism) as well as a common history: until the signature of the Treaty of Tientsin with France, hardly more than a century ago (1885), China had suzerain rights and sovereignty over Vietnam (and the Indo-China peninsula). Vietnam also used Chinese ideograms up until the early twentieth century.[1] Since independence (1945), Vietnam has maintained a close political and economic relationship with China (only interrupted, temporarily, from the end of the 1970s to the beginning of the 1990s). Finally, China and Vietnam are among the last countries in the world where the Communist Party still has a monopoly of power.

It is therefore unsurprising that economic reform in Vietnam followed that of China relatively closely: facing economic difficulties, both countries had to adopt some principles of market economy. Although reform in Vietnam was (as in the case of China) gradual, results came quickly in terms of economic growth and integration in the world economy.

VIETNAM'S 'DOI MOI'

At the beginning of the 1980s, Vietnam faced alarming economic difficulties: acute shortage of basic consumer goods (even for staple food products), growing external debt, increasing macroeconomic imbalances (inflation, public sector and trade deficits), and a slowdown of economic growth.

In December 1986—eight years after China (December 1978)—Vietnam reacted by embarking on a radical reform programme called 'doi moi' ('renewal') that marked the adoption of 'market socialism' (Figure 6.1). As in China, the reforms started in the rural areas where agriculture was virtually decollectivized, farmers were given more autonomy, and prices were liberalized. A private sector was authorized, consisting mainly of small and medium-sized enterprises. Major elements of central planning were dismantled.

The external liberalization process was also very rapid. The state monopoly of foreign trade was abandoned. Tariff exemptions were introduced for inputs

---

[1] At the beginning of the twentieth century, Vietnam abandoned Chinese ideograms and shifted to the Latin alphabet.

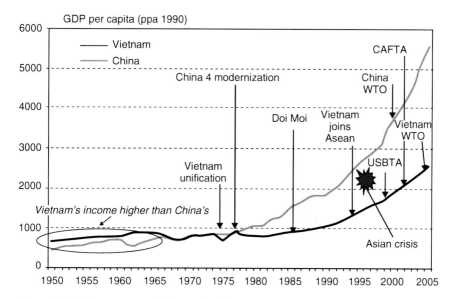

Figure 6.1. *Vietnamese and Chinese development trajectories*

Source: For years 1950–2000 Maddison n.d.; from 2000, national statistics (China and Vietnam).

used in the production of export goods; the non-tariff barriers were reduced. Progress was made in a number of areas, including reduction in maximum import tariff rates, the implementation of tariff reductions associated with membership of ASEAN (in 1997), and so on.

Since the adoption of doi moi, and following the East Asian 'Dragons' model (World Bank 1993), Vietnamese trade policy has mixed import substitution measures and export subsidies to promote an export-led growth strategy. As had previously been the case in East Asian emerging countries (Amsden 2001), export subsidies have played a key role in the export surge, especially for textiles and clothing products.

Following the end of the US embargo in 1994, Vietnam speeded up its process of international integration. Three trade agreements have had a major impact on trade liberalization and increased market access.

After joining ASEAN, tariffs on imports from ASEAN countries were reduced to below 5 per cent in 2006 under the Asian Free Trade Area (AFTA). This tariff reduction was also applied by other ASEAN countries to Vietnamese exports, which benefited from improved market access in the area.

In 2000, Vietnam signed a bilateral trade agreement with the United States (USBTA), opening the doors of the American market to Vietnamese products (submitted to quotas). As Vietnam's exports to the US have been granted most-favoured nation (MFN) status since 2002, the average tariff on Vietnamese imports into the USA dropped from some 40 per cent to 3–4 per cent.

Vietnam eventually joined the WTO at the beginning of 2007 (five years after China), almost exactly twenty years after the adoption of doi moi. As it is now a member of the WTO, Vietnam benefits from the MFN status in all member countries (which also means that quotas will no longer be applied to Vietnamese exports) and has to apply WTO rules. Consequently, the MFN tariff will be reduced, on average, to below 15 per cent by 2019 and the maximum tariff applied will decrease from 150 per cent to 85 per cent (IMF 2007). However, after its accession to the WTO, Vietnam will not be immune from new trade frictions as it is considered (as is China, also) to be a 'non-market economy'.

INCREASING FLOWS OF FDI

Although financial liberalization has been slow and modest, Vietnam has received important foreign funding: according to the balance of payment figures, foreign direct investment (FDI) amounts to around US$2 billion per year (that is, 4 per cent of GDP) and Development Aid to around US$1.5 billion per year. FDI comes mostly from Asian countries (Table 6.1): the first five foreign investors (Singapore, Taiwan, Japan, Korea, and Hong Kong)

Table 6.1. *Cumulative amount of foreign investment projects in Vietnam (1988–2006)*

Rank		Number	Investment (disbursed)		Investment (committed)	
			Amount (US$ billion)	Share of total (percentage)	Amount (US$ billion)	Share of total (percentage)
	Total	6,761	25.4	100.0	57.3	100.0
1	Japan	724	4.8	18.9	7.1	12.3
2	Singapore	447	3.6	14.2	8.0	14.0
3	Taiwan	1,547	2.9	11.4	8.0	14.0
4	Korea	1,246	2.6	10.2	6.1	10.6
5	Hong Kong	375	2.1	8.3	4.6	8.0
	Total Top 5	4,339	16.0	62.9	33.8	59.0

Source: Ministry of Planning and Investment.

contributed to nearly two-thirds (63 per cent) of total disbursed investment up until 2006.

FDI has become a significant contributor to domestic investment (more than 10 per cent of gross investment) and exports, and picked up with the completion of the WTO negotiation. Up until 2000, the oil and gas sectors were the principal recipients of FDI but since then light and heavy industries have received the lion's share.

For Asian firms, Vietnam is increasingly perceived as an alternative to China with regard to labour-intensive industries. It is notably the case for Japanese multinationals: Vietnam ranks third in their intentions for investment behind India and China, according to a survey of the Japan Bank for International Cooperation (JETRO 2007). Labour costs in Vietnam are slightly lower than in China and both countries share the same work ethics. Compared with low-income countries, Vietnam also has an excellent education record: the primary completion rate is almost 100 per cent and the secondary school enrolment ratio is as high as 76 per cent (World Bank 2007).

EXPORT BOOM SUSTAINED BY FOREIGN FIRMS

In Vietnam, economic and export growth rates have been impressive: since the mid-1980s, GDP has grown at the rate of nearly 8 per cent per year and foreign trade has expanded at the rate of nearly 20 per cent per year (the respective figures for China are nearly 10 per cent and 15 per cent per year). For the last two decades, Vietnam and China have been the fastest growing Asian economies. Thanks to the low level of its financial openness, Vietnam was relatively spared from the 1997 crisis. As the dollar has been depreciating since 2003, Vietnamese competitiveness has been helped by an exchange rate policy that follows a crawling peg to the US$. At the national level, between 1993 and 2006, the proportion of the population living in poverty was considerably reduced from 54 per cent to 16 per cent.

The growth of the Vietnamese share of the world market for goods has been remarkable since the mid-1980s, even when compared with China (Figure 6.2). Its growth is by far the most dynamic of all Asian exporters (although the current level of 0.3 per cent is far behind Thailand's market share of 1 per cent and, of course, China's 8 per cent). The Vietnamese market share on the world and EU markets has almost tripled between 1995 and 2004. The ratio is 14 on the US market, where Vietnamese exports were totally insignificant in 1995 (as the US embargo had only ended in 1993). The gain on the Japanese market is important but much lower than that on the European market.

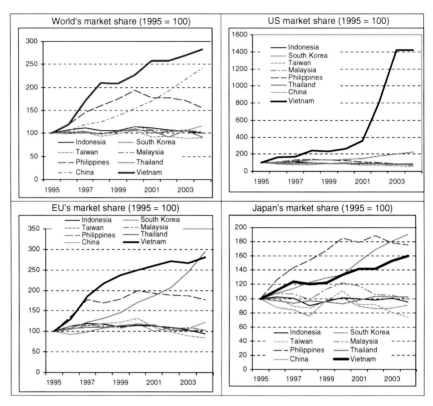

Figure 6.2. *Evolution of market shares of Vietnam compared with major Asian exporters*
Source: CEPII/CHELEM.

According to the General Statistical Office, foreign investors (which are mostly Asian) exported a total value of US$22.8 billion in 2006 (including oil); that is, 57 per cent of total exports. Foreign firms export over 50 per cent of total garment exports (this share is probably even larger in the case of electronics). The role of export processing is similar to that in China, where Asian subsidiaries account for around 50 per cent of total exports (Gaulier, Lemoine, and Unal-Kesenci 2005).

The structure of exports has also changed dramatically in recent years. Since 2002, manufactured products have contributed to the majority of exports (Figure 6.3). This 50 per cent threshold was reached by the Philippines in 1984, by China in 1986, by Thailand and Malaysia in 1989, and by Indonesia in 1995. Being an oil exporter (as is Indonesia, but on a smaller scale) tends to reduce the share of manufactured exports. However, crude oil exports will go down in the next few years as Vietnam is building oil refineries

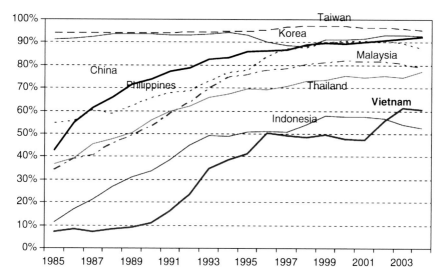

Figure 6.3. *Share of manufactured products in total exports (percentage)*
Source: CEPII/CHELEM.

for domestic consumption (the first refinery will start operating in 2009 in Dung Quat).

Vietnam still has the trade specialization pattern of a low-income country In spite of its rapid progress, Vietnam is still in the early stages of industrialization and international integration. The study of its trade specialization conducted in this section confirms this situation. Contrary to other Asian emerging countries, Vietnam is not yet part of the Asian production network (except, to a certain extent, in clothing) which is dominated by China. Its trade with China corresponds to a 'South–North' trade pattern: it exports raw materials and imports manufactured products from its sizeable neighbour.

NEW COMPARATIVE ADVANTAGES

The specialization in Vietnamese foreign trade is analysed here using the indicators of revealed comparative advantage, drawn from Balassa 1965. The advantage of using these indicators is that we do not restrict ourselves to analysing the breakdown of Vietnamese trade independently from the rest of the world, but we analyse Vietnam's specialization relatively to the structure of world trade.

Table 6.2. *Five main revealed comparative advantages/disadvantages of Vietnam and China in 2004 (in 1/1000 of GDP)*

Vietnam		China	
Comparative advantage		Comparative advantage	
1. Oil (crude)	104.5	1. Computers	27.8
2. Shoes and leather products	84.7	2. Manufactured products NEC	19.7
3. Clothing	53.4	3. Shoes and leather products	19.1
4. Knitwear	32.9	4. Clothing	14.9
5. Meat	29.2	5. Knitwear	12.6
Comparative advantage		Comparative advantage	
1. Oil (refined)	−64.0	1. Electronic components	−27.8
2. Yarn and fabric	−46.7	2. Oil (crude)	−20.3
3. Iron and steel	−32.7	3. Specialized machinery	−11.9
4. Plastic products	−24.7	4. Chemical organic products	−10.7
5. Specialized machinery	−21.2	5. Plastic products	−10.1

Source: CEPII/CHELEM databases.

Vietnamese specialization, which is highly concentrated on a few products, is characteristic of a low-income country rich in natural resources (Table 6.2): oil (20 per cent of its exports in 2004, according to CEPII/CHELEM) is its first comparative advantage, followed by textiles and clothing products (shoes, followed by clothing and knitwear) and by meat products. On the import side, refined oil is the first comparative disadvantage (12 per cent of imports), followed by yarn and fabric used by the textiles and clothing industry and by other intermediate products (iron and steel, plastic products) and specialized machinery.

Among Asian emerging countries, Vietnam's specialization is only comparable to Indonesia's (Table 6.3). All the other countries participate in the Asian electronic regional network and, therefore, have a strong revealed comparative advantage in electronic and computer products. Only China, Indonesia, and the Philippines are still specializing in clothing products, whereas the more advanced economies (Korea, Malaysia, Taiwan, and Thailand) have moved up the ladder.

Chinese specialization is much more diversified than the Vietnamese. Exports, contrary to Vietnam, do not rely on raw materials at all: the comparative advantages are found in computers, other manufactured products, and textiles and clothing (shoes, clothing, and knitwear, in the same order as Vietnam). The comparative disadvantages correspond to inputs for the computer industry (electronic components), raw materials (crude oil),

Table 6.3. *Revealed comparative advantages of Vietnam and major Asian exporters (2004) (in 1/1000 of GDP)*

	Indonesia	Malaysia	Philippines	Thailand	China	Vietnam	Korea	Taiwan
Cement	0.4	0.1	0.4	0.7	0.9	0.2	-0.6	0.3
Ceramics	-0.4	-0.5	-1.9	0	1.7	2.9	-0.6	-0.9
Glass	0.4	-1.4	-0.5	0.4	0.3	-0.7	-1.1	-2
Iron Steel	-10.5	-18.5	-14	-21.2	-8.4	-32.7	-3.9	-4.3
Tubes	-1.9	-4.2	-0.7	-1.6	-0.1	-4.6	1.3	1.3
Non ferrous metals	0.9	-15.6	-1.1	-9.7	-4.7	-10.3	-5.3	-11.6
Clothing	-0.2	-1.9	-10	-1.6	-0.1	-46.7	8.2	23.5
Knitwear	8.5	1.5	13.4	5.8	14.9	53.4	-0.7	0.6
Carpets	6.6	5.3	11	10.4	12.6	32.9	0.9	2.6
Leather	0.1	-0.7	0.4	1.5	5.4	3.7	1.2	2.6
Wood articles	5	6.4	1.5	8.1	19.1	84.7	-0.1	1.3
Furniture	8.5	13.6	1.7	2	1.5	0.4	-1	-0.9
Paper	5.8	10.4	3.5	5.2	9.3	26.8	-0.5	3.3
Printing	2.7	-8.7	-5	-2.7	-3.9	-7.1	0	-2.3
Miscellaneous manufacturing articles	-0.2	-1	-1.2	-0.5	0.4	-1.4	0.1	0.1
Metallic structures	0.6	-2.6	-1.4	-0.5	19.7	0.9	-1.3	11.4
Miscellaneous hardware	0	0.8	-1.4	1.1	0.4	-0.8	0.4	-0.1
Engines	-7.1	-12.7	-6.4	-9	7	-6	0.5	20.9
Agricultural equipment	-11.1	-10.1	-5.9	-3.8	-4.4	-13.8	-2.2	-8.9
Machine tools	-0.4	-0.6	-0.2	-0.9	0	-0.9	-0.1	0.1
Construction equipment	-2.7	-7.5	-3.2	-8.6	-5.2	-8.7	-2	-0.3
Specialized machinary	-5	-4.5	-1.4	-4.1	-1.7	-8.6	2.4	-2.4
Arms	-8.6	-13.5	-9.4	-16.4	-11.9	-21.2	-4	-12.4
Precision instruments	-0.2	-0.1	0	-0.1	0.1	0	-0.5	-0.6
Clock-making	-2.1	-4.3	-6.5	-5.8	-3.1	-6.1	-6.5	-13
Optics	-0.1	-0.3	0.8	0.9	1.1	0.1	-0.1	-0.5
Electronic components	0.6	-6.1	0.5	1.5	-8.8	-0.2	-2.1	8.8

(continued)

Table 6.3. Continued

	Indonesia	Malaysia	Philippines	Thailand	China	Vietnam	Korea	Taiwan
Consumer electronics	-3.4	-36.2	64.8	-14.1	-27.8	-3.6	-0.6	-3.2
Telecoms equipment	8.3	41.5	3.4	13.1	14.1	-0.5	4.8	4.6
Computer equipment	-3.9	30.3	5.5	8.1	5.9	-8.5	32.6	10.8
Domestic electric appliances	7.3	88.7	61.9	34.9	27.8	-10.5	18.1	38.1
Electrical equipment	-0.6	1.8	-0.5	4.6	6.7	-0.2	3	0.4
Electrical apparatus	-0.1	-6.7	7.4	2.3	1.1	-0.2	-1.9	1.5
Vehicle components	-1.5	-25.7	2.2	-6.7	2.6	-2.7	-6.8	14.5
Cars/cycles	-4.6	-10.1	-1.7	-9.6	-3.7	-4.9	3.7	2.3
Commercial vehicles	-5.9	-13.5	-5.1	1.3	-0.2	-7.6	33	3.5
Ships	-2.5	-5	-2.2	4.8	0.3	-9.9	2	-2.1
Aeronautics	-1.5	-6.2	-0.4	-0.3	0.2	-0.7	18.5	0.7
Bulk inorganic chemicals	-1.2	-8.9	-3.4	-3.7	-3.8	-18.6	-2.3	-4.5
Fertilizers	-1.5	-4.7	-2.2	-2.6	1.6	-2.5	-2.2	-2.9
Bulk organic chemicals	-1.6	-3.2	-2.7	-2.7	-0.5	-9.4	-0.1	-0.2
Paints	-10.3	-0.9	-6.5	-5.7	-10.7	-6	0.1	-11.5
Toiletries	-2.5	-2.1	-3.8	-4.6	-1.2	-7.8	-2.1	-3.8
Pharmaceutical products	-2.9	2.6	-5.1	-3.2	-1.6	-4.1	-2.6	-5.9
Plastics	-1.2	-5.4	-5.7	-4.1	0.4	-8.7	-2.1	-4
Plastic articles	-2	-1.4	-1.4	-0.4	-1.9	-6.3	1.5	3.9
Rubber/tyres	-6.3	-9.3	-12.4	-1.3	-10.1	-24.7	9.6	18.3
Iron ores	0.7	0.9	-1.3	3.4	0.9	1	2.4	2.1
Non ferrous ores	-1.4	-5.2	4.5	-1.7	-7.7	0	-4.7	-5.3
Unprocessed minerals	9.5	-0.1	-3.2	-0.2	-5.3	1.1	-4.8	-2.4
Coals	-1	-1.2	-0.3	0	0.1	0.2	-0.8	-1.7
Crude oil	13.2	-3.3	-1.9	-0.3	1.8	8.1	-6.4	-9.4
Natural gas	3.4	16.8	-20.9	-2.3	-20.3	104.5	-47.5	-43.4
Coke	27.3	38.2	-2.7	0.6	-1.3	-0.4	-13	-8.3
Refined petrol products	-0.1	-0.1	-0.1	0	2.2	-0.1	-0.3	-0.2
Electricity	-17.8	-17.2	-23.6	3.6	-4	-64	1.7	7
Cereals	0	0.1	0	-0.1	0.2	0	0	0

Other agricultural products	−2.1	−4.7	−6.2	5.5	−0.6	3.2	−3.1	−3.4
Cereal products	−0.9	−10.3	6.2	3	−2.3	23.5	−1.9	−3.3
Fats	4.4	15.4	0.1	7.9	−5.8	0	−3.5	−3.7
Meat	−0.4	0.1	−0.7	−0.2	0.2	−1.4	−0.1	−0.2
Processed meat	12.1	28.9	−0.9	−1.8	−2.7	−4.7	−1.1	−1.6
Processed fruits	3.6	−2.9	0.8	5.1	0.4	29.2	−3.4	1.7
Sugar	1.1	−0.1	2.1	11.4	1.5	8.5	−0.1	0.2
Animal food	0	−3	−0.9	3.2	1.3	−0.8	−0.3	−1.3
Beverages	−0.5	1	−0.9	2.9	0	0	−0.5	−0.6
Manufactured tobacco	−2.9	−1.6	−3.5	−0.4	−0.2	−3.5	−1	−0.8
Jewellery/w. art	−0.1	−0.6	0	−0.2	0.2	−0.3	−0.3	−1
Non monetary gold	0.2	0.1	−1.3	−0.2	0	−2.6	0.2	−1.4
Not elsewhere specified products	0.5	3.8	0.6	5.8	1	1	0.7	−1.8

Source: CEPII/CHELEM databases.

specialized machinery, and other intermediate products (chemical organic and plastic products).

In both countries, the evolution of trade specialization over the last two decades is striking. Vietnam has built up its revealed comparative advantages in textiles and clothing from scratch (in knitwear but not in clothing, which already existed at the end of the 1980s). This is also the case for shoes and for furniture. Inversely, the specialization of exports in agricultural products has been progressively reduced. As Vietnam has started producing pharmaceutical products, the relative weight of this product in imports has also strongly decreased.

China already had a specialization in textiles and clothing two decades ago but did not export any computers, electronic products, or telecommunication equipment: the specialization in these products has increased progressively.

BILATERAL TRADE WITH CHINA: SOUTH–NORTH PATTERN

In 2004, China became the first supplier to Vietnam and its fourth client.[2] According to Vietnam's trade statistics, total bilateral trade amounted to US $7.5 billion in 2006 (the real amount is larger due to widespread smuggling). Applying a gravity model taking into account usual variables (the distance between the two countries, the size of their economies, and so on), Tumbarello (2006) shows that bilateral trade is in line with the amount predicted by the model. Bilateral trade is expected to double and rise to US$15 billion in 2010.[3]

Vietnam's bilateral trade with China shares three common characteristics with its least-developed country (LDC) neighbours (Cambodia, Laos, and Myanmar).

In contrast to middle-income Asian countries, which all enjoy a large surplus in their trade with China, Vietnam (as well as these other LDCs' neighbours) runs a trade deficit with China. According to Vietnam's trade statistics, this bilateral deficit amounted to US$3 billion in 2006 (4 per cent of GDP), and the ratio of exports to imports was 41 per cent. The deficit has sharply increased over time. In 2001, the bilateral trade was still almost

---

[2] Bilateral trade was completely marginal when both countries re-established diplomatic relations in 1991.

[3] Vietnam and China joint press communiqué, 19 May 2007 <http://english.vietnamnet.vn/politics/2007/05/696637>.

balanced (the deficit amounted to US$200 million only, and the export: import ratio to 87 per cent).

In Vietnam, as in Cambodia and Myanmar (but not in Laos, where Thailand is the largest supplier), China is by far the largest supplier. This is not the case for middle-income Asian countries, where China's market share is much smaller.

Finally, as is the case for Cambodia, Vietnam's export structure to China is different from the structure of its world exports. Indeed, manufactured goods represent a small percentage of Vietnamese exports to China (18 per cent), much inferior to the share of these products in Vietnam's total world exports (Figure 6.4); the same discrepancy is observed in the case of Cambodia and Bangladesh, which are both LDCs.

This third characteristic is in sharp contrast to the structure of trade between other Asian countries and China. The low flow and the structure of Chinese investment in Vietnam are consistent with this characteristic. Although China is the largest supplier to Vietnam its share of FDI in Vietnam is low and Chinese FDI is concentrated in natural resources.

The imbalance of bilateral trade reflects a division of labour that is usually observed in trade relationships between low-income countries and developed countries. As shown in Table 6.4, Vietnam mainly exports raw

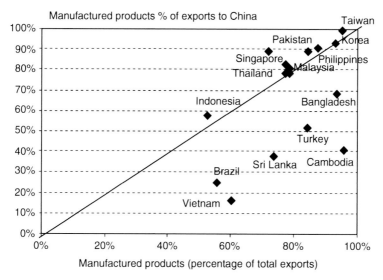

Figure 6.4. *Share of manufactured products in total exports and in exports to China for Vietnam and selected countries (percentage)*

Source: CEPII/CHELEM.

Table 6.4. *Ten main products traded between Vietnam and China in 2004 (percentage)*

Exports to China			Imports from China		
Products	percentage	Cumulative percentage	Products	percentage	Cumulative percentage
1. Crude oil	57.7	57.7	1. Refined oil	14.5	14.5
2. Coal	7.3	65.0	2. Yarn and fabric	11.7	26.2
3. Rubber products	4.5	69.5	3. Fertilizers	10.9	37.1
4. Other edible agricultural products	3.4	72.9	4. Iron and steel	10.7	47.8
5. Non-edible agricultural products	3.3	76.2	5. Engines	5.1	52.9
6. Non-ferrous ore	2.5	78.7	6. Specialized machinery	2.9	55.8
7. Organic chemical products	2.2	80.9	7. Other edible agricultural products	2.7	58.5
8. Iron ore	1.9	82.8	8. Hardware	2.7	61.2
9. Leather	1.6	84.4	9. Leather	2.4	63.6
10. Yarn and fabric	1.0	85.4	10. Electrical appliances	2.1	65.7

Source: CEPII/CHELEM.

products to China: oil, minerals, agricultural products, rubber, and so on. In return, it imports mainly processed and manufactured products from China: refined oil, yarn, and fabric used as input for its clothing industry, other intermediate products, and machinery.

This analysis of trade specialization and bilateral trade with China confirms that Vietnam is not (yet?) part of the Asian production network in which China plays a central role. This network is characterized by two main elements: on the one hand, an increasing vertical specialization, corresponding to the splitting up of the value-added chain (Athukorala 2006); on the other hand, a growing importance in intra-Asian flows of trade of intermediate goods (mostly parts and components), especially for electronic products (Gaulier, Lemoine, and Unal-Kesenci 2005). However, this situation will probably evolve once the recent large projects in the electronics sector come on stream.

FREE TRADE AGREEMENT WITH CHINA

In 2004, ASEAN and China signed a free trade agreement (ACFTA), which will be implemented by most participants in 2010, and by the new ASEAN member countries, including Vietnam, in 2015. Some 'early harvest' agreements have been signed by China with its partners (mostly for agricultural goods), especially with Vietnam.

The impact of the ACFTA on Vietnam is somewhat uncertain (Nguyen and Tran 2007; Vo 2005). The FTA will stimulate bilateral trade with China. It will create a huge market of 1.7 billion people, which will attract foreign investment and might bring dynamic gains from trade. But, in comparison with China, Vietnam might become less attractive for FDI. Competition with China will increase and there is a risk of Vietnam exploiting its static comparative advantage in labour (and natural resources) and falling into a 'low-waged labour trap'.

One benefit from increased trade integration is already appearing, as huge investments in infrastructure (roads, energy, and so on) are being implemented within the regional economic corridors (Ishida 2005). Among these new projects, one can mention the construction of a new highway between Kunning (China) and Haiphong (Vietnam), which will make the Vietnamese harbour play a key role for Southern China's access to foreign markets. Electrical interconnection between China and Vietnam is also planned.

VIETNAM AND CHINA: MORE COMPLEMENTARY THAN COMPETITORS

In order to assess the potential for further growth of Vietnamese exports, it is essential to measure the degree of competition with China, which has become the first exporter of goods in the world. In this section, we analyse the proximity of the Vietnamese export structure with that of China and its evolution, and study the particular case of textiles and clothing.

Making inroads in an increasing number of sectors

The USA is, by and large, the largest market for both Vietnam and China; they account for one-fifth of their exports (respectively 20 per cent and 21 per cent of exports in 2006, according to Vietnamese and Chinese trade statistics). While the Chinese share of the US market increased from 8.9 per cent (2001) to 15.5 per cent (2006), Vietnam's share increased from 0.09 per cent to 0.46 per cent.

In order to compare the performance of China and Vietnam on the US market, trade shares have been computed for the period 2001 to 2006 at the three-digit industry level. Table 6.5 confirms that China has emerged as a

Table 6.5. *Number of industries where the share of the US market has increased/decreased between 2001 and 2006*

Exporter evolution	China	Vietnam	Thailand
Increase	210	175	137
Decrease	7	15	33
Not relevant	46	73	93
Total	263	263	263

Source: Computed by the authors from USITC data.

significant exporter across virtually the entire spectrum of industries: its share of the US import market has increased in 210 out of 263 industries and decreased in only 7. To assess Vietnam's performance, one has to take into account the fact that Vietnamese exports were facing strong trade obstacles up until the USBTA came into force in 2002. Nevertheless, Table 6.5 shows that, between 2001 and 2006, Vietnam has made inroads on a very large number (175 out of 263) of markets.

As Vietnamese exports diversify rapidly on the US market, their structure could well be rapidly coming to resemble that of China; such evolution might represent a threat for the future of Vietnamese exports. In order to appreciate this evolution, we measured the proximity of the export structure of China on the US and the EU markets with the export structures of Vietnam from 2001 to 2006 (Figure 6.5). We use the indicator proposed by Finger and Kreinin (1979), which was calculated by desegregating exports between 230 products, using the SITC classification at three-digit levels (see methodology in Appendix 1).

On both markets, the structures of Vietnamese and Chinese exports are very different,[4] but register different evolutions. On the EU market, the Vietnamese export structure is very different from the Chinese structure, and this difference has not evolved significantly since 2001. Vietnam exports mostly shoes (around 50 per cent of total exports) and textiles and clothing products, whereas China exports mostly electronic and computer products together with a relatively small proportion of textiles and clothing. The evolution is somewhat different on the US market. In 2001, the Vietnamese structure used to be rather dissimilar to the Chinese, but appears to be a little closer in 2006. This increased proximity is due to the export boom of

---

[4] For Thailand (which has the most similar export structure to China) the value of the index amounts to more than 0.6, which is about twice as high as Vietnam.

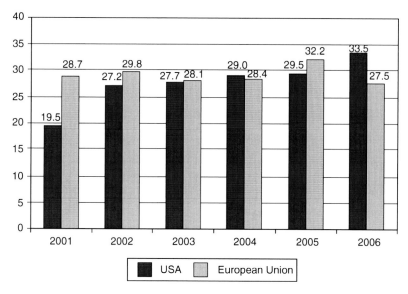

Figure 6.5. *Proximity of China's export structure with Vietnam, 2001–6 (Finger–Kreinin index)*

Note: The indicator evolves between 0 (total dissimilarity) and 100 (total similarity).

Sources: Computed by the authors from USITC and Eurostat (three-digit SITC).

Vietnamese exports of textiles and clothing (which were previously insignificant) since the opening of the US market (USBTA).

As stated by Lall and Albaladejo (2004), these similarities, or their absence, reveal either a lack of competition or a potential for competition. They do not demonstrate that competition actually exists as product categories are still broad (for example, in our classification in 230 products, all shoe exports are grouped into one category) and might include products that do not compete with each other. Even if the products were comparable, it would be possible that countries specialized in differentiated versions. Even in the same product, countries may complement each other by performing different functions within an integrated production system. Vietnamese and Chinese textiles exports are both benefiting from joining the WTO and from the cessation of quotas.

As mentioned before, Vietnamese manufactured exports consist mostly of textiles and clothing (as well as shoes). This structure is characteristic of a developing country in the early stages of its industrialization process. As shown in Figure 6.6, the share of these products in total exports of goods is still growing (the decrease in 2004 was due to quotas and has reversed since

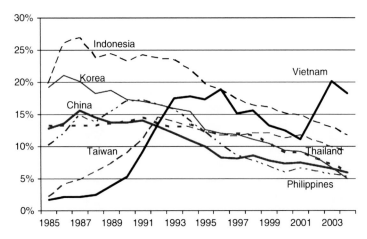

Figure 6.6. *Share of textiles and clothing in total exports (percentage)*
Source: CEPII/CHELEM.

2005). This trend is in comparison with other major Asian exporters, where the share of textiles and clothing in exports peaked around 1985–1990 and has been progressively declining since then.

Indeed, as happened with Japan a few decades earlier (and with European countries and the USA during the nineteenth-century industrial revolution), textiles and clothing has historically been the core industrial sector for all countries starting a take-off process. Many reasons explain why this key role is still valid at the beginning of the twenty-first century: clothing is the first industrial product consumed; it is a sector that requires light investment; the technology is simple; it mostly uses unskilled labour; poor countries have a huge supply of cheap labour and, therefore, are the most competitive in this labour-intensive sector.

It is therefore important to assess recent Vietnamese performance in this sector together with future potential. This is all the more important as international competition has increased in this sector following the final dismantling of quotas imposed on Asian countries since the beginning of 2005.[5]

Having been a member of the WTO since the end of 2001, China appears to be the main beneficiary from the cessation of quotas (Table 6.6): its exports to

---

[5] The Multi-Fibre Arrangements (MFAs) were established in 1974. They imposed quotas on Asian exports of textile and clothing to industrialized countries. The Agreement on Textile and Clothing (ATC) signed in 1994 organized the progressive dismantling of these quotas during a ten-year period which ended at the beginning of 2005.

Table 6.6. *US, EU, and Japanese clothing imports from Vietnam and major Asian exporters (in million dollars)*

	2001	2002	2003	2004	2005	2006	Variable 2006/1 (percentage)	Market share (percentage) (2006)
1. China								
Total	28,069	29,098	35,254	41,869	55,315	62,476	+122.6	
EU	7,486	8,810	11,578	14,322	21,092	23,934	+219.7	31.4
USA	6,416	7,070	8,667	10,685	16,774	19,865	+209.6	27.1
Japan	14,167	13,218	15,009	16,862	17,448	18,678	+131.8	83.4
2. Bangladesh								
Total	4,471	4,359	5,302	6,518	6,686	8,636	+93.2	
EU	2,527	2,583	3,515	4,621	4,400	5,811	+130.0	7.6
USA	1,929	1,757	1,759	1,871	2,268	2,808	+45.6	3.8
Japan	15	18	28	26	18	18	+20.0	0.0
3. India								
Total	3,862	4,208	4,839	5,443	7,233	8,229	+113.1	
EU	1,979	2,186	2,688	3,079	4,028	4,824	+143.8	6.3
USA	1,774	1,939	2,059	2,256	3,064	3,235	+82.4	4.4
Japan	109	83	92	107	141	171	+56.9	0.2
4. Hong Kong								
Total	4,382	6,129	6,131	6,354	5,672	6,052	+38.1	
EU	2,328	2,208	2,379	2,440	2,121	3,200	+37.5	4.2
USA	1,994	3,873	3,708	3,863	3,507	2,799	+40.4	3.8
Japan	60	48	44	51	45	53	−11.7	0.2
5. Indonesia								
Total	4,016	3,590	3,815	4,169	4,476	5,613	+39.8	
EU	1,607	1,391	1,537	1,662	1,492	1,812	+12.8	2.4
USA	2,203	2,050	2,153	2,390	2,868	3,666	+66.4	5.0
Japan	205	149	125	117	115	135	−34.1	0.2
6. Vietnam								
Total	1,261	1,988	3,413	3,839	4,110	5,052	+300.6	
EU	689	656	591	788	857	1,285	+86.5	1.7
USA	47	873	2,337	2,503	2,664	3,152	+6,606.4	4.3
Japan	525	459	484	548	588	616	+17.3	0.8

Notes: 'Total' means the sum of total exports to the EU, USA, and Japan.
Sources: Eurostat, USITC, and Global Trade Statistics.

the EU and the USA have almost doubled between 2004 and 2006 (despite new restrictions being quickly reimposed on Chinese exports until the end of 2008); export growth has been slower on the Japanese market, which was already 'quota free'. China is now, by far, the first exporter of textiles and clothing on all major industrialized markets.

However, Vietnam has also benefited (as have other major Asian exporters) from the new international context for these products (although the USA has imposed quotas within the USBTA): it now ranks sixth (even fifth, if Hong Kong is considered to be part of China) amongst Asian exporters to the EU + USA + Japanese market and its exports have grown at a strong pace over recent years (as has its market share).

As Vietnam joined the WTO at the beginning of 2007, it can be expected that its exports growth rate could even increase, as they will no longer be subject to quotas (although the EU has applied anti-dumping measures to Vietnamese shoe exports since 2006 and the USA has threatened to do the same on textiles and clothing). However, joining the WTO also means eliminating all export subsidies. Thus, as from June 2006, when Decision 126 replaced Decision 55 (2003), the textiles and garment industry has no longer been eligible to receive preferential state credits from the Vietnam Development Bank (VDB).

In any case, the Asian low-income countries' gain on textiles and clothing confirm that these countries have relatively similar low labour costs and high overall competitiveness for these products. This is not the case for other important exporters (Mexico and North African countries), which are generally middle-income countries that have lost considerable ground in recent years.

CONCLUSION

At the beginning of the 1980s, Vietnam was still recovering from three decades of devastating war—first with France, then with the USA—followed by a rising tension with China that culminated in a war at the border in 1979. It was also suffering from an embargo imposed by the USA (which lasted until 1994) which also prevented the World Bank (as well as other donors) from bringing aid to the country. The 'boat people' leaving Vietnam at the turn of the 1970s because of political pressure and the disastrous economic situation contributed to reinforcing the country's isolation.

A quarter of a century later, the economic improvement is remarkable, as is the integration into the world economy. Vietnam has been able to make inroads on world markets and can no longer be considered a 'sitting duck' waiting to be picked off by China, armed with a huge pool of cheap labour (Bhalla 1998, quoted by Ahearne, et al. 2006). As has always been the case, the sustainability of Vietnam's growth path is intimately linked to the economic situation in China and to the evolution of China's economic specialization.

China is undoubtedly both a serious competitor and a very important economic partner (Vo 2005). One of the main challenges for Vietnam's industry, therefore, is to pursue a more offensive strategy towards China, as its neighbour will probably be the main engine of the world economy in the coming years. Vietnam needs to diversify its exports to China (which currently consist of oil and agricultural products only), while industrial goods dominate imports.

However, the impact of Vietnam's WTO accession on its industrialization strategy must not be underestimated. In order to add greater value to its exports, this country needs to invest heavily in new technologies and raise productivity. It also needs to improve domestic support industries in order to provide inputs to the rapidly growing industries. While private and foreign firms are very active in labour-intensive industries, they import a significant part of their inputs. The government plans to reinforce the state-owned sector in order to stimulate the production of upstream industries (steel, petrochemicals, refining, and fertilizers) as well as to develop industrial chains (Cao and Tran 2005). This strategy will have to abide by the rules of the WTO, and exports and import substitution subsidies will be totally eliminated in the next few years.

In order to strengthen their position, state-owned enterprises will have to attract foreign investment. This could prove difficult in the case of scale-intensive industries where these enterprises are more exposed to international competition from Japan, Korea, and, increasingly, China.

Ultimately, although WTO regulations and the competition from China might make it more difficult for Vietnam to follow the East Asian path, Vietnam might none the less enjoy the benefit of being a late starter (especially at the Asian level), as stated by Gerschenkron (1966): 'One can say that in a backward country, there exists a prerequisite to industrial development which the advanced countries did not have at its disposition, that is the existence of the more advanced countries as source of technological assistance, skilled labour and capital goods.'

At the moment, unlike other Asian emerging countries, Vietnam does not participate actively in the swiftly developing regional production networks, a situation that might change with the rise of electronics exports. Vietnam increasingly emerges as an alternative destination for the multinationals of this sector, as illustrated by Intel's decision to build a chip assembly and testing plant in this country, and the appearance of outsourcing activities. This move could help Vietnam to join Asian countries in the 'Asian integrated circuit', which could prove Gerschenkron right.

APPENDIX 1: METHODOLOGY

Finger–Kreinin indicator

The Finger–Kreinin export similarity index for two countries' i and j exports is defined as:

$$FK_{ij} = \sum_k \min(S_{ik}, S_{jk}) \times 100$$

Where S_{ik} represents country i's share of export of product k to the third market in its total exports toward the third market and S_{jk} country j's share of export of product k to the third market in its total exports toward the third market. The indicator varies between 0 (total dissimilarity) and 100 (similarity).

Revealed comparative advantage

The comparative-advantage indicator answers the question: 'what are the strong points and the weak points of an economy?' Instead of relative export structures, as in the classic Balassa (1965) method, the analytical indicator used here is based on the share of the total trade balance and takes into account the size of each country's market.

The formulas are described below, with V_{ijk} indicating the flow from exporting country i to importing country j for product k. The summations of the various indices are given as:

$$X_{ik} = V_{i.k} \quad \text{Exports from country i of product k}$$
$$X_{i.} = V_{i..} \quad \text{Exports from country i of all goods}$$
$$M_{jk} = V_{.jk} \quad \text{Imports by country j of product k}$$
$$M_{j.} = V_{.j.} \quad \text{Imports of country j of all goods}$$
$$W_k = V_{..k} \quad \text{World trade of product k}$$
$$W_. = V_{...} \quad \text{World trade of all goods}$$

For country i and product k, the balance is first calculated in relation to GDP at current exchange rate Y, giving (in thousandths):

$$y_{ik} = 1000 * \frac{X_{ik} - M_{ik}}{Y_i}$$

The contribution of product k to the trade balance, in relation to GDP, is defined by:

$$f_{ik} = y_{ik} - g_{ik} * y_i$$

where:

$$g_{ik} = \frac{X_{ik} + M_{ik}}{X_{i.} + M_i} \text{ AND } y_{i.} = 1000 * \frac{X_{i.} - M_{i.k}}{Y_i}$$

In addition, it is necessary to eliminate the influence of changes that are not specific to the country in question but result from the evolution of the importance of the product in world trade. In relation to a base year (r), the flows X and M in the other years (n) are adjusted by multiplying them all by:

$$e^n_i = \frac{W^r_k}{W^r} : \frac{W^n_k}{W^n}$$

The comparative advantage indicator f′ is therefore calculated using world weights for the base year (r). For this year, it is identical to the relative contribution f. For the other years (n), the difference is all the greater the more world trade in product k diverges from the average tendency for all merchandise.

Comparative advantages are calculated for individual products at the most detailed level of the CHELEM sectoral classification. The advantage by chain or by stage or production is then calculated by summing.

Source: www.cepii.fr (accessed 10 May 2007).

APPENDIX 2: STATISTICAL SOURCES

Foreign trade

Three types of foreign trade data are used in this chapter: international databases, industrialized countries' imports, and foreign direct investment.

International databases

We use the CHELEM-IT database built by CEPII (Centre d'études prospectives et d'informations internationals, Paris). CHELEM-IT brings together trade flows (goods) which are broken down into seventy-one product categories. These trade figures are given in current US$ (millions), and are available from 1967. Trade statistics for flows between geographic zones (countries and country groups) are provided for each year, and for each product category, in a single, 'harmonized' matrix.

Industrialized countries' imports

European Union (15): Eurostat, HS 2 Classification
  <http://ec.europa.eu/eurostat/ramon/relations/index.cfm?TargetUrl=LST_REL>.
USA: US International Trade Commission: CTCI 3 digit Classification
  <http://www.usitc.gov>.
Japan: Global Trade Atlas <http://www.gtis.com/gta/>.
Vietnam: General Statistical Office (GSO).
China: Statistical Yearbook.

Foreign direct investment

Ministry of Planning and Investment: statistics on FDI (committed and disbursed), with breakdown by country origin of investors.

REFERENCES

Ahearne, A., J. Fernald, P. Loungani, and J. Shindler (2006) *Flying Geese or Sitting Ducks: China's Impact on the Trading Fortunes of other Asian Countries*, Board of Governors of the Federal Reserve System, International Finance Working Paper 887 (Dec.).

Akamatsu, K. (1962) 'A Historical Pattern of Economic Growth in Developing Countries', *Developing Economies*, 1: 3–25.

Amsden, A. (2001) *The Rise of the Rest* (Oxford: Oxford University Press).

Athukorala, P. (2006) *Product Fragmentation and Trade Patterns in East Asia*, Asian Economic Papers 4 (New York and Cambridge, Mass.: Columbia University/MIT).

Balassa, B. (1965) 'Trade Liberalization and "Revealed" Comparative Advantage', *Manchester School of Economics and Social Studies*, 33: 99–123.

Bhalla, S. S. (1998) *Chinese Mercantilism: Currency Wars and How the East was Lost*, ICRIER Paper 45 (July) (New Delhi: Indian Council for Research on International Economics).

Cao, X. D., and T. A.-D. Tran (2005) 'Transition et ouverture économique au Vietna une différenciation sectorielle', *Economie Internationale*, 104: 28–43.

Chang, H. A. (2002) *Kicking Away the Ladder: Development Strategy in Historical Perspective* (London: Anthem Press).

Cling, J.-P., M. Razafindrakoto, and F. Roubaud (eds) (2009) 'Vietnam's WTO accession and export-led growth', *Economie Internationale/International Economics*, special issue on Vietnam, No. 118, 2009–2.

Eichengreen, B. J. (2004) 'The Impact of China on the Exports of Other Asian Countries', NBER Working Paper 10768 (Sept.) (Cambridge, Mass.: NBER).

—— (2005) *How China is Reorganizing the World Economy*, Asia Economic Policy Panel.

—— and H. Tong (2005) *Is China's FDI Coming at the Expense of Other Countries*, NBER Working Paper 11335 (Cambridge, Mass.: NBER).

Finger, J. M., and M. E. Kreinin (1979) 'A Measure of Export Similarity and its Possible Use', *Economic Journal*, 89: 905–12.

Gaulier, G., F. Lemoine, and D. Unal-Kesenci (2005) *China's Integration in East Asia: Production Sharing, FDI and High-Tech Trade*, Working Paper 2005–09 (June) (Paris: Centre d'études prospectives et d'informations internationales).

Gerschenkron, A. (1966) *Economic Backwardness in Historical Perspective* (Cambridge, Mass.: Harvard University Press).

Humphrey, J., and H. Schmitz (2006) *The Implication of China's Growth on Other Asian Countries* (Brighton: Institute of Development Studies).

IMF (2007) *Regional Economic Outlook: Asia and Pacific* (Apr.) (Washington, DC: IMF).

Ishida, M. (2005) *Effectiveness and Challenges of Three Economic Corridors of the Greater Sub-region*, Discussion Paper 35 (Tokyo: Institute of Developing Economies).

JETRO (2007) *2006 Survey of Japanese-Affiliated Firms in ASEAN and India* (Tokyo: Japan External Trade Organization).

Kwan, C. H. (2002) 'The Rise of China and Asia's Flying Geese Pattern of Economic Development: An Empirical Analysis Based on US Import Statistics', RIETI Discussion Paper 02 E 003 (Tokyo: RIETI).

Lall, S., and M. Albaladejo (2004) 'China's Competitive Performance: A Threat to East Asian Manufactured Exports?', *World Development*, 32: 1441–66.

Maddison, A. (n.d.) <http://www.ggdc.net/maddison/>.

Nguyen, B. D., and T. A.-D. Tran (2007) 'Insertion internationale et intégration régionale: le Vietnam doit-il craindre la concurrence chinoise?' (Paris: Université Paris-Nord). mimeo.

Okita, S. (1985) 'Special Presentation: Prospect of Pacific Economies', Korea Development Institute, *Pacific Cooperation: Issues and Opportunities*. Report of the Fourth Pacific Economic Cooperation Conference, Seoul, Korea, 29 Apr.–1 May: 18–29.

Ravenhill, J. (2006) 'Is China an Economic Threat to Southeast Asia?', *Asian Survey*, 46 (Sept.).

Tumbarello, P. (2006) 'Does Vietnam Overtrade with its Neighbouring Countries? A Regional Investigation using a Gravity Model'. IMF Country Report No. 06/20, Vietnam: Selected Issues. (Washington, DC: IMF).

Vo, T. T. (2005) 'Vietnam's Trade Liberalization and International Economic Integration; Evolution, Problems and Challenges', *ASEAN Economic Bulletin*, 22: 75–94.

World Bank (1993) *The East Asian Miracle: Economic Growth and Public Policy* (New York: Oxford University Press).

—— (2007) *World Development Indicators* (Washington, DC: World Bank).

Part III

The Role of Capital Flows, Investment, and Trade

7

The Liberalization of Capital Outflows in China, India, Brazil, and South Africa: What Opportunities for Other Developing Countries?

Ricardo Gottschalk and Cecilia Azevedo Sodré[1]

INTRODUCTION

China, India, Brazil, and South Africa (CIBS) are becoming major players in the global economy due to their trade relations with the rest of the world and their growing political assertiveness on the international stage. Moreover, China and India also matter because they have accumulated large amounts of international reserves, thereby becoming major sources of official capital to the rest of the world.

In each CIBS country, the opening of trade has been followed by the liberalization of the capital account. However, capital account liberalization (CAL) has not been completed. Although liberalization on the side of capital inflows by non-residents has been significant, in some CIBS countries the liberalization of capital outflows by residents has been fairly limited. It will be seen later in this chapter that this has especially been the case in China. What will happen if these countries promote further CAL on the outflow side? For China, from its current position as a holder of massive amounts of international reserves, the most likely outcome will be that it will increasingly export private capital, rather than official. Thus, in China, and in CIBS more broadly,

[1] The authors would like to thank Gustavo Bagattini for his effective research assistance. Comments from the participants of the UNU-WIDER Conference on Southern Engines of Global Growth: China, India, Brazil, and South Africa, held 7–8 September 2007 in Helsinki; the book editors; Adam Swallow; and three anonymous referees are also greatly acknowledged. The usual caveats apply.

it will not be Central Bank officials but private agents who will decide where, how, and for how long to invest abroad.

Who will gain and who will lose from this shift from official to private capital flows, and from capital invested domestically to capital invested abroad? Can we predict the future destination of private capital flows from these countries? Which countries will be able to attract such flows, by how much, and in what form?

This chapter examines the implications of the liberalization of capital outflows in CIBS for other developing countries. It focuses on their prospects of attracting not only FDI, but also portfolio capital flows from CIBS. It asks the question: will developing countries have the ability to attract part of the portfolio capital flowing from CIBS or will these flows go only to developed countries? Will CIBS capital flows be invested in other developing countries from the same region—for example, China's capital flows being invested in developing Asia—or will these be invested in other developing regions as well? What initiatives could developing countries take to obtain access to these flows? Would such flows be desirable in the first place? These questions are about future developments, which, in turn, depend on an array of factors, including future policy decision-making and portfolio allocation decisions made by domestic private investors in the CIBS countries. Thus, to address these questions, this chapter takes an exploratory approach, with the aim of offering a preliminary idea of potential trends in private capital flows from CIBS towards the rest of the world.

The chapter's approach consists of two parts: first, it briefly describes capital account liberalization undertaken by CIBS to date and intended liberalization in order to have a more concrete idea of what sort of capital flows might come from this group of countries in the future. Second, it maps geographic distribution of outward FDI, and foreign portfolio equity and debt assets held by the CIBS countries in the recent past, so as to give us indications of the possible direction of capital flows in the future.

The next section describes capital account liberalization for each of the four CIBS countries. This is followed by an analysis of trends in the stocks of assets held abroad by the CIBS countries and the changes in their composition in the period 1990–2004. The chapter goes on to examine the direction and location of FDI and portfolio assets held abroad in the early 2000s, and then provides a summary analysis and suggests a few policy ideas to enhance developing country ability to attract portfolio flows from the CIBS countries. The chapter closes with an overview and conclusions.

CAPITAL ACCOUNT LIBERALIZATION IN CIBS

This section describes the steps CIBS have undertaken towards liberalization on the side of capital outflows by residents.[2] It shows that the liberalization in these countries has occurred in diverse ways and at different speeds, but all have been sequenced. In discussing sequencing, the categorization used is the type of resident—not the type of flows, as usually is the case in analysis of liberalization of capital inflows.

Of the four countries under analysis, Brazil began liberalization first (in the early 1990s) and has gone furthest in opening the capital account for residents to invest abroad, especially corporations and individuals. South Africa and India can be considered intermediate cases, in that they have been somewhat more cautious than Brazil. South Africa pursued gradual financial liberalization including institutions and private investors in the process. India has adopted a gradual approach linked to meeting preconditions. China was the last to commence liberalization and has been the slowest, liberalizing in only a very limited way, although the process has been speeded up more recently.

Despite the differing rates of liberalization, CIBS have signalled their intention of further liberalizing outflows to a major degree in the future, Brazil again going furthest in considering full capital account convertibility. As in the past, India has signalled that further liberalization will be dependent on meeting key preconditions, such as the strengthening of its financial system. In China, it is probable that further liberalization will continue to be not only gradual, but also experimental and responsive to the country's macroeconomic circumstances.[3]

In what follows, liberalization on capital outflows is described for each of the CIBS countries in a summarized form. The summary begins with Brazil, followed by South Africa, India, and China.

---

[2] The analysis comprises the liberalization of bank lending and portfolio flows only, thus excluding FDI. It draws on Gottschalk and Sodre 2008.

[3] Zhao (2006) argues that in China liberalization of the capital account has not been gradual but, rather, experimental. The difference between the two forms of liberalization is that the latter is not committed to an end goal of full liberalization, is based on experiments with small liberalization steps, and can be reversed when it is shown that such steps do not work well.

BRAZIL

Brazil took major steps towards liberalization, especially on the side of capital inflows, during the Collor government from 1990 to 1992.[4] On the outflows side, which is our interest here, in early 1992, the government permitted foreign banks to transfer resources abroad through a mechanism called Carta-Circular No. 5 (CC-5). The CC-5 was, until very recently, the main means by which residents could invest abroad. It was created in 1969 to allow non-residents with business in Brazil to send money abroad.[5] Specifically, the CC-5 established that non-residents could only use national currency to buy foreign currency and send this abroad if the resources in domestic currency were the result of previous conversion from foreign currency brought by the non-resident to the country.

In February 1992, the Brazilian government deepened the liberalization process by permitting foreign banks to create a sub-account in order to send dollars abroad without the need for previous internalization of an equivalent amount of resources.[6] The additional relevant element was that corporations and individual residents in Brazil could use these sub-accounts to make a direct investment abroad or to send money to their own account abroad.

The liberalization of capital outflows took further steps in 1994 with the creation of the special investment funds abroad, known as Fiex (now called *Fundos de Divida Externa*).[7] The Fiex is a fund that domestic institutional investors, financial institutions, non-financial corporations, and individuals can use to invest abroad. The rules that initially governed the fund were that at least 60 per cent of the total resources had to be invested in Brazilian foreign debt, with the remainder permitted to be invested in other securities, derivatives, or held in the form of bank deposits abroad (in January 1999, the limit was increased to 80 per cent).[8] The fund clearly represented an additional mechanism through which resources could be sent abroad. Besides investments made through Fiex, residents could invest in stocks

---

[4] These steps included further opening of the domestic capital markets to foreign portfolio investment involving both the stock and derivative markets and fixed income following limited opening in 1987, and permission given to Brazilian companies to issue different types of securities abroad (Prates 1998).

[5] See Carta-Circular No. 5, 27 Feb. 1969.

[6] Cartas-Circulares 2.242, 7 Oct. 1992.

[7] Fiex is the acronym for *Fundos de Investimento no Exterior*, which we translate into English as 'special investment funds abroad'. *Fundos de Divida Externa* can be translated as 'external debt funds'.

[8] See Circular of the Central Bank of Brazil 2.111 (22 Sept. 1994) and Circular 2.714 (28 Aug. 1996).

from Mercosur countries. Institutional investors were also permitted to invest in the Fiex; however, they could only invest 10 per cent of their total resources.

In March 2005, the Central Bank brought the CC-5 to an end. In its place, it authorized individuals and corporations to transfer resources abroad through their own bank accounts, with no quantitative limits. In September 2006, further liberalization for residents took place. Corporations and individuals have been allowed to send resources abroad through the foreign exchange market in order to acquire stocks, derivatives, and other investments in the international capital markets. Until then, explicitly, residents could only acquire stocks from Mercosur countries and securities issued by Brazilian corporations abroad (for example, ADRs) by foreign corporations domestically (BDRs), or through Fiex.

SOUTH AFRICA

Since 1994, when the South African economy was reintegrated into the world economy, the liberalization of capital outflows by residents has been gradual and sequenced. As from mid-1995, institutional investors were granted permission to invest abroad by means of an asset exchange mechanism, amounting to 5 per cent of their total assets. According to this mechanism, the resident investor had to find an external counterpart interested in investing in South Africa's financial assets, and this investment had to be equivalent in value to the financial investment of the South African investor abroad. The aim was to ensure balance of payments neutrality (National Treasury 2001). The 5 per cent limit was increased to 10 per cent in 1996, coupled with the option that investors could transfer resources abroad amounting to 3 per cent of the net inflows of funds during the previous year.

Since then, significant steps have been taken regarding the liberalization of capital outflows. The limit on institutional investors' external assets was increased to 15 per cent of total assets in 1999, with the limit of foreign exchange purchase increasing from 3 per cent to 5 per cent of the net inflows of funds during the previous year. In 2001, the asset exchange mechanism was eliminated, as were restrictions relative to annual inflows. This applied for long-term insurers, pension funds, and fund managers. Unit trusts could hold external assets up to 20 per cent of their total assets, subject to the upper limit of 10 per cent of annual net inflows in the previous period (Hviding 2005; IMF 2002; National Treasury 2001).

INDIA

India has taken steps towards CAL since June 1997, when the first Tarapore Committee (Tarapore I) recommended a timetable for implementation (Reserve Bank of India 2000). Until then, India's capital account was fairly restricted, as a result of a very slow liberalization process that had started back in the early 1990s. According to the proposed timetable by Tarapore I, the capital account in India would be liberalized gradually, in three phases over the course of three years: 1997–8 (phase 1); 1998–9 (phase 2); and 1999–2000 (phase 3). The proposed liberalization included both capital inflows and outflows.

With regard to capital outflows—the focus of this chapter—the proposal made by the committee involved the following categories of residents: (i) corporations; (ii) the Security Exchange Board of India (SEBI), which registers Indian investors (including mutual funds); and (iii) individuals. Corporations would initially be permitted to transfer up to US$25,000 of financial capital abroad. Later, this limit would be raised to US$50,000 and US$100,000 in the second and third phases of the proposed liberalization. Banks, in turn, would be permitted to invest up to US$10 million in overseas money markets, mutual funds, and/or debt instruments. This limit was increased to US$25 million in November 2002.

For the Security Exchange Board of India (SEBI), from an initial position in which no investment abroad was permitted, Tarapore I proposed that investors be permitted to invest in overseas financial markets, subject to an overall ceiling of US$500 million in the first phase, US$1 billion in the second phase, and US$2 billion in the third phase. The committee observed that it was important to ensure that the total amount was not met by just a few large-sized funds. Similarly to institutional investors, until 1997 individuals were not permitted to invest abroad. Tarapore I changed this by proposing that individuals be able to invest in financial markets and/or hold deposits abroad up to US$25,000 per annum in the first phase, US$50,000 in the second phase, and US$100,000 in the third phase.

It is widely known that the timetable proposed by Tarapore I was not fully implemented. Admittedly, the main reason for this was the fact that the East Asian crisis occurred shortly after the Tarapore I report was released. Indeed, the Asian crisis led to a change in the whole situation.

More broadly, with regard to the effective capital controls observed in the 1990s, which do not necessarily correspond with Tarapore I intentions, Nayyar (2000) emphasizes the existence of a complex and asymmetrical structure of capital controls: asymmetry between capital inflows and outflows, with a wide range of controls on capital outflows compared with the more liberalized capital inflows; asymmetry between residents and non-residents, with more liberalization of capital by non-residents and strict controls by residents (showing that this was an area where the Tarapore I guidelines were not really implemented); and asymmetries between individuals and corporations, with individuals facing more controls, while corporations benefited from significant liberalization.

The macroeconomic conditions in India have improved in recent years and the financial system has become stronger and less repressed. Reflecting this, a new Tarapore Committee on CAL (Tarapore II) was set up in March 2006 and a report was made public at the end of July 2006. It recommended a phased increase in the ceilings on outward transfers of resources according to the different types of investors. As in the previous report, Tarapore II recommended a three-phase approach over a five-year period for further CAL in India: 2006–7 (phase 1); 2007–9 (phase 2); 2009–11 (phase 3). As established by Tarapore I, the latest report has included further liberalization of outflows.

Corporations will initially be permitted to invest up to 25 per cent of their net worth in overseas corporations having at least a 10 per cent shareholding in listed Indian corporations and in rated bonds/fixed-income securities. It is intended that this restriction should be abolished at the end of phase 1. Banks should maintain the same limits previously established by Tarapore I without any changes.

SEBI-registered Indian investors (including mutual funds) should be allowed to invest from an overall ceiling of US$2 billion to US$3 billion in phase 1. It is anticipated that an overall ceiling of US$4 billion will be observed in phase 2 and of US$5 billion in phase 3.

The annual limits of transfers of money abroad by *individuals* should be raised to US$50,000 in phase 1 from the existing limit of US$25,000 per annum, to US$100,000 in phase 2 and to US$200,000 in phase 3. The present rule regarding limitless investments in overseas corporations listed on a stock exchange (and having a shareholding of at least 10 per cent in an Indian company) should be banned in the context of the large increase in the new limits. Should there be any difficulties in managing the new scheme, it is anticipated that Tarapore II will review the situation.

The Tarapore II report also suggests a road map for fuller capital account convertibility (FCAC), which does not necessarily mean zero capital restrictions.

CHINA

Since the commencement of the 'open door' policy in 1978, China has undergone significant capital liberalization. This has occurred mainly on the inflow side, initially with the liberalization of FDI and bank lending, followed by portfolio flows. On the outflow side, liberalization only really started, very timidly, in 2004, when domestic insurance companies were permitted to invest their own foreign exchange in the international capital markets. The next liberalization move took place soon afterwards, with a foreign firm being allowed to list on the Shanghai stock exchange (Zhao 2006).

In 2006, further relaxation took place. Qualified domestic financial institutions were permitted to invest in international capital markets—in both fixed income and stocks, on behalf of domestic institutions and individuals (Lane and Schmukler 2006; Zhao 2006). This latest liberalization took place in response to pressure to ease outflows of capital in the context of rapid accumulation of international reserves. The expectations are that China will continue to liberalize outflows by residents. However, as argued by Zhao (2006), this will be done in a controlled manner and according to the macroeconomic circumstances at the time, as has always been the case in the past with the liberalization steps undertaken for capital inflows by non-residents.

SUMMARY

Table 7.1 summarizes the main liberalization measures for each of the CIBS countries.

It is interesting to observe that the liberalization experiences between the four countries have been gradual and sequenced. With regard to financial outflows by institutional investors, Brazil and India have both maintained some restrictions, including end-use restriction in the case of Brazil, while in South Africa, liberalization has been less restrictive. It will be seen that, in the case of Brazil, such restrictions have clearly affected the direction of capital flows. In India, mutual funds face overall upper limits to investment abroad, while institutional investors (such as pension funds) are public owned, investing mainly in domestic assets, and the insurance industry is almost totally public owned, only very recently being subject to reforms involving privatization.[9] From an

---

[9] Interview material.

Table 7.1. *Liberalization of financial outflows by residents*

	Institutional investors	Corporations	Individuals
Brazil	Investment funds have no limits to investment abroad; end-use restrictions. Pension funds can invest up to 10% of total assets abroad; end-use restrictions.	Until 2005, investment through CC-5 accounts beyond US$5 million required previous authorization from the Central Bank. Since then, transfer can be made directly, and restrictions have been removed. Need to specify purpose of transfers.	Until 2005, transfers could be made through CC-5 accounts. Since then, transfers can be made directly, with no limits. Need to specify purpose of transfer.
China	Domestic insurance companies permitted to invest their own foreign exchange in the international capital markets. Permitted to invest abroad both in fixed income and stocks, via qualified domestic financial institutions.	Not specified.	Permitted to invest in the international capital markets, via qualified domestic financial institutions.
India	Aggregate limit of US$2 billion per annum set by Tarapore I. Recommended by Tarapore II to be increased to US$5 billion by 2009–11. This is, in practice, valid for investment funds, but not pension funds or insurers, which are mainly public owned.	Restrictive quantitative limits. Tarapore II indicates they will be permitted to invest up to 25% of their net worth in overseas companies having at least 10 per cent shareholding in listed Indian companies and in rated bonds/fixed-income securities. In 2002, Banks permitted to invest up to US$25 million.	Current limit of US$25,000 per annum to be increased to US$50,000, US$100,000, and US$200,000 by 2006–7, 2007–9, and 2009–11, as recommended by Tarapore II. Existing permission to invest without limits in overseas companies listed on a stock exchange, and having at least 10% shareholding in an Indian company should be banned.
South Africa	Pension funds, insurers, and mutual funds permitted to invest abroad subject to the aggregate limit of 15% of total assets (20% for unit trust industry). Limits of up to 5% of total net inflows in the previous year (but removed since 2001, except for unit trusts, which still face a higher limit, of up to 10%).	Allowed to expand their offshore investments with profits generated abroad or financed abroad.	Quantitative limits; they can also maintain foreign-earned income. Residents permitted to invest in foreign instruments listed on South African exchange

Source: Modified from Gottschalk and Sodre 2008.

initial position of very limited liberalization, China has more recently taken a significant step towards liberalization for institutions and individuals.

Today, all four countries are either signalling or effectively undertaking further liberalization steps. Brazil has done so in the recent past, India is proposing a timetable to further the process, and China is debating possible further liberalization to ease macroeconomic pressures arising from the accumulation of large reserves.

TRENDS IN ASSETS AND LIABILITIES STOCKS

CIBS began to liberalize capital outflows by residents from the early 1990s, as noted earlier. In the early 1990s, Brazil was the first to begin liberalization, followed by South Africa in the mid-1990s, India in 1997–8, and China in 2004.

We commence the analysis by looking at the trajectories of stocks of assets held abroad by these countries in the period 1970–2004. The aim is to see how liberalization of capital outflows affected such trajectories. For that purpose, we use the data set on stocks of foreign assets and liabilities constructed by Lane and Milesi-Ferretti (2006) (hereafter L-M).[10] The L-M estimates of assets and liabilities comprise FDI, portfolio equity investment, external debt, and international reserves.[11] We plot the data on assets together with liabilities (and international reserves) to gather a sense of proportion, and because over certain periods both trends are strongly correlated—for example, in China since the early 1990s.

Figures 7.1A–7.1D show that stocks of assets grew strongly for CIBS in the period 1990–2004, although less so in Brazil—229 per cent against 559 per cent in South Africa, 1,728 per cent in China, and 1,721 per cent in India. Growth of total assets in Brazil was driven mainly by FDI; in China and India, by international reserves, with a far smaller contribution from debt assets; and in South Africa, by portfolio equity assets, and to a lesser extent, debt, and FDI. Table 7.2 shows the contribution of each type of asset stock to total asset stock accumulation for each country. Figures 7.1A–7.1D

---

[10] The database for Lane and Milesi-Ferretti 2006 is available at <http://www.imf.org/external/pubs/ft/wp/2006/data/wp0669.zip>.

[11] The cut-off point to differentiate FDI from portfolio equity is holdings of at least 10 per cent of an entity's equity; in turn, debt comprises portfolio debt securities, bank loans and deposits, and other debt instruments.

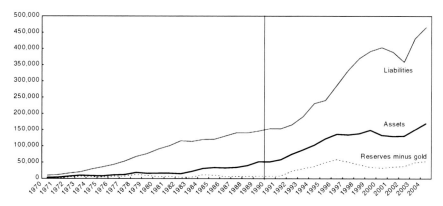

Figure 7.1.A. *Brazil: assets, reserves, and liabilities, 1970–2004 (US$ million)*
Source: Authors' elaboration, based on data from Lane and Milesi-Ferretti 2006.

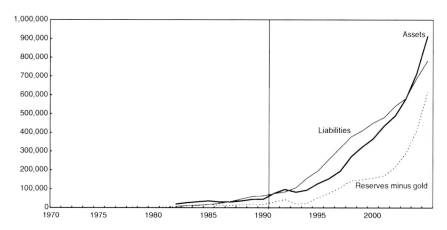

Figure 7.1.B. *China: assets, reserves, and liabilities, 1981–2004 (US$ million)*
Source: Authors' elaboration, based on data from Lane and Milesi-Ferretti 2006.

and Table 7.2 thus show that accumulation of total assets in China, and especially India, mirrors accumulation of international reserves, while in Brazil and South Africa accumulation of total assets is driven by non-reserves assets. This indicates that capital account liberalization during 1990–2004 was more significant in Brazil and South Africa than in China and India.

As one might expect, growth of assets has been accompanied by a change in their composition. Figures 7.2A–7.2D show that between 1990 and 2004

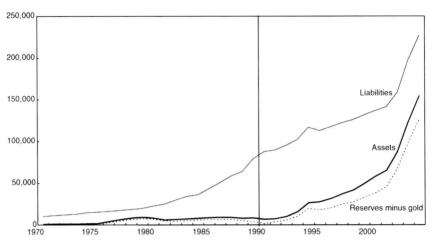

Figure 7.1.C. *India: assets, reserves, and liabilities, 1970–2004 (US$ million)*

Source: Authors' elaboration, based on data from Lane and Milesi-Ferretti 2006.

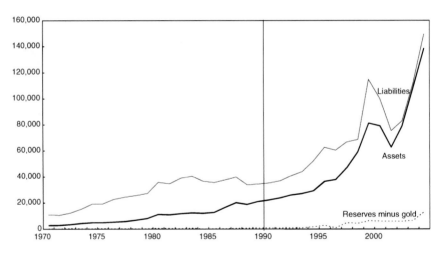

Figure 7.1.D. *South Africa: assets, reserves, and liabilities, 1970–2004 (US$ million)*

Source: Authors' elaboration, based on data from Lane and Milesi-Ferretti 2006.

the main change in Brazil has been a shift towards FDI assets; in China and India, towards international reserves; and in South Africa, portfolio equity. Table 7.3 displays growth of total assets in the period 1990–2004, which includes international reserves and growth of the non-reserves assets. It shows that accumulations in China and especially India were smaller when

Table 7.2. *Contribution of different categories of assets to growth of total asset stocks (1990–2004 percentage)*

	Brazil	China	India	South Africa
FDI	43.8	3.7	6.4	21.6
Portfolio equity	7.0	0.7	0.6	43.9
Debt	10.9	27.0	9.2	24.2
International reserves	38.2	68.7	83.8	10.4

Source: Authors' elaboration based on data from Lane and Milesi-Ferretti 2006.

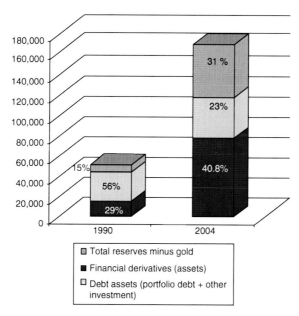

Figure 7.2.A. *Brazil: composition of assets, 1990 and 2004 (US$ million)*

Source: Authors' elaboration, based on data from Lane and Milesi-Ferretti 2006.

international reserves are excluded, although still high, partly because of initial low levels of non-reserves assets held abroad by these two countries. For Brazil and South Africa, accumulation of assets, both with and without international reserves, took place at similar growth rates, especially for South Africa.

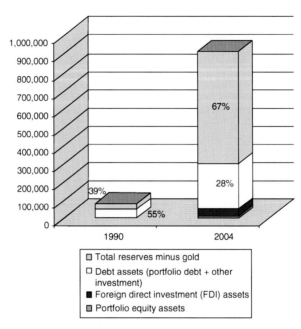

Figure 7.2.B. *China: composition of assets, 1990 and 2004 (US$ million)*

Source: Authors' elaboration, based on data from Lane and Milesi-Ferretti 2006.

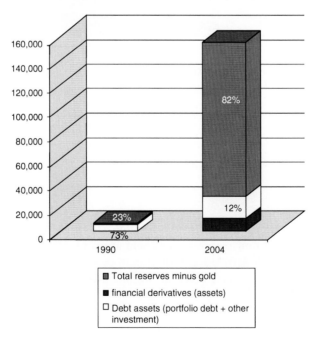

Figure 7.2.C. *India: composition of assets, 1990 and 2004 (US$ million)*

Source: Authors' elaboration, based on data from Lane and Milesi-Ferretti 2006.

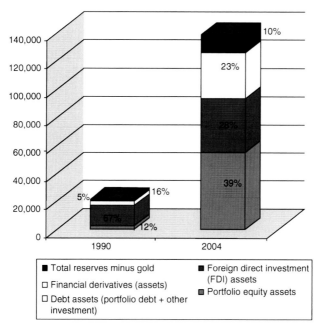

Figure 7.2.D. *South Africa: composition of assets, 1990 and 2004*

Source: Authors' elaboration, based on data from Lane and Milesi-Ferretti 2006.

Table 7.3. *Accumulation of total and non-reserves assets, 1990–2004 (growth rates percentage)*

	Total assets (includes international reserves)	Non-reserves assets
Brazil	229.2	165.8
China	1927.8	1003.8
India	1721.8	509.6
South Africa	558.5	524.6

Source: Authors' elaboration, based on data set from Lane and Milesi-Ferretti 2006.

DISTRIBUTION OF ASSETS/FLOWS ACROSS REGIONS AND GROUPS OF COUNTRIES

Accumulation of non-reserves assets has been strong among CIBS, as noted. What has been the geographic distribution of these assets? This section analyses how the different types of assets have been distributed across different regions and/or groups of countries. Most of the analysis that follows focuses on the distribution of assets in the 2000s, although in some cases information on flows is used instead. We start with FDI, followed by portfolio equity stocks and then portfolio debt stocks. FDI is used in addition to portfolio stocks for comparative purposes, and because we are also interested in possible distribution patterns of bank lending and believe FDI may be used as an indicator of where bank lending from CIBS might be heading.

Data on FDI for China and India are displayed in flows and are obtained from the UNCTAD's World Investment Report (WIR). For Brazil and South Africa, data are in stocks and have been obtained from Brazil's Central Bank database and WIR, respectively.[12] Data on portfolio equity and debt stocks are obtained from the Coordinated Portfolio Investment Survey (CPIS), which is available on the IMF website. This data set is available for India, Brazil, and South Africa, but not China.

For the analysis of distribution, the categorization used is hybrid: first, countries are divided between OECD and non-OECD countries; Korea, Mexico, and Turkey have been included as non-OECD countries. A separate category is then created—offshore financial centres (OFCs)—which includes both OECD and non-OECD countries. Finally, we use the World Bank classification to group the non-OECD countries in the following categories: Asia and Pacific, Latin America and the Caribbean, Europe, sub-Saharan Africa (SSA), and the Middle East and North Africa.

DISTRIBUTION OF FDI

Starting the analysis of direction of FDI for Brazil, given that information used is in stocks, we focus on distribution of the FDI stocks position in 2005, which is the most recent year for which data are available.

Figure 7.3A shows that of a total FDI stock of US$65 billion held abroad 49 per cent is located in offshore financial centres (OFCs), a further 42 per cent is in the OECD countries, and the remaining 9 per cent is distributed between Latin America and the Caribbean (8 percent) and developing Europe (1 per cent).[13] It is reported that nearly all of the FDIs

---

[12] We consider data inflows preferable as these better reflect recent patterns of FDI direction. However, data are in stocks for Brazil and South Africa, as only these were available.

[13] This subsection is limited to describing directions of FDI from the CIBS countries. For a thorough discussion of the main drivers and motivations of Brazil's outward FDI, and also of China's and India's, see Sauvant 2005. For a recent discussion of outward FDI from emerging economies more broadly, see OECD 2007.

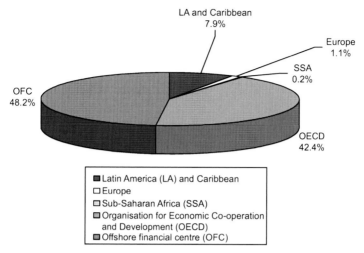

Figure 7.3.A. *Distribution of Brazil's outward foreign direct investment (FDI) stocks, 2005*
Source: Authors' elaboration, based on data from Central Bank of Brazil.

in the OFCs are invested in the tertiary sector, specifically in services provided to companies and financial intermediation (Central Bank of Brazil 2007). In reality, these resources probably go, first, to the OFCs, because of tax exemptions, and are redirected to other countries to support expansion of large corporations abroad and export operations through funding the establishment of offices, technical assistance, and distribution centres in the importing countries (Barros 2007). If we exclude these and focus on the remaining 51 per cent of FDIs, we can see that 82 per cent goes to the OECD countries, 15 per cent to Latin America and the Caribbean, and 2 per cent to Europe. The distribution is therefore still skewed towards the OECD group of countries.

Of the FDIs in the OECD countries, about 50 per cent is located in just two countries: the USA and Denmark.[14] In Latin America, most of the FDIs are in Argentina (40 per cent) and Uruguay (34 per cent). The concentration of FDIs in these two countries reflects the existence of South America's Mercosur trade area.[15] Most of the FDIs in SSA are in Liberia and Angola.

---

[14] The high level of FDI in Denmark is explained by the acquisition of Canada's Labatt Brewing Company by Brazil's Ambev in 2004 and the fact that Labatt's controlling company had its headquarters in Denmark (Tavares 2006).

[15] Sauvant 2005 notes that Brazil's FDI in Latin America reflects the country's increasing role promoting regional integration through investment and production in the region.

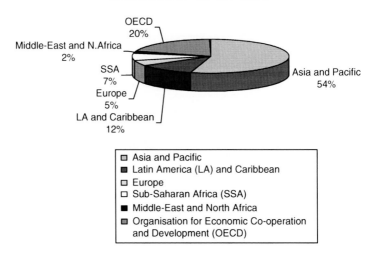

Figure 7.3.B. *Destination of China's outward foreign direct investment (FDI) flows, 1999–2002*

Source: Authors' elaboration, based on data from UNCTAD's World Investment Report.

Next, we look at China's FDI flows abroad. Taking the average of FDI flows over 1999–2002, we can see that of US$708 million of total flows, 54 per cent went to the Asia and Pacific region, a further 20 per cent to the OECD, 12 per cent to Latin America, and 7 per cent to SSA (see Figure 7.3B). The largest recipient by far is Hong Kong, followed by the USA, and then several developing countries both from Asia and Latin America, plus Russia. Australia also features among the main recipients of China's FDI. However, the destination patterns are changing very rapidly. Using the classification in Cheng and Ma 2007, in 2005 over half of China's FDI (nearly 53 per cent) went to Latin America. The main factor driving China's FDI towards Latin America is the need for natural resources to sustain her high growth path. In 2005, Asia as a whole attracted 36 per cent of total FDI, Europe 4 per cent, and Africa 3 per cent.

India's FDI destination is better distributed across the different groupings and regions. Of the total average flows of US$1.7 billion over 2001–4, 34 per cent went to the OECD countries. The remaining flows went to developing Europe (28 per cent), SSA (24 per cent), Asia and Pacific (9 per cent), the Middle East and North Africa (3 per cent), and OFCs (2 per cent) (see Figure 7.3C).

In terms of countries, the largest recipients are Russia (over 25 per cent of the total flows), the USA (nearly 22 per cent), and Sudan (over 13 per cent). Most of the flows to Asia went to Vietnam, Singapore, Hong Kong, and China (7.4 per cent of the total) and less than 1 per cent to the neighbouring Nepal and Sri Lanka in South Asia.

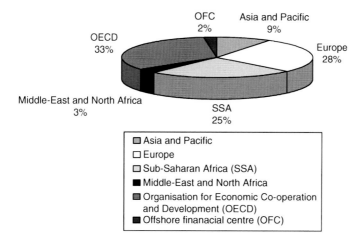

Figure 7.3.C. *Destination of India's outward foreign direct investment (FDI) flows, 2001–4*

Source: Authors' elaboration, based on data from UNCTAD's World Investment Report.

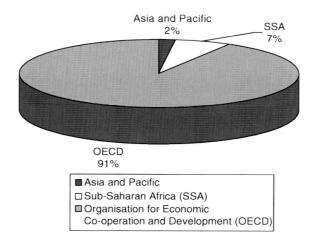

Figure 7.3.D. *Distribution of South Africa's outward foreign direct investment (FDI) stocks, 2002*

Source: Authors' elaboration, based on data from UNCTAD's World Investment Report.

In contrast to India, South Africa's outward FDI is highly concentrated. Using stock data for 2002, it is possible to see that 91 per cent of total FDI is located in the OECD countries, and 7 per cent in SSA (see Figure 7.3D). Among the OECD grouping, the main recipients are the UK, Luxembourg, and Austria, followed by Belgium, Switzerland, and the USA. In SSA, the bulk of FDI can be found in Mozambique and Mauritius, with the remainder distributed among other Southern African countries.

The analysis of the destination of FDI from CIBS shows that for Brazil and South Africa most FDIs are located in the OECD, although some are in the neighbouring countries. For China, most FDI flows go to Asia, including neighbouring countries such as Cambodia, Laos, and Vietnam in addition to Hong Kong. India, which has its FDI better distributed worldwide, invests very little in her neighbours from South Asia's sub-region.

DISTRIBUTION OF FOREIGN PORTFOLIO EQUITY ASSETS

We now look at the distribution of foreign portfolio equity assets held by residents from Brazil, India, and South Africa. How similar or different are their distribution? Figure 7.4 depicts the geographic distribution of portfolio equity assets for these three countries.

Figure 7.4 shows that, in Brazil, the distribution of foreign portfolio equity assets is highly concentrated, with 70 per cent of the total held in the OECD

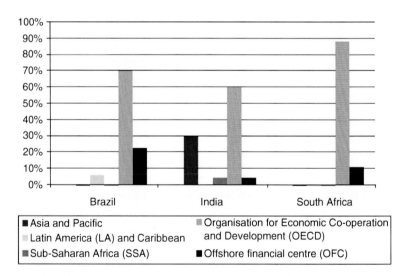

Figure 7.4. *Distribution of Brazil's, India's, and South Africa's foreign portfolio equity asset holdings, 2005*

Source: Authors' elaboration, based on data from IMF, Portfolio Investment: Coordinated Portfolio Investment Survey (CPIS).

grouping in 2005, a further 23 per cent in the OFCs, and 6 per cent are in Latin American countries. Among the OECD countries, most of the assets are in the USA; within the OFC countries, most assets are registered in the British Virgin Islands and Cayman Islands.[16] Within Latin America, most portfolio equity assets are in Argentina and Uruguay. This bias towards these two countries, and the fact that some of the investment took place in Latin America at all, reflects capital account regulation in place during the period, which determined that Brazilians could only invest in portfolio securities abroad if these were from Mercosur member countries, in addition to ADRs and BDRs or through Fiex.

In India, whilst most of portfolio equity investment went to OECD countries (60 per cent of the total), nevertheless 30 per cent went to Asia and the Pacific region and 5 per cent to SSA.[17] Very little went to OFCs, in contrast to Brazil, and, as will be seen, also South Africa. Among the OECD grouping, the main recipients were the USA, followed by Japan and the UK. In Asia, the largest recipients were Singapore and Hong Kong, followed by Malaysia and Thailand. Neighbouring Nepal and Sri Lanka, taken together, attracted less than 1 per cent of total portfolio equity from India.

Finally, nearly all portfolio equity held abroad by South Africans in 2005 was located in the OECD and the OFCs (88 and 11 per cent, respectively).[18] The UK and USA have been the main recipients among the OECD countries; Jersey and Bermuda the main recipients among the OFCs. Thus, although South Africa's equity assets are substantial, relative to Brazil's and India's, they are highly concentrated, as with Brazil but unlike India.

What can be seen, thus far, is that distributional patterns for portfolio equity are much more concentrated than for FDI. India's portfolio equity is distributed slightly more geographically, but the value of total stocks that serve as a basis for information on distribution is very low.

DISTRIBUTION OF PORTFOLIO DEBT

Figure 7.5 depicts distribution of portfolio debt for Brazil, India, and South Africa. Unlike in the case of portfolio equity assets, nearly half of total portfolio debt held by Brazilians abroad[19] is located in Latin America and

---

[16] The distribution analysis is based on a total of US$2.8 billion in 2005, as reported by the CPIS, IMF.

[17] Based on a total of US$35.6 million in 2005.

[18] Based on a total of US$60.8 billion in 2005.

[19] The total value is US$6.8 billion in 2005.

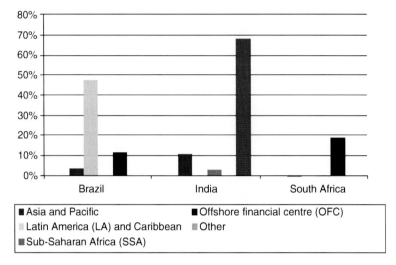

Figure 7.5. *Distribution of Brazil's, India's, and South Africa's foreign portfolio debt, 2005*

Source: Authors' elaboration, based on data from IMF Portfolio Investment: Coordinated Portfolio Investment Survey (CPIS).

the Caribbean region (48 per cent), with the remainder located in the OECD countries (37 per cent), OFCs (12 per cent), and Asia (3 per cent). The reason why so much debt is held in Latin America is that most of it is Brazil's debt, acquired internationally, and reflecting regulation on capital account in Brazil which until recently determined that 80 per cent of Fiex funds were invested in Brazil's debt. The other major location of debt assets is the USA, as would be expected. If Brazil's bonds are excluded, then debt assets are highly concentrated in just the USA, with small portions distributed among the UK, Austria, and a few other OECD countries.

In India, most of debt that is specified is held in the OECD countries, and the rest in Asia and the Pacific.[20] However, the largest share (69 per cent of the total) has no specified destination.

Finally, for South Africa, as with the distribution of portfolio equity, the distribution of portfolio debt is highly concentrated in the OECD (81 per cent of the total) and OFCs (19 per cent); 0.1 per cent is held in SSA countries, chiefly in Angola.[21]

---

[20] Based on a total of US$45 million in 2005.
[21] Based on a total of US$3.9 billion in 2005.

Table 7.4. *Distribution of flows/stocks in total (percentage)*

	Foreign direct investment			Portfolio equity			Portfolio debt		
	Offshore financial centre	OECD	Developing countries	OFC	OECD	Developing countries	Offshore financial centre	OECD	Developing countries
Brazil	48.2	42.4	9.4	22.8	70.1	7.0	11.7	37.3	51.0
China	0.2	19.8	80.0	N/A	N/A	N/A	N/A	N/A	N/A
India	2.2	33.2	64.6	4.4	60.1	35.4	N/A	N/A	N/A
South Africa	0.0	91.5	8.5	11.3	88.4	0.3	19.0	80.8	0.1

Sources: Authors' elaboration, based on Central Bank of Brazil 2007; IMF Coordinated Portfolio Investment Survey; and UNCTAD 2004.

SUMMARY ANALYSIS

In the previous sections, we have analysed the flows and stocks of assets held abroad by CIBS residents. These are the recorded flows and stocks, which in some cases may be a gross underestimate of the actual flows and stocks. However, the focus of the analysis is not on levels but, rather, on geographic distribution—in that it is assumed that the distribution of the unrecorded flows and stocks is similar to those recorded.

There is, however, no reason to believe that has been the case. The recorded flows tend to be those that leave the countries through specific legal mechanisms, and these mechanisms usually specify how such flows should be invested, both in terms of type of assets and countries. It is likely that those unrecorded flows will follow a different investment pattern. Moreover, much of the flows and stocks registered in OECD countries and OFCs are probably redirected to other countries. This is especially the case of portfolio assets, which are acquired with resources put in the hands of international investment funds based in OECD countries and OFCs, which are then reinvested by such funds following their own investment strategies.

Having these caveats in mind, we turn to Table 7.4, which summarizes the distribution of different forms of capital by CIBS. The table shows that the ability of developing countries to attract capital from CIBS varies according to the type of capital and country. In what follows, we analyse distribution by type of capital.

FDI

A significant share of FDI flows from China and India go to developing countries (80 and 65 per cent, respectively). However, very little of the total

FDI assets from Brazil and South Africa's residents are located in developing countries (that is, less than 10 per cent).

Portfolio equity

Most of foreign portfolio equity assets held by CIBS are located in the OECD and OFCs, with only 7 per cent of the total from Brazil and a mere 0.3 per cent from South Africa located in developing countries. Although most of India's portfolio equity assets also are located in the OECD, a significant share of 35 per cent is invested in developing countries. This somewhat mirrors the more widely diversified pattern of India's FDI.

Portfolio debt

Data for debt with complete information on direction are available only for Brazil and South Africa. Although 51 per cent of Brazil's portfolio debt is located in developing countries, if we subtract from this total the portion that corresponds to Brazil's assets issued internationally, then most assets are located in the OECD countries and OFCs, with 7 per cent in Asia. In the same way as Brazil, South Africa's portfolio debt is highly concentrated in the OECD and OFCs, with less than 1 per cent located in SSA.

In all, developing countries are not a major destination of capital from the CIBS countries. This is particularly true for portfolio equity. Of course, this result probably partly reflects the fact that capital restrictions on portfolio flows in developing countries as a whole are still significantly higher than in OECD countries.[22] Moreover, stock exchanges in developing countries, particularly low-income ones, are still very thin to attract foreign capital, with very few listed companies and lacking liquidity. That makes it difficult not only for CIBS but for any country including OECD countries to invest in low-income countries. What about the ability of neighbouring countries to attract capital from the CIBS countries?

Table 7.5 summarizes the share of total flows/stocks from CIBS grabbed by neighbouring countries, and the share they have within the group of developing countries. It shows that, in the case of FDI, China's neighbours grab 53 per cent, with 66 per cent of all Chinese FDI going to developing countries. Neighbouring countries to Brazil and South Africa grab just around 7 per cent

---

[22] Asiedu and Lien (2004) show that capital account restrictions can affect the flow of FDI as well.

Table 7.5. *Share of flows/stocks to neighbouring countries in total/developing countries (percentage)*

	FDI		Portfolio equity		Portfolio debt	
	Of total	Of developing countries	Of total	Of developing countries	Of total	Of developing countries
Brazil	7.1	75.5	5.0	71.4	0.1	0.3
China	52.6	65.8	N/A	N/A	N/A	N/A
India	0.8	1.2	0.6	1.6	N/A	N/A
South Africa	6.5	76.5	0.2	59.3	0.0	0.0

Notes: The neighbouring countries are specified as follows. Brazil: Argentina, Bolivia, Chile, Colombia, Paraguay, Peru, Uruguay, Venezuela; China: Cambodia, Hong Kong, Laos, Korea, Myanmar, Mongolia, Thailand, Vietnam; India: Nepal, Sri Lanka; South Africa: Botswana, Lesotho, Mauritius, Mozambique, Namibia, Swaziland, Zambia, Zimbabwe.

Sources: Authors' elaboration, based on Central Bank of Brazil 2007; IMF Coordinated Portfolio Investment Survey, and UNCTAD 2004.

of these countries' total FDI. However, they grab over 75 per cent of these countries' FDI going to developing countries. India's neighbours are the worst performers; they grab less than 1 per cent of India's total FDI, and a little more than 1 per cent of Indian FDI going to developing countries.

In the case of portfolio assets, the story is somewhat different. Of the total assets, very little is located in the neighbouring countries (less than 1 per cent, in general), although the share in the case of Brazil's portfolio equity is somewhat higher (5 per cent). However, compared with other developing countries, the neighbouring countries of Brazil and South Africa do rather well in attracting investment in portfolio equity (71 per cent in the case of Brazil, and 59 per cent in the case of South Africa). Moreover, in the case of portfolio debt, if one excludes Brazil from the group of developing countries holding debt from Brazil, the share moves up from 0.3 per cent (displayed in Table 7.5) to 3.7. In the case of South Africa, while no debt holdings in developing countries were registered for the year 2005 (see Table 7.5), data for the year 2002 that we do not display here show that at that time South Africa had debt holdings in developing countries, all of these in just one country: Zimbabwe. But, as the data suggest, a massive pull-out took place between 2002 and 2005.

On the whole, although neighbouring countries do not do well in attracting foreign capital from CIBS, they do far better than other developing countries. This suggests that proximity matters in attracting foreign capital, both FDI and portfolio assets. Of course, this assessment should be tempered by the fact that capital account regulations sometimes bias the direction of capital towards neighbouring countries, as was the case with Brazil until recently, concerning regulation specifying that Brazilians could only hold securities abroad from Mercosur countries.

LOOKING FORWARD

What about the ability of developing countries to attract portfolio flows from CIBS in the future? As CIBS continue to liberalize the capital account on the side of outflows, it is possible that any existing incentives and rules to invest in neighbouring countries will disappear, as was the case in Brazil when, in early 2006, Brazilians were granted permission to invest in securities abroad. It is therefore possible that future assets data for Brazil from 2006 will show changes in distribution patterns, against neighbouring countries and in favour of OECD and OFCs. However, because, for CIBS, neighbouring countries are able to attract flows from them regardless of existing regulation in their favour, these countries will probably continue to attract flows from CIBS, on the whole.

In the longer term, if neighbouring countries and developing countries more broadly wish to attract larger amounts of private capital flows from CIBS, it is important that they create investment opportunities—in addition, of course, to liberalizing further their capital accounts for portfolio flows, which typically face higher restrictions than FDI. In the specific case of portfolio equity flows, efforts should be made to make their stock exchanges more attractive to CIBS, through encouraging listing of domestic companies and increasing liquidity. Another possible initiative is to encourage regional stock exchanges. In the case of portfolio debt, neighbouring countries could think of issuing bonds on a regional basis. Moreover, the fact that CIBS do invest more in neighbouring countries than in other developing countries indicates that the knowledge they hold on their neighbours is an important factor in their investment decisions. Developing countries could therefore promote their countries among CIBS (for example, by making relevant information available to them) thereby further enhancing the informational advantage CIBS has about them.

It is therefore possible that neighbouring countries will be able to attract larger amounts of private capital from CIBS. This will also happen, to the extent that, with further liberalization of portfolio flows, such flows could follow FDI, which already are invested in neighbouring countries in relatively large proportions. However, while it is possible that their share in total CIBS flows might increase in the future, this probably will not happen to any major degree. As CIBS further liberalize their capital account, domestic investors will probably place their resources so as to be managed mainly by investment funds based in the OECD countries and OFCs. Although these are only intermediaries, and these resources might end up spread across the globe, the distribution pattern will be not much different from the way it is today—that is, capital invested mainly in developed countries, with less than 2 per cent going to developing countries.

Is there any advantage in attracting capital from CIBS than elsewhere? To the extent that CIBS-based investors have more knowledge on their neighbours it is possible that they will be able to take better-informed investment decisions and hold their assets, even during times of financial turbulence (thus acting as contrarians), thereby contributing to more stable capital flows. Of course, this argument does not hold for developing countries more broadly, as CIBS do not have a particular informational advantage about these countries.

CONCLUSIONS

This chapter shows that from 1990 to 2004 CAL on the outflows side has been significant in Brazil and South Africa but limited in India and especially China. The chapter also shows that CIBS have accumulated large amounts of foreign assets during that period. In Brazil, foreign asset accumulation has been mainly in the form of FDI and in South Africa, portfolio equity. In the cases of China and India, accumulation has been mainly in the form of international reserves invested abroad, partly due to their limited degree of CAL.

Further CAL in China and India will probably lead to rapid growth of private capital outflows, with these flows gradually replacing official outflows. This change in the composition of flows will certainly have an impact on the direction of flows. Further CAL in Brazil and South Africa, involving the removal of remaining CAL regulations (including end use restrictions), will also influence future directions of capital outflows from these countries. This chapter then asks the question: where will these flows go?

Drawing on the analysis of geographic distribution of FDI and foreign portfolio asset holdings during the 2000s, the chapter shows that FDI from China and India have been invested in the developing world to a considerable degree. However, this was not the case with Brazil or South Africa. The analysis of distribution patterns of portfolio asset holdings, in turn, shows that in nearly all cases for which data were available most holdings are in OECD countries and OFCs, with very little (within the range of 1 per cent to 2 per cent) in developing countries. This level is similar to portfolio investment abroad by developed countries. Portfolio asset holdings in developing countries are only higher when there is explicit capital account regulation determining country-specific destination. There is therefore a clear bias of direction of portfolio capital from CIBS towards OECD and OFCs.

What about the distribution of FDI and portfolio assets within the group of developing countries? In this case, the data show that a clear bias exists towards capital holdings in neighbouring countries and against other developing countries, especially from outside CIBS regions. This applies especially to portfolio equity assets. For example, Brazil invests very little in Africa or Asia, India invests very little in Latin America, and so on.

All this suggests that CIBS do draw on their informational advantage to invest relatively more in neighbouring countries. There is therefore potential for this latter group of countries to attract more portfolio and other types of capital from CIBS—for example, by reducing obstacles to investment, by encouraging more flows through increasing liquidity in their stock exchanges, and by issuing bonds at the regional level. As for developing countries more broadly, natural resource rich countries have great opportunities to attract more FDI from China and India in the future. To the extent that bank loans and portfolio flows might follow FDI, they might furthermore be able to attract these latter forms of flows.

REFERENCES

Asiedu, E., and D. Lien (2004) 'Capital Controls and Foreign Direct Investment', *World Development*, 32: 479–90.

Barros, J. R. M. (2007) 'O investimento brasileiro no exterior é recorde', Valor Economico (11 Jan.).

Bhalla, S. S. (2006) 'Dissent Note on the Report on Fuller Capital Account Convertibility', in 'Report of the Committee on Fuller Capital Account Convertibility', Reserve Bank of India (31 July). <http://rbidocs.rbi.org.in/rdocs/PublicationReport/Pdfs/72250.pdf>.

Central Bank of Brazil (2007) 'Capitais Brasileiros no Exterior (CBE)', Central Bank website. <http://www4.bcb.gov.br/?CBERESULT>.

Cheng, L. K., and Z. Ma (2007) 'China's Outward FDI: Past and Present' (July) unpub.

Gottschalk, R., and M. C. Sodre (2008) 'The Liberalisation of Capital Outflows in Brazil, India and South Africa Since the Early 1990s', in P. Arestis and L. de Paula (eds), *Financial Liberalisation and Economic Performance in Emerging Countries* (Basingstoke: Palgrave Macmillan).

Hviding, K. (2005) 'Liberalizing Trade and Capital Transactions: An Overview', in M. Nowak and L. A. Ricci (eds), *Post-apartheid South Africa: The First Ten Years after Apartheid* (Washington, DC: IMF).

IMF (2002) International Financial Statistics (Washington, DC: IMF) (July).

——(2005) 'Annual Report on Exchange Arrangements and Exchange Restrictions' (Aug.) (Washington, DC: IMF).

——(2006) 'South Africa: 2006 Article IV Consultation—Staff Report', Country Report 06/237 (Sept.).

——(var.) Coordinated Portfolio Investment Survey (CPIS): Portfolio Investment. <http://www.imf.org/external/np/sta/pi/cpis.htm>.

Lane, P., and G. M. Milesi-Ferretti (2006) 'The External Wealth of Nations Mark II: Revised and Extended Estimates of Foreign Assets and Liabilities, 1970–2004'. IMF Working Paper WP/06/69 (Mar.) (Washington, DC: IMF).

——and S. Schmukler (2006) 'The International Financial Integration of China and India', in L. A. Winters and S. Yusuf (2006) *Dancing with Giants: China, India and the Global Economy* (Washington, DC and Singapore: World Bank/Singapore Institute of Policy Studies).

National Treasury (2001) 'The Role of the National Treasury in the Economy'. South African National Treasury. mimeo.

Nayyar, D. (2000) 'Capital Controls and the World Financial Authority: What Can We Learn from the Indian Experience?'. CEPA Working Paper Series III, Working Paper 14 (Mar.).

OECD (2007) 'Trends and Recent Developments in Foreign Direct Investment' (June) (Paris: OECD).

Prates, D. M. (1998) 'Investimentos de Portfolio no Mercado Financeiro Domestico', in FUNDAP, *Abertura Externa e Sistema Financeiro. Relatorio Final* (May) (São Paulo: FUNDAP): chap. 1.

Reserve Bank of India (2000) 'Recommendations of Tarapore Committee on Capital Account Convertibility'. <http://iic.nic.in/iic3_j.htm>.

——(2006) 'Report of the Committee on Fuller Capital Account Convertibility' (31 July). <http://rbidocs.rbi.org.in/rdocs/PublicationReport/Pdfs/72250.pdf>.

Sauvant, K. P. (2005) 'New Sources of FDI: The BRICs', *Journal of World Investment and Trade* (Oct.): 639–710.

Tavares, M. (2006) 'Investimento brasileiro no exterior: panorama e consideracoes sobre politicas publicas'. CEPAL Serie Desarrollo 172 (Nov.) (Santiago: CEPAL).

UNCTAD (2004) 'World Investment Report' (Geneva: United Nations).

Zhao, M. (2006) 'External Liberalisation and the Evolution of China's Exchange System: An Empirical Approach' (Beijing: World Bank). unpub.

8

China, India, Brazil, and South Africa: Capital Flows and Exchange Rates. What Lessons Have Been Learnt since the East Asian Crisis of 1997–8?

Marion Pircher[1]

INTRODUCTION

China, India, Brazil, and South Africa (CIBS) are considered to boost world economic growth as, over the past few years they experienced and continue to experience large GDP growth rates. The source and facts leading to these high growth rates in the four emerging economies have already been the topic of various studies; hence, this will not be the main question of this chapter. Instead, this study focuses on a different approach and will try to answer the following questions. What implications does a liberalization of the capital account in CIBS have for the economy? Are there any important lessons for CIBS from the East Asian Crisis of 1997–8? Are there any remaining threats in CIBS financial systems?

The chapter will show that the timing and speed of capital account liberalization have to be chosen *carefully* and with *prudence*, thereby reducing financial vulnerability. Furthermore, it is important to note that all countries have to be aware of the so-called 'impossible trinity' and the resulting implications. Table 8.1 presents an overview of the macroeconomic situation in the economies being analysed.

---

[1] The views expressed in this chapter are solely those of the author.

Table 8.1. *Macroeconomic data*

	2002	2003	2004	2005	Projected 2006
(Annual percentage changes, except otherwise indicated)					
Real GDP					
Brazil	1.9	0.5	4.9	2.3	3.5
China	9.1	10.0	10.1	9.9	10.0
India*	5.8	3.8	8.5	7.5	8.4
South Africa	3.0	4.5	4.9	4.2	4.2
Population (mid-year, in millions)					
Brazil	179.246	181.787	184.318	186.831	189.323
China	1,288.4	1,296.84	1,304.98	1,312.98	1,320.86
India	1,081.9	1,099.49	1,116.99	1,134.4	1,151.75
South Africa	46.580	47.088	47.540	47.938	48.282
GDP per capita (in US$)					
Brazil	2,868	3,085	3,654	4,789	5,715
China	1,132	1,275	1,490	1,742	2,070
India	491	568	650	746	843
South Africa	2,430	3,610	4,640	5,130	5,390
Consumer Price Index					
Brazil	8.4	14.8	6.6	6.9	4.9
China	−0.8	1.2	3.9	1.8	1.5
India	4.3	4.0	3.9	3.8	4.4
South Africa	9.2	5.8	1.4	3.4	4.7
GDP Deflator					
Brazil	10.2	15.0	8.2	7.2	4.0
China					
India	2.8	3.6	4.1	4.2	4.1
South Africa	10.5	4.4	5.6	4.7	5.8
(In per cent of GDP)					
Overall balance public finance					
Brazil	−4.6	−5.1	−2.7	−3.3	−2.4
China	−3.0	−2.4	−1.5	−1.3	−1.2
India	10.1	9.7	9.1	7.3	7.4
South Africa	−1.2	−2.0	−1.7	−0.6	−1.2
Public sector debt					
Brazil	65.5	58.7	54.2	51.7	50.6
China	18.9	19.2	18.5	17.9	17.3
India	81.4	86.1	85.9	82.7	80.8
South Africa	37.0	35.6	35.4	34.4	32.8
(End of period percentage changes)					
Broad money (M2)					
Brazil	23.2	3.7	18.6	18.9	N/A
China	16.8	19.6	10.9	13.6	N/A
India	14.1	14.7	16.7	12.3	21.2
South Africa	18.1	12.9	13.1	14.0	13.2

(continued)

Table 8.1. Continued

	2002	2003	2004	2005	Projected 2006
(Annual percentage changes, except otherwise indicated)					
(In US$ billion)					
Current account balance					
Brazil	−7.6	4.2	11.7	14.2	11.1
China	35	46	69	161	179
India	3.4	6.3	14.1	−2.5	−10.6
South Africa	0.7	−2.2	−7.4	−10.1	−12.5
Capital and financial account					
Brazil	8.0	5.1	−7.5	−9.6	5.7
China	32	53	111	63	41
India	8.6	10.8	16.7	28.0	24.7
South Africa	0.8	1.6	13.2	15.5	16.9
Outstanding external debt (in % of GDP)					
Brazil	44.9	42.1	33.3	21.1	18.1
China	12.8	12.7	12.8	12.6	12.7
India	21.1	20.4	17.8	17.3	15.8
South Africa	29.7	23.0	20.2	19.3	18.8

Notes: * For India: 2000–1, 2001–2, 2002–3, 2003–4, 2004–5, 2005–6.

Sources: IMF, Article IV Consultation Staff Reports, var. issues; DataStream.

THEORETICAL ISSUES

This section will discuss some theoretical issues, starting with the concept of the 'impossible trinity' and followed by a rough overview of the 'third-generation' crisis model.

'IMPOSSIBLE TRINITY'

The trilemma in open economies shows that of the three goals that most countries share—that is, independence in monetary policy, stability of exchange rate, and free movement of capital—only two can be reached simultaneously. This is the trilemma that policymakers face as they have to decide which one to relinquish. In their empirical study, Obstfeld, Shambaugh, and Taylor (2004) show that the constraints imposed by the trilemma—that is, the choice of exchange rate and its trade-off with monetary policy—are tight and apply in practice, which means that policymakers should be aware of it.

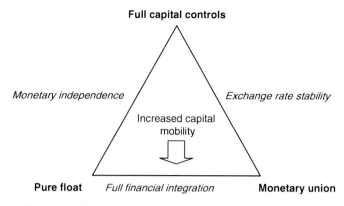

Figure 8.1. *The impossible trinity*

Source: Frankel 1999 © copyright J. A. Frankel.

A graphical representation of the choices of the trilemma and the consequences of choosing an appropriate exchange rate system can be seen in Figure 8.1. This figure shows the three policy instruments in an open economy (full capital controls, pure float, and monetary union) on the three corners of the triangle, while three goals are listed on the three sides of the triangle (monetary independence, exchange rate stability, and full financial integration). A movement from the top to the bottom of the triangle means increased capital mobility. Policymakers can only choose to pursue two policies contemporaneously—that is, monetary independence and exchange rate stability (which lead to full capital controls), monetary independence and full financial integration (leading to a pure float), or exchange rate stability and full financial integration (which lead to a monetary union). Figure 8.1 shows that it is not possible to achieve any combination of all three policies at the same time without creating instability within the system.

As Obstfeld (2000) argues in his research summary, the trilemma is often associated with Robert A. Mundell but goes back to earlier writers such as John Maynard Keynes. By starting from the Mundell–Fleming model for open economies, one has to consider its drawbacks—for example, assuming perfect capital mobility or neglecting inter-temporal constraints—and, therefore, over the years the model was adjusted and extended.

The CIBS economies and their policymakers could consider various policies in situations where advantages and disadvantages have to be weighed against each other.

FLOATING EXCHANGE RATE

The governments could maintain monetary policy autonomy and free capital movements. According to theory (that is, a simple Mundell–Fleming model), monetary policy is very effective in a floating exchange rate system. With regard to monetary policy, it has been argued that emerging countries do not have the institutional requirements with which to implement effective monetary policies (Summers 2000) and, according to this opinion, countries with floating exchange rates would not be able to implement an effective and complex feedback rule in order to have an effective inflation targeting system (Eichengreen and Masson 1998: 18–19). Additionally, another objection to floating exchange rates in emerging countries has been raised; that is, the 'fear of floating' (Calvo and Reinhart 2000). Calvo and Reinhart argue that in a world of high capital mobility incomplete information, fads, rumours, and dollar-denominated liabilities the authorities are afraid to float their currency as the exchange rate will move significantly and large depreciations will have a negative impact on inflation and on corporate debt. However, as Edwards (2003: 75) argues, this criticism seems to be based on a small number of historical episodes or underestimated difficulties with super-fixed systems. Furthermore, studies of Mexico after the collapse of 1994 and its floating exchange rate show that emerging countries could have a floating exchange rate but that the monetary authorities need to communicate their policies (Edwards and Savastano 1999).

A further question is whether capital mobility should be free. The advantage is that this policy is regarded as a positive sign in the international financial community, and that the government could use monetary policies for intervention in the economy. The costs of free capital movements could be large outflows of funds, which could hurt the private sector, leading to a credit crunch, bankruptcies in the economy, and to a further drop in aggregate demand and recession of the economy. This situation applied in the case of the East Asian Crisis of 1997–8, where the private sector had dollar-denominated debt and mismatches of debt in their balance sheets.

Other advantages of a flexible exchange rate include the fact that governments retain seigniorage and that the float allows smooth adjustments to real shocks, even in the presence of price frictions (Frankel 1999). The other cost that might come with a floating exchange rate is the exchange rate risk; however, this could be limited by introducing and using appropriate hedging instruments.

ESTABLISHING A MONETARY UNION
OR A CURRENCY BOARD

The establishment of a monetary union or a currency board implies that the authorities keep stable exchange rates and free capital movements. The main advantages of a fixed exchange rate are the reduction of transaction costs and exchange rate risk, providing a credible nominal anchor for monetary policy (by pegging to a hard currency and thereby exhibiting strong monetary policy). Also, to a lesser degree, competitive depreciations or appreciations are not possible (Frankel 1999). Monetary policy under a fixed exchange rate system with free capital movements is, in some sense, not beneficial, as domestic interest rates will be tied to foreign interest rates and, for example, an expansion of money supply would have no impact on the economy as the new money would flow out of the economy through a balance of payments deficit. Therefore, the drawback of this exchange rate system is that the authorities lose, in the case of necessity, one important instrument of intervention in the economy: monetary policy. They have to resort to fiscal policy in order to intervene effectively in the economy, with the disadvantage of building up government indebtedness, which is not desired in the CIBS economies.

Another disadvantage associated with this exchange rate system could be that corporations and so on will not hedge against currency risks, leaving their balance sheets with foreign currency debts and, in a period of a speculative attack (a bubble or some similar situation that involves the abandonment of the fixed exchange rate), would end badly and drive the economy into bad equilibrium (Frankel 1999).

The discussion on free capital movement is very controversial, leading to opposing views about the pertinence of free capital movements for the countries.

IMPOSITION OF CAPITAL CONTROLS

The discussion on capital controls is also controversial. By imposing capital controls, governments can enjoy the benefits of autonomy of monetary policy and stable exchange rates. The benefits of autonomy of monetary policy include the opportunity to respond swiftly and effectively to sudden shocks in the economy.

The considerably more controversial discussion is about capital controls. Isard (2005: 246) argues that the main arguments against capital controls are derived from economic theory and historical experience. Theory suggests that markets allocate resources better (that is, profit incentives of firms, income allocation of households) and experience suggests that such systems are relatively efficient in encouraging technological innovation and economic growth over time. It has also been observed that leaving allocation of capital to the government could lead to corruption and the financing of unproductive activities. Additionally, capital controls provide an incentive to delay or try to avoid fiscal or monetary policy actions in order to deal with macroeconomic imbalances.

Furthermore, Isard (2005: 246–8) claims that these arguments against capital controls have to be balanced against arguments in favour of them. The arguments for capital controls are based on the theory of 'the second best'—that is, if the market allocates the resources with distortions, the imposition of capital controls (thereby imposing a further distortion) will lead to a welfare improvement. Distortions in the market could arise in financial markets due to informational frictions (that is, costs of screening borrowers and monitoring their behaviour) resulting in incomplete and asymmetric information for lenders and to an adverse selection of borrowers, which could ultimately result in excessive volatility in financial markets (as a result of herding behaviour). Additionally, Isard (2005: 246–8) argues that capital controls might be beneficial if the government wishes to provide macroeconomic stability, which leads to an accumulation of foreign exchange reserves (thereby smoothing national consumption) and provides an explicit or implicit insurance to the domestic financial system. A further argument in favour of capital controls is that governments care about national welfare while financial markets do not ('greed and fear' motivation); therefore, the imposition of capital controls could give authorities breathing space in times of panic or pressure from financial markets. An alternative point of view is that long-term capital flows are beneficial for the growth of an economy and in order to keep economic growth economies should open themselves to free capital movement.

Overall, one problem with capital controls is that implementation and enforcement have to be ensured. Capital controls are not effective for highly developed countries; however, empirical evidence suggests that capital controls are effective in countries without highly developed financial sectors (Isard 2005: 249). The relationship between opening a capital account and growth is rather mixed, but growth and liberalization tend not to be strongly, positively correlated (Jomo 2005).

There are different types of capital controls: dealing with capital controls can be problematic, as investors might try to evade capital controls and authorities might not give incentives for the promotion of long-term capital investments, which usually are excluded from controls. There is wide agreement that market-based capital controls (such as interest rate ceilings or reserve requirements) are preferred to quotas, licences, or other controls that require administration (Isard 2005: 255).

The distinction on controls in inflows and outflows is usually much more controversial: while there is broad agreement that controls on inflows are effective (Edwards 2003: 49; Isard 2005: 255), the effectiveness of controls on outflows is much more controversial (for example, against effectiveness: Eichengreen, et al. 1998; suggesting effectiveness: Kaplan and Rodrik 2001). A theoretical approach that should discourage short-term capital flows was Tobin's (1978) proposal: the imposition of the so-called 'Tobin tax' should, in theory, limit short-term flows; in practice, it would only work if all countries agreed to adopt this measure.

As can be seen, the discussion on the imposition of capital controls is very controversial in academic debates. The international community, especially the Bretton Woods institutions, would not appreciate impositions of capital controls, although the combination of autonomy of monetary policy and a stable exchange rate might be preferable to the other two choices in some cases (for example, if the business sector had non-hedged foreign currency denominated liabilities combined with the threat of a large currency depreciation).

During the 1980s, the so-called 'Washington Consensus' emerged and this led to the view that financial liberalization would contribute to economic growth, although theory leaves no unambiguous prediction of whether opening the capital account helps in the promotion of growth or not. It seems that opening the capital account has a positive influence on economic growth if the domestic financial markets are well developed and regulated, and the operation of the international financial system is smooth and stable, while it might be more negative if domestic and international financial markets are subject to crises (Eichengreen and Leblang 2002).

The discussion of the advantages and disadvantages of the options of the 'impossible trinity' leads to fundamental questions for policymakers who have to choose between fixed or flexible exchange rates, monetary policy autonomy or stronger fiscal policy intervention, and capital account liberalization or capital controls.

While the choice between fixed or flexible exchange rates is the subject of theoretical discussions, capital account liberalization has to be considered very carefully as it could indirectly harm the economy (that is, in the case of a financial system that was not fully developed, a precipitate opening of the capital account could increase the risk of an economic slump). No general rule on capital account liberalization exists. However, as previously mentioned, it is widely recognized in economic theory that liberalization of long-term capital flows (that is, foreign direct investments (FDI)) is beneficial for economic growth. More controversial is the impact of short-term capital flows (that is, portfolio flows), which seem to be beneficial in highly developed financial markets but not in financial markets that do not have a fully developed financial infrastructure and are controlled by relatively weak regulatory bodies. Therefore, a general recommendation regarding the speed of opening the capital account cannot be given; however, a stepwise liberalization of different types of capital flows seems to be appropriate in most cases. Emerging markets, such as CIBS, are in a conflict situation as foreign investors are attracted by the high growth rates in their economies and therefore wish to invest in different assets in the country (long- and short-term). On the other hand, the financial industries of these economies are in a transition period; that is, they have relatively good and sound financial institutions and supervision, but have not yet completed the move to a developed financial market. Furthermore, some investments from outside are usually welcome in these economies (for example, with regard to technology spillovers, or higher liquidity of capital markets). However, the policymakers have to decide whether the market could allocate them efficiently or whether intervention is required. Policymakers are facing a trade-off where the principle of the 'impossible trinity' should be kept in mind. The next section discusses the 'third generation' crisis model.

'THIRD-GENERATION' CRISIS MODEL

Since the breakdown of the Bretton Woods system, different types of crises occurred. Many economists tried to understand why these events happened and created some models describing the crises. The different crisis models evolved over time in order to match the specific features of the crisis. According to the convention introduced by Eichengreen, Rose, and Wyplosz (1995), they were grouped into 'first generation' and 'second generation' and with the rise of the East Asian crisis the 'third generation' has been added. One shortcoming of these models is that they failed to predict an upcoming crisis. The first generation crisis models help to explain the crisis in the 1970s and early 1980s, while not giving insights into speculative attacks on currencies of the European monetary system in 1992–3. For that crisis, academics developed the second-generation crisis models, which, again, did not predict the rise of the crisis in East Asia. The theoretical models trying to explain the East Asian Crisis are the so-called 'third-generation' crisis models.

The East Asian crisis was in contrast to the preceding crises in that it was not driven by mismanagement of economic actions by the government or by a lack of credibility of government actions. As Ahgion, Bacchetta, and Banerjee (2001) argue, most of the affected countries enjoyed balanced government spending and increasing foreign exchange reserves, low unemployment, and a booming export sector; however, there seems to be evidence that the financial sector in these countries was not very well regulated. Furthermore, the authors argue that a lack of transparency in the financial sector was known among market participants and most of the countries recovered very quickly, not experiencing interest rates significantly higher than in the period before the crisis and without a significant overhaul of the financial sector.

According to Ahgion, Bacchetta, and Banerjee (2001), the third-generation models, developed after the East Asian crisis, have in common the idea that a shock can be amplified by the so-called 'financial accelerator mechanism' (Bernanke, Gertler, and Gilchrist 1999). Some models (for example, Aghion, Bacchetta, and Banerjee 1999a; Aghion, Bacchetta, and Banerjee 1999b) introduce a real shock that is amplified, while other models introduce multiple equilibria and the crisis is caused by a pure shift in expectations (for example, Chang and Velasco 1999; Krugman 1999a). As Ahgion, Bacchetta, and Banerjee (2001: 1121) point out, the common feature of the models is that 'a real currency depreciation can have a large effect on output if it affects the credit access of some subset of agents; moreover this effect on output may in turn affect the exchange rate, further amplifying the shock and causing it to persist'.

The main contributions to the third-generation crisis models are Ahgion, Bacchetta, and Banerjee 2000; 2001; 2004; Céspedes, Chang, and Velasco 2000; Chang and Velasco 1998a; 1998b; and Krugman 1999a; 1999b; 2001: only the last will be discussed, in brief, by giving an overview. Krugman (1999a; 1999b; 2001) proposed a so-called 'cartoon version' of a third-generation crisis model (a more-detailed version of this model can be found in Krugman 1999a).

According to Krugman (1999b), the Mundell–Fleming model could be used to describe the crisis. The basic model consists of the following three equations.

$$y = D(y, i) + NX(eP^*/P, y) \qquad (8.1)$$

Aggregate demand equation relating domestic spending (D) to real income (y) and interest rate (i) and net exports (NX) that depend on the real exchange rate (eP^*/P)

$$M/P = L(y, i) \qquad (8.2)$$

Money demand equation

$$i = i^* \qquad (8.3)$$

Interest arbitrage equation (with risk-neutral investors and static expectations about the exchange rate).

As this model is too simple to describe the situation in East Asia in a satisfactory way, Equation 8.1 can be modified by adding a strong, open economy Bernanke–Gartler effect,

$$y = D(y, i, eP^*/P) + NX(eP^*/P, y) \qquad (8.1')$$

where firms are highly leveraged, a substantial part of their debt is denominated in foreign currency, and their investment will be constrained by their balance sheets. In this modified equation, domestic demand also depends directly on the real exchange rate.

The modified model implies that, at favourable real exchange rates, only few firms have constrained balance sheets and the direct effect on aggregate demand would be small. However, at unfavourable real exchange rates, companies would be unable to invest and the direct effect on aggregate demand would be substantial, resulting in a corporate sector that is basically bankrupt, unable to invest, and where only small firms and farmers would be benefiting from a weak currency. The middle course would outweigh the direct effect of the competitive position on exports and, as such, the depreciation would lead to a contraction rather than an expansion of the economy (Krugman 1999b). These results lead to no clear policy prescription and suggest difficulties in choosing the right policies (which was true in the real world, as there are many discussions upon the adequacy of the policies imposed by the IMF).

Summing up, the commonality of the third generation models is that they include a Bernanke–Gertler effect and are monetarist models for small, open economies. It can be seen that the financial leverage of corporations and the exposure to foreign exchange movements is important in these models. This is important for CIBS, as it shows that possible threats might arise in *corporate balance sheets*, combined with unhedged foreign exchange stocks in the respective countries and *weak financial infrastructures* (for example, bank balance sheet mismatches, poor regulation, underdeveloped bond, and financial markets).

A DEEPER LOOK AT CIBS

Let us now turn to some key data in CIBS: the exchange rate system and movements, government spending, balance of payments, interest rates, and other relevant macroeconomic data. All data are from Thomson Financial Datastream and deal with the period 1995–2006 (or the latest available data).

EXCHANGE RATE

The actual exchange rate arrangements and monetary policy framework of CIBS (as at 31 July 2006: IMF 2006) can be summarized as follows:

China: 'Other conventional fixed peg arrangements' and the target of monetary policy framework is monetary aggregate. (On 21 July 2005 China announced the move to a managed floating exchange rate based on an undisclosed basket of currencies.)

India: 'Managed floating with no predetermined path for the exchange rate' and other targets of monetary policy; that is, monitoring various indicators in conducting monetary policy.

Brazil: 'Independently floating' with a monetary policy framework to target inflation.

South Africa: 'Independently floating' with a monetary policy framework to target inflation.

This shows that two countries have a floating exchange rate regime (Brazil and South Africa) and can therefore, according to the impossible trinity, reach the targets of monetary independence and full financial integration (that is, inflation targeting and free capital movements). The remaining two countries (China and India) experience some 'hybrid' exchange rate arrangements, where the Chinese exchange rate regime is closer to a fixed exchange rate regime and India's exchange rate regime is in between the two courses of action.

China, in order to have an effective monetary policy, should therefore, according to the impossible trinity, have a lower degree of capital mobility (China is closer in this case to the 'full capital controls' corner in Figure 8.1) than Brazil or South Africa (both of which countries are close to the 'pure float' corner). India is facing a mid-course in exchange rate regimes. It is therefore difficult to categorize China and India in accordance with Figure 8.1. The commitment to more exchange rate flexibility could increase India's integration into world financial markets. Studying Figures 8.2–8.5, it can be seen that the Indian rupee is not fixed, neither does it seem to be fully floating; it does, however, appear that the Indian exchange rate experienced some smooth movement over recent years. China experienced large changes in exchange rate policies for two years, while the movement of the Brazilian real and South African rand shows that these currencies are floating and few interventions might have occurred over the period showed here.

Following the concept of the impossible trinity, the current situation of exchange rate movement and system in China and India seems unclear and could, therefore, bear some risks. (Movement to full financial integration without the accompanying change of exchange rate system is not feasible; for example, a high interest rate spread (US to local interest rates) and a fixed exchange rate could attract more portfolio flows than desired and lead to troubles in the local financial markets.)

At best, all nominal exchange rates with regard to the US$ achieved appreciation and relative stability over the period 2002–6. This means that in nominal terms the countries' competitive positions worsened slightly.

Studying the real effective exchange rate index, which is a better approximation for international competitiveness, shows that since 2003, CIBS experienced an increase of the index with regard to stability. This means that the fixed or relatively fixed nominal exchange rate (as is true for China and India) has increased the strength of the domestic economies

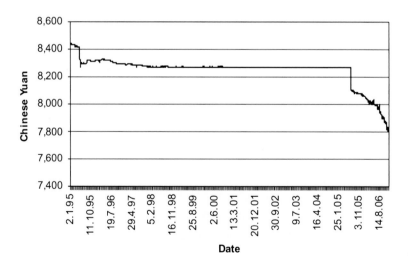

Figure 8.2. *Chinese yuan to US$*

Source: Datastream.

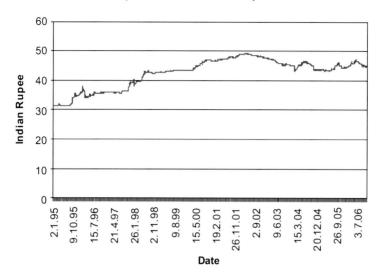

Figure 8.3. *Indian rupee to US$*

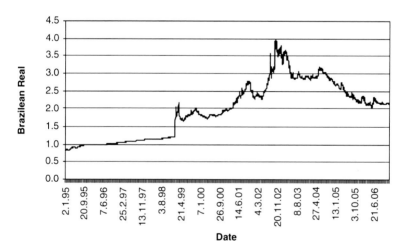

Figure 8.4. *Brazilian real to US$*

Source: Datastream.

over the period analysed here, which would imply an appreciation of the nominal exchange rate. The current level of the nominal exchange rate seems to be relatively costly (due to its undervaluation) and the so-called shadow exchange rate might become significantly different from the nominal exchange rates. Furthermore, Figure 8.6 shows that international CIBS

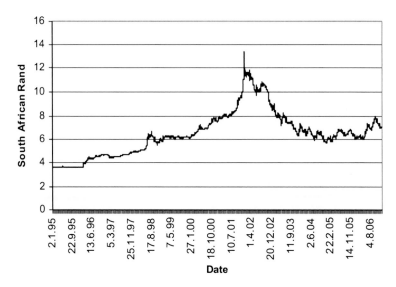

Figure 8.5. *South African rand to US$*

Source: Datastream.

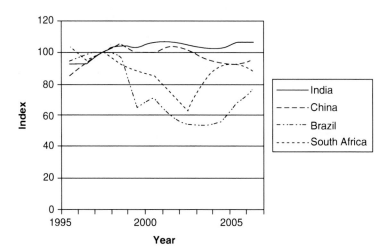

Figure 8.6. *Real effective Exchange Rate Index*

Source: Datastream.

competitiveness worsened slightly for Brazil and India (an increase of the index), while it remained relatively stable for China and South Africa since 2005.

GOVERNMENT SPENDING AND BALANCE OF PAYMENTS MOVEMENTS

Table 8.1 shows that between 2002 and 2006 CIBS reduced public sector debt (as a percentage of GDP). This implies that the governments are aware of

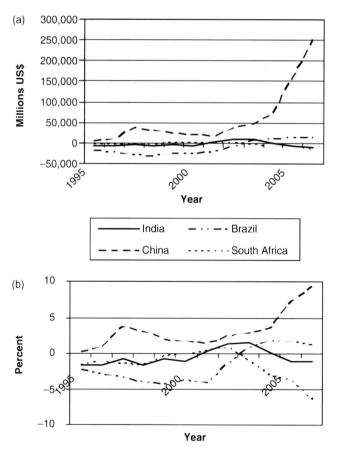

Figure 8.7. *Current account balance, in US$ (millions) and as percentage of GDP*
Source: Datastream.

government indebtedness and that the threat of a first- or second-generation crisis is very low. Turning to different parts of the balance of payments, two datasets are of main interest: the direction of the current account (comprising the flows of goods and services) and the composition of the capital account (comprising flows of capital to and from a country).

From Figure 8.7(a) it can be seen that the direction of the current account balance differs in CIBS. While India and South Africa experience a negative current account balance, Brazil experienced a slight increase, and China a sharp increase and strong positive current account balance (the same results can be drawn from Figure 8.7(b)). The causes of this different direction of current account movements can be found for three countries by the directions of trade. China and Brazil are net exporters, while India is a net importer of goods and services (Figure 8.8). For South Africa, the situation is slightly different, as the trade balance is almost balanced (slightly negative); therefore the remaining items (services, income, and transfers) are the contributing elements to the negative current account balance.

Next, the flows of the capital account should be considered. It can be seen from Figure 8.9 that net direct investment flows are positive for China and India, which means that these economies experience long-term and stable capital inflows, which should contribute to economic growth. It can be seen that India still has capital account controls, as the flows are stable and relatively small over the whole period analysed, while China has experienced capital account liberalization in recent years. Net direct investment flows for South Africa and Brazil became negative in 2005 and 2006. For South Africa,

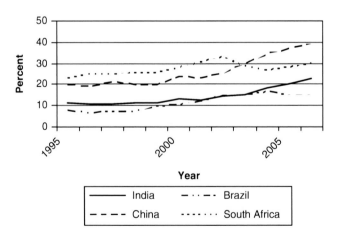

Figure 8.8. *Exports of goods and services (as percentage of GDP)*

Source: Datastream.

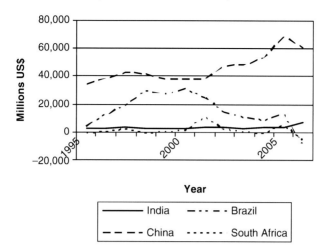

Figure 8.9. *Financing: net direct investment flows*

Source: DataStream.

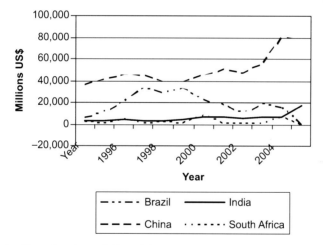

Figure 8.10. *Financing: inward direct investment*

Source: Datastream.

this reversal of long-term capital flows could be explained by the increasing investments of South African corporations in neighbouring economies. Brazil experienced a decline in long-term inward flows, which seems to be a result of the last major financial market crisis in 1997–8, which also affected Brazil (Figures 8.10 and 8.11).

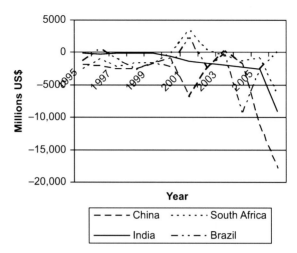

Figure 8.11. *Financing: outward direct investment*

Source: Datastream.

Now let us turn to an analysis of portfolio flows. Inward portfolio investment (Figure 8.12) increased for all economies in recent years. While outflows (Figure 8.13) remained stable for India, Brazil, and South Africa, they increased for China (that is, short-term portfolio investments abroad—a negative sign means an outflow). Short-term inflows remained stable for India but increased for the remaining countries (in China, to a higher degree in absolute values than in the other countries). China experienced the largest outflow of portfolio flows, which can be explained by the cross-border activities of Chinese citizens and onshore foreign currency deposits (BIS 2002) as well as the recent changing of rules for domestic financial institutions, which allow portfolio investments overseas and, therefore, the opening of specific actions and capital account movements.

The risk with increasing portfolio investment, as mentioned, is that these could be very harmful in the case of liberalization of capital accounts. However, even if, officially, capital accounts are not fully liberalized (as in the case of China), some cross-border activities and onshore foreign currency deposits are a risk for the Chinese economy if the principles of the impossible trinity are not respected. Allowing a relatively high interest rate spread combined with a relatively fixed (effectively 'pegged') exchange rate is dangerous and could lead to a higher than desired level of capital inflows, as this spread attracts foreign investors and gives an illusionary assurance to domestic corporations who borrow in foreign currency without appropriate hedging.

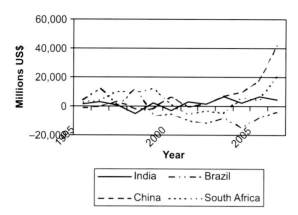

Figure 8.12. *Financing: inward portfolio investment (net of foreign currency (FC) bonds)*
Source: Datastream.

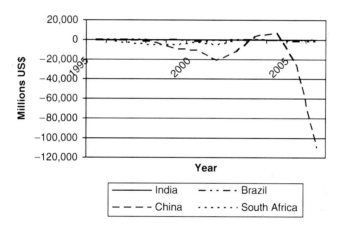

Figure 8.13. *Financing: outward portfolio investment*
Source: Datastream.

The last figure of this section, Figure 8.14, shows the current foreign exchange reserves of the four countries over the past ten years. It can be seen that all countries tended to build up stocks of foreign exchange reserves. Most impressive is the increase of foreign exchange reserves in China, almost quintupling between 2002 and 2006. One cause of this huge increase in Chinese foreign exchange reserves is China's increasing share of exports of goods and services, and the current account surplus. Furthermore, Asian central banks are well known to build up foreign exchange reserves for 'bad' times; that is, for intervention in the foreign exchange market and in order to

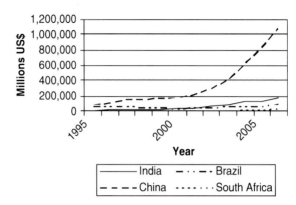

Figure 8.14. *Current foreign exchange reserves*
Source: Datastream

be less dependent for assistance on international organizations (for example, the IMF).

It is interesting that India has built up the second-highest current foreign exchange reserves in the group analysed here, although not experiencing large current account surpluses in recent years. This could be a sign of the intention of Asian central banks to have sufficiently large reserves for intervention in the foreign exchange market. The other two economies, Brazil and South Africa, experienced a very small increase of their foreign exchange reserves when compared with China.

DEBT

This section will look at CIBS debt structure. It can be seen from Figure 8.15 that net foreign debt as a percentage of GDP decreased in all countries over recent years, becoming negative even for China and India, and moving towards zero for Brazil and South Africa. (Net foreign debt is defined as claims owned by foreigners in the domestic economy minus claims by domestic holders owned in foreign economies.) China and India are, therefore, net creditors to the world, while Brazil and South Africa are net debtors. Brazil records a very impressive turnaround of net foreign debt: from almost 40 per cent in 1999–2002 (that is, the period when Brazil experienced economic problems after the East Asian crisis of 1997–8) to an almost single-digit figure in 2002–6 (since 2003, Brazil experienced a current account surplus). Brazil's position as a net creditor to the world, and especially to the USA, is discussed almost daily in the press. Even more impressive is the large share of net debt to GDP, which is in double digits. The rule that developed economies should be creditors to emerging economies seems not to apply for India and China—in fact, the reverse seems to be true. The same pattern can be seen from Figure 8.16, which shows the same pattern as net foreign debt as a percentage of GDP.

Figure 8.17 shows foreign debt per capita, which is highest for Brazil and South Africa and lowest for India and China. While Brazil has decreased its foreign debt per capita since the late 1990s, South Africa and China have experienced a slight increase in foreign debt per capita. In sum, China is a net creditor and South Africa and Brazil have been decreasing their share of net foreign debt over the past few years.

Looking at the ratio of international reserves to total debt, it can be seen that this ratio is increasing for CIBS (Figure 8.18). This might be explained by the increase of international reserves (especially for China and India). Furthermore, it shows that foreign debt is backed in China and India by at least the same amount of international reserves, thereby providing insurance against bad times. Brazil and South Africa have a double-digit ratio, which is increasing over time and showing that both countries are experiencing a decrease in risk of foreign indebtedness.

The last part of this section is dedicated to the composition of debt. Figures 8.19–8.21 show different pictures for CIBS. While medium- and long-term debt is mostly owed to private creditors and decreasingly stable over time,

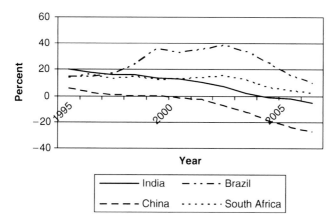

Figure 8.15. *Net foreign debt (as percentage of GDP)*
Source: Datastream.

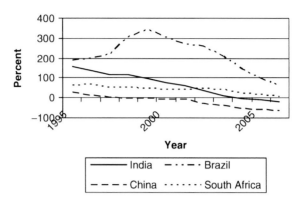

Figure 8.16. *Net foreign debt to exports of goods and services ratio*

Source: Datastream.

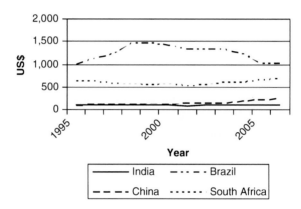

Figure 8.17. *Foreign debt per capita*

Source: Datastream.

short-term debt is stable for India, Brazil, and South Africa while sharply increasing for China.

Before looking at the share of non-performing loans in CIBS, there are some BIS figures to study. Figure 8.22 shows BIS's undisbursed credit commitments,[2] which decreased sharply for CIBS in 2004 and might indicate that

---

[2] According to the OECD Glossary of Statistical Terms, 'credit commitments' are: 'Funds committed by the creditor but not yet utilized by the borrower. In BIS terminology, this refers to open lines of credit that are legally binding on lending banks. A transaction in the balance of payments or a position in the international investment position (IIP) is only recorded when an actual disbursement takes place.'

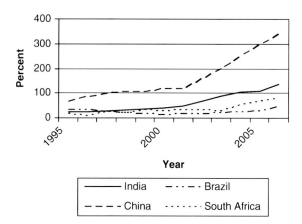

Figure 8.18. *International reserves to total debt ratio*

Source: Datastream.

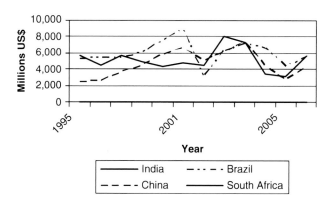

Figure 8.19. *Foreign debt service: medium- and long-term (official creditors)*

Source: Datastream.

corporations resort to the credit lines as short-term debt increased in CIBS over recent years, too.

Looking at the time structure of foreign debt owed to BIS Banks (Figures 8.23–8.25), it can be seen that debts with maturity below one year have increased sharply in China and India since 2003 while staying constant in Brazil and South Africa. The volume of foreign debt with maturity of one to two years is small when compared with the other two categories (below one year and above two years). This kind of debt increased for China and Brazil while staying constant for India and South Africa. Compared with China,

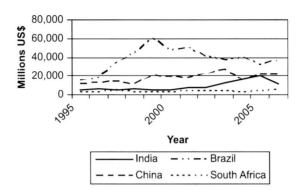

Figure 8.20. *Foreign debt service: medium- and long-term (private creditors)*
Source: Datastream.

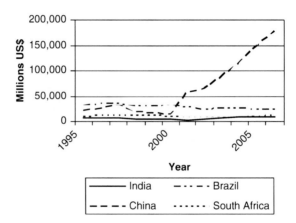

Figure 8.21. *Foreign debt stock: short term*
Source: Datastream.

India, and South Africa, Brazil relied most on foreign debt with a maturity of more than two years, and all four countries experienced an increase of this type of debt over recent years.

Finally, it is important to look at the non-performing loans (or bad loans) in the four economies in order to see whether the share of outstanding debt might become harmful to the economies in the future. An increasing share of non-performing loans indicates problems in the corporate sector and a higher risk for banking institutions (which have to write off these loans in their balance sheets and might, therefore, experience problems in specific capital adequacy ratios; for example, Basel II tier capital adequacy ratios). Unfortunately, it is

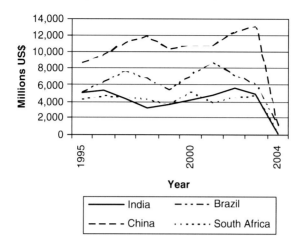

Figure 8.22. *Bank for International Settlements (BIS) banks undisbursed credit commitments*

Source: Datastream.

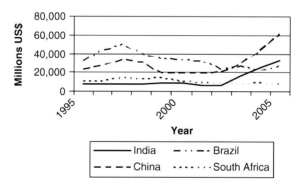

Figure 8.23. *Foreign debt owed to Bank for International Settlements (BIS) banks with maturity 0–1 years*

Source: Datastream.

difficult to find any specific numbers showing the behaviour of domestic bank institutions that could indicate mismatches in lending (mismatches, in this context, means time mismatches; that is, foreign short-term debt will be lent to domestic corporations as medium- to long-term debt). The high share of foreign short-term debt in China indicates some vulnerability, although it is, by itself, not a sign of financial crisis. In the case of China, the build-up of international reserves is positive: these might buffer smaller shocks but, again, they are no guarantee in times of crisis. More interesting and controversial is

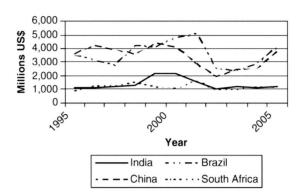

Figure 8.24. *Foreign debt owed to Bank for International Settlements (BIS) banks with maturity 1–2 years.*

Source: Datastream.

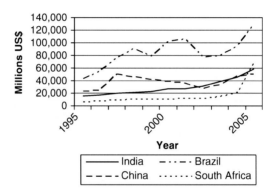

Figure 8.25. *Foreign debt owed to Bank for International Settlements (BIS) banks with maturity over 2 years*

Source: Datastream.

the fact that India and China are net foreign creditors: assets owned overseas could be considered as a type of insurance and risk diversification for domestic corporations. However, on the other hand, these are flows that are not invested in the domestic economy (and, therefore, not used for domestic investment opportunities) and are exposed to foreign market risk (for example, the mortgage market of the United States). There are difficulties in analysing these opaque financial flows. The new and various forms of financial flows, and indirect linkages between the domestic and overseas economies, make any attempt at analysis of possible threats in this section almost impossible. Additionally, available data are very limited, which increases the problems of interpretation, too.

Table 8.2. *Non-performing bank loans to total loans (percentage)*

	2001	2002	2003	2004	2005	2006
China	29.8	26.0	20.4	12.8	9.8	7.5
India	11.4	10.4	8.8	7.2	5.2	3.3 (Mar.)
Brazil	5.6	4.8	4.8	3.8	4.4	N/A
South Africa	3.1	2.8	2.4	1.8	1.5	1.2 (June)

Source: IMF 2007.

Looking at non-performing loans (Table 8.2), it can be seen that in CIBS the ratio decreased over the period of 2001 to 2005 in respective of 2006. South Africa's very low ratio is impressive, which might indicate a sounder financial industry, while the ratio for China is high (these are official numbers and some other sources, for example, the US Department of State reports even higher numbers). The combination of an increasing reliance on short-term debt and a relatively high share of non-performing loans could be an indicator of financial vulnerability in China and should be analysed in greater detail. However, as mentioned, this might be difficult owing to a lack of data. The average bank non-performing loans to total loans ratio in developed financial markets is between 1 and 2 per cent. Therefore, based on these official figures, three countries, China, India, and Brazil, can be considered as being relatively more risky and exposed to financial instability when compared with South Africa. Lastly, China seems to be exposed more than the other countries owing to its relatively larger share of short-term debt in comparison with the other three countries.

INTEREST RATES AND EQUITY MARKETS

This last section deals with interest rate and equity market developments in CIBS. It can be seen from Figures 8.26 and 8.27 that between 2001 and 2005 the lending interest rate and discount rate in China, India, and South Africa were below 10 per cent. In contrast, Brazil experienced very high lending interest rates (reaching even more than 80 per cent) and a discount rate above 20 per cent. Both indicators are decreasing for Brazil over the period, which shows that the problems after the economic shock in the late 1990s seem to be resolved.

Since 2004, stock market indices (Figures 8.28–8.31) for CIBS increased sharply (in China's case, since 2005), which could be a sign of economic growth. This is also a sign of attractiveness to foreign investors. This upward trend can be

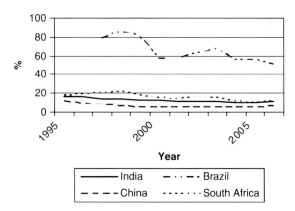

Figure 8.26. *Lending interest rate*

Source: Datastream.

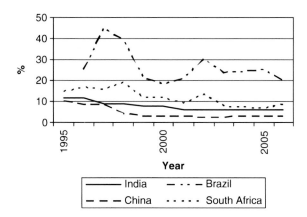

Figure 8.27. *Discount rate*

Source: Datastream.

seen from major developed market indices (for example, Dow Jones, S&P500, FTSE). An increasing and unsustainable level of stock market growth leading to a 'bubble' that could burst in the event of a crisis could become problematic; for example, in the proprietary market (as happened in Thailand in 1997). A well-regulated equity market with independent supervision could limit the risk of harmful bubbles and the spread of crisis among different economic branches.

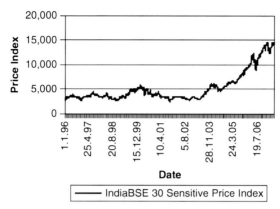

Figure 8.28. *Stock market index: India*

Source: DataStream.

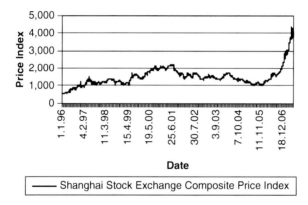

Figure 8.29. *Stock market index: China*

Source: Datastream.

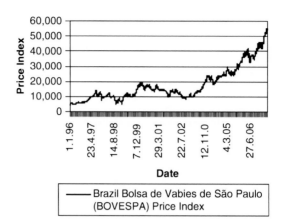

Figure 8.30. *Stock market index: Brazil*

Source: Datastream.

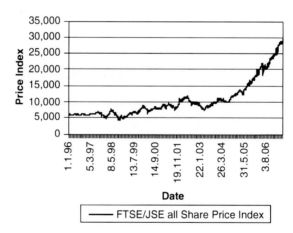

Figure 8.31. *Stock market index: South Africa*

Source: Datastream.

SUMMARY

Looking at the individual findings presented in this chapter, it can be seen that the results are mixed and interpretation is not straightforward. In some countries, exchange rate regimes are flexible; in others they are 'hybrid'. Short-term debt is higher in one country than another; however, if combined with high international reserves or employed to ease short-term disequilibria and temporary mismatches in financial markets, this should be less problematic. Some countries are net creditors while others are net debtors, and so on.

CIBS have in common the fact that they all experienced a high growth rate; however, considering the capital flows, exchange rates, and debt structure, four different stories emerge. Commonalities are the high real GDP growth rates, stock market and export growth, some improvements in the financial industry, and stable macroeconomic indicators (for example, interest rates, inflation rate). On the other hand, differences can be observed.

China is a net creditor to the world and has built up huge international reserves, a strong current account surplus, and gains from FDI inflows. At the same time, however, China has a relatively high share of short-term debt and non-performing loans (NPLs), as well as a high level of stock in short-term capital flows.

India is also a net creditor, has lower international reserves and a current account surplus such as China's but is, however, exposed to less short-term debt and fewer NPLs. Also, its capital account is relatively closed.

Brazil and South Africa have had different experiences, as both countries are not building up a high share of debt and international reserves. They do, however, have to deal with other situations and experience a lower share of short-term debt and NPLs. For example, South Africa is experiencing some capital outflow, seemingly due to investments in neighbouring countries; Brazil still has a level of burden resulting from economic troubles in the late 1990s. Both Brazil and South Africa experience a relatively high share of foreign debt per capita when compared with India and China and a current account deficit (South Africa) and a relatively small surplus (Brazil).

LESSONS FROM THE EAST ASIAN CRISIS OF 1997–8 AND CONCLUDING REMARKS

The East Asian Crisis of 1997–8 has shown that even economies with seemingly sound macroeconomic fundamentals and high growth rates are not safe from a sudden financial economic crisis. Lessons from the East Asian Crisis are as follows.

The economies and policymakers have to be aware of the concept of the 'impossible trinity'. This is difficult for situations in which economies shift from one exchange rate regime to another (for example, fixed to flexible) and when, indirectly, all three goals might be reached. The result would be an increasing risk in the economy. As discussed, it seems that China, due to its exchange rate system and the large share of capital flows (short- and long term), is exposed to a higher degree to a third-generation crisis. The other three countries seem to have chosen policies that are in line with the impossible trinity: Brazil and South Africa are using a floating exchange rate system combined with free capital flows and monetary independence; India has chosen a hybrid exchange rate system but has very low capital mobility. Furthermore, the high rate of NPLs in China, combined with macroeconomic policy (a seemingly fixed exchange rate, portfolio capital inflows, sharp increase of the stock market indices, and other policies as discussed), could increase the risk of a third-generation crisis. Remember, in East Asia, high NPLs and the sharp reversal of short-term capital inflows were some of the factors leading to the crisis. Although these factors are present in China, this does not necessarily guarantee such a crisis. India, Brazil, and South Africa, according to the 'impossible trinity', do not seem to be affected by the threat of a third generation crisis.

The introduction of prudent regulations in the financial industry benefits the whole economy. Regulations that increase the health of the corporate and the banking sectors (for example, international accounting standards, independent supervisory agencies) indirectly improve the strength of the economies and lower the risk of crises related to problems in corporations' and banks' balance sheets (for example, third-generation crisis models).

The timing of the liberalization of the capital account has to be chosen carefully. As discussed, studies show that the liberalization of capital accounts is not as beneficial for economic growth as the opening of the current account, although long-term capital inflows are considered to benefit the economy. Short-term capital flows are considered to be more risky because of their time structure (for example, the problem of sudden reversals) and are therefore sometimes referred to as 'hot money'. Furthermore, timing of the liberalization of the capital account has to be accompanied by improvements in the domestic financial industry (for example, improvement of regulations). Policymakers have to be aware of the sudden reversals and other problems that can occur in financial markets (for example, herding behaviour) by opening up domestic finance markets for foreign investors.

Policymakers in CIBS should be aware of these possible threats. As with all crisis models, this might not predict a third-generation crisis; however, it might give a hint of some problems and help to identify new ones. Unfortunately, it is not possible to predict the emergence of any new type of crisis model or their form. Therefore, policymakers should be aware of potential known risks and invest some effort in crisis prevention.

REFERENCES

Aghion, P., P. Bacchetta, and A. Banerjee (1999a) 'Financial Liberalization and Volatility in Emerging Market Economies', in P.-R. Agénor, M. Miller, D. Vines, and A. Weber (eds), *The Asian Financial Crisis: Causes, Contagion and Consequences* (Cambridge: Cambridge University Press): 167–90.

—— —— ——(1999b) 'Capital Markets and the Instability of Open Economies'. CEPR Discussion Paper 2083 (London: CEPR).

—— —— ——(2000) 'A Simple Model of Monetary Policy and Currency Crises', *European Economic Review*, 44: 728–38.

—— —— ——(2001) 'Currency Crises and Monetary Policy in an Economy with Credit Constraints', *European Economic Review*, 45: 1121–50.

—— —— ——(2004) 'A Corporate Balance-sheet Approach to Currency Crises', *Journal of Economic Theory*, 119: 6–30.

BIS (Bank of International Settlement) (2002) 'China's Capital Account Liberalisation in Perspective'. Speech by André Icard, Deputy General Manager of the BIS, on the occasion of the joint BIS/SAFE seminar on 'Capital Account Liberalisation in China: International Perspectives', Beijing, 12–13 Sept.

Bernanke, B. S., M. Gertler, and S. Gilchrist (1999) 'The Financial Accelerator in a Quantitative Business Cycle Framework', in J. Taylor and M. Woodford (eds), *Handbook of Macroeconomics*: 1341–93.

Calvo, G. A., and C. M. Reinhart (2000) 'Fear of Floating'. NBER Working Paper 7993 (Cambridge, Mass.: NBER).

Céspedes, L. F., R. Chang, and A. Velasco (2000) 'Balance Sheets and Exchange Rate Policy'. NBER Working Paper 7840 (Cambridge, Mass.: NBER).

Chang, R., and A. Velasco (1998a) 'Financial Fragility and the Exchange Rate Regime'. NBER Working Paper 6469 (Cambridge, Mass.: NBER).

—— ——(1998b) 'Financial Crises in Emerging Markets: A Canonical Model'. Working Paper 98-10, Federal Reserve Bank of Atlanta.

—— ——(1999) 'Liquidity Crises in Emerging Markets: Theory and Policy'. NBER Working Paper 7272 (Cambridge, Mass.: NBER).

Edwards, S. (2003) 'Exchange Rate Regimes, Capital Flows and Crisis Prevention', in M. Feldstein (ed.), *Economic and Financial Crises in Emerging Market Economies* (Chicago: University of Chicago Press): 31–78.

——and M. A. Savastano (1999) 'Exchange Rates in Emerging Economies: What Do We Know? What Do We Need to Know?' NBER Working Paper W7228 (Cambridge, Mass.: NBER).

Eichengreen, B. J., and D. Leblang (2002) 'Capital Account Liberalization and Growth: Was Mr Mahathir Right?' NBER Working Paper 9427 (Cambridge, Mass.: NBER).

——and P. Masson (1998) 'Exit Strategies: Policy Options for Countries Seeking Greater Exchange Rate Flexibility'. IMF Occasional Paper 168 (Washington, DC: IMF).

——M. Mussa, G. Dell'Ariccia, et al. (1998) 'Capital Account Liberalization: Theoretical and Practical Aspects'. Occasional Paper 172 (Washington, DC: IMF).

——A. Rose, and C. Wyplosz (1995) 'Exchange Market Mayhem: The Antecedents and Aftermath of Speculative Attacks', *Economic Policy* (Oct.): 251–96.

Frankel, J. A. (1999) 'No Single Currency Regime is Right for all Countries or at all Times'. Working Paper 7338 (Cambridge, Mass.: NBER).

IMF (2006) 'De Facto Classification of Exchange Rate Regimes and Monetary Policy Framework (Data as of 31 July)'. <http://www.imf.org/external/np/mfd/er/2006/eng/0706.htm>.

——(2007) *Global Financial Stability Report: Market Developments and Issues* (Apr.) (Washington, DC: IMF).

Isard, P. (2005) *Globalization and the International Financial System: What's Wrong and What Can Be Done?* (Cambridge: Cambridge University Press).

Jomo, K. S. (2004) 'Were Malaysia's Capital Controls Effective?', in K. S. Jomo (ed.), *After the Storm: Crisis, Recovery, and Sustaining Development in Four Asian Economies* (Singapore: Singapore University Press): 173–203.

——(2005) 'Malaysia's September 1998 Controls: Background, Context, Impacts, Comparisons, Implications, Lessons'. G-24 Discussion Paper Series 36 (Mar.) (New York and Geneva: UN).

Kaplan, E., and D. Rodrik (2001) 'Did the Malaysian Capital Controls Work?' NBER Working Paper 8142 (Cambridge, Mass.: NBER).

Krugman, P. (1999a) 'Balance Sheets, the Transfer Problem, and Financial Crises', in P. Isard, A. Razin, and A. K. Rose (eds), *International Finance and Financial Crises: Essays in Honor of Robert Flood* (Norwell, Mass.: Kluwer Academic).

——(1999b) 'Analytical Afterthoughts on the Asian Crisis' (Cambridge, Mass.: MIT). mimeo.

——(2001) 'Crises: The Next Generation?' Draft prepared for Razin Conference, Tel Aviv University, 25–6 Mar.

Obstfeld, M. (2000) 'Globalization and Macroeconomics'. NBER Research Summary (Fall) (Cambridge, Mass.: NBER).

—— J. C. Shambaugh, and A. M. Taylor (2004) 'The Trilemma in History: Trade-offs among Exchange Rates, Monetary Policies, and Capital Mobility'. Working Paper 10396 (Cambridge, Mass.: NBER).

OECD *Glossary of Statistical Terms* (Paris: OECD).

Summers, L. H. (2000) 'International Financial Crises: Causes, Preventions, and Cures', *American Economic Review*, 90: 1–16.

9

Foreign Direct Investment from China, India, and South Africa in sub-Saharan Africa: A New or Old Phenomenon?

John Henley, Stefan Kratzsch,
Mithat Külür, and Tamer Tandogan[1]

INTRODUCTION

The literature on outward foreign direct investment (OFDI) from emerging markets usually adopts the position that the universe of motives behind a firm's decision to undertake foreign direct investment (FDI) is, in principal, the same as that of a firm from a developed market economy. However, because the ownership-specific advantages of different investors are shaped by the context from which firms originate and the period in which investment occurs, the specific features of OFDI from emerging markets—such as China, India, or South Africa (CISA)—might be expected to reflect the social, political, and economic history of the country of origin (Filatotchev, et al. 2007).

For example, Wells (1977; 1981; 1983) suggests that the reason why what he styles as third-world multinational enterprises (TWMNEs) are able to invest abroad successfully is because their growth path typically provides them with four 'new' advantages. These are: a less costly management team; technology adjusted to the typical factor endowments of developing countries; the ability to purchase low-cost raw materials locally; and a range of products developed in the setting of a third world economy. Lall, in a similar vein in 1983, claimed that TWMNEs were able to benefit from localization of technology that more accurately matched the requirements

[1] The authors gratefully acknowledge the contribution of the research team that generated the data used in this chapter.

of developing host countries, particularly smaller-scale production units to service the small consumer markets of developing countries.

These kinds of arguments were certainly plausible in the 1980s with regard to Africa (where markets were generally heavily protected by tariff and non-tariff barriers). The subsidiaries of large transnational corporations (TNCs), mostly European and many tracing their origins back to the colonial era, were well entrenched as clones of their parents. By the end of the 1980s—after a decade of economic stagnation in Africa, the beginnings of economic liberalization, and increased competition in the major markets of Europe and North America—many of these older TNCs were beginning to look for exits from the region. The scale factors identified by Lall as a competitive advantage of TWMNEs became a major weakness of TNCs from the North as increased concentration of fast-moving consumer goods (FMCG) companies progressed and larger production units located in key markets became the norm.

Corporate strategy groups restructuring TNC parent companies in the North during the 1990s increasingly could no longer accept the high transaction costs associated with operating small, low-growth production units in Africa, especially as margins were under pressure from reductions in tariff protection. Moreover, supplying many of these African markets through exports was becoming more attractive as liberalization began to drive down trade barriers. This evolution created new opportunities for smaller, more-nimble investors able to serve local markets from a lower cost base, much as Wells and Lall had proposed in 1983, although this occurred more than a decade later.

This chapter, first, briefly reviews the literature on theories of outward foreign investment and their relevance for understanding FDI from CISA. Second, the chapter examines the descriptive statistics generated from a survey of 1,216 foreign owned firms and subsidiaries operating in fifteen sub-Saharan Africa (SSA) countries carried out by UNIDO in 2005 (UNIDO 2007). The subset of data from foreign investors declaring their country of origin as being China, India, or South Africa is compared with investors from the North (Europe, North America, and Japan) and three regions of the South: the Middle East and North Africa (MENA); SSA (excluding South Africa); and emerging Asia (excluding China and India). The final section of the chapter attempts to answer the question posed in the introduction: are the characteristics of foreign investors from China, India, and South Africa in SSA significantly different from each other, or is there some meaningful category 'FDI from the South'?

THEORIES OF FDI

Theories of OFDI have been dominated by the work of John Dunning for more than thirty years. His original eclectic theory, first proposed in 1977, has undergone several modifications. Dunning identifies three variables: owner-ship-specific advantage, location-specific advantage, and internalization-specific advantage; he states that these can be used to explain why a firm chooses to expand into foreign markets through FDI rather than through other less-capital intensive means, such as licensing or exporting.

More recently, Dunning (2000) has proposed that the eclectic paradigm should be treated as 'an envelope for economic and business theories of MNE activity'. Perhaps rather wisely, the issue of how the three variables interrelate and, in particular, which of the advantages weighs more in the FDI process is not addressed directly (Moosa 2002). There is an inevitable survivor bias in any population of successful foreign investors and, therefore, an element of circularity in any attempt to extract normative advice from surveys of firms in order to identify successful combinations of Dunning's three 'advantages'. Successful FDI is rarely a one-off event; it is more usually a stream of resource flows, to a greater or lesser extent, stimulated by the interactive relationship between the investor and the host economy, and dependent on the changing motivation of the investor. An important empirical question for host author-ities is the extent to which policy interventions can influence an investor's location decision with positive benefits for the host economy.

The specific ownership advantages required to exploit a given set of location advantages are likely to change over time, not least because of changing economic conditions as well as policy interventions by the host authorities. The World Bank, for example, has invested significant resources through its Doing Business Reports and its Business Environment and Enter-prise Performance Survey (BEEPS) activity in encouraging governments in emerging markets to adopt a business-friendly investment environment. UNIDO has been actively supporting national investment promotion agen-cies in SSA since 2001 through AfrIPANet. Thus, with increasing liberaliza-tion of investment policy regimes in many African countries, newcomers face much lower barriers to FDI than their more established rivals, mostly origin-ating from the North (Mathews 2006; Yin and Choi 2005).

Another approach to explaining FDI is founded on a process theory of internationalization (PTI) and focuses on the processes that firms undertake when embarking on FDI, originally stimulated by the work of Johanson and Vahlne (1977). The basic assumption of this approach is that lack of foreign market knowledge is a major problem for foreign investors, especially for firms at the very early stages in the internationalization process. Johanson and Vahlne (1990) make the distinction between objective knowledge about a given business environment, such as that imparted by the World Bank's Doing Business Reports, and operational experience gained from investing and working in a foreign market. The Johanson–Vahlne formulation implies that firms have to reach a certain size before they can invest internationally, and that the requisite experiential knowledge is accumulated through superior organizational processes.

The organizational cloning approach adopted by TNCs from the North to exploit highly protected markets in post-colonial Africa in the 1960s and 1970s fits well with the PTI model. The import substitution industrialization policies widely adopted during the period reduced risk and competition for investors through import tariffs, quotas, and investment licensing. Protection helped to offset the diseconomies of operating in small markets. FDI from emerging markets was largely unable to exploit the competitive advantages identified by Wells (1983) and Lall (1983) for, although by following Johanson and Vahlne (1977) managers from the South should have experienced less psychological and cultural distance from the business environment in SSA markets, their organizational resources were less developed than TNCs from the North.

The global business environment has changed radically since the 1970s. As Autio (2005) points out, the costs of managerial control over foreign operations has dropped dramatically with the development of telecommunications technology enhancing information flow and reducing psychological distance, with falling transportation costs and the increased availability of high-level managerial expertise in emerging markets. This now enables less-well-resourced investors to be confident in employing a range of governance mechanisms as an alternative to operating wholly owned subsidiaries. As a consequence, it has become possible for smaller firms to internationalize by leveraging resources through alliances and informal networks rather than through full ownership. Nevertheless, the original insight of Johanson and Vahlne (2003)—that internationalization is basically a process of learning and reacting—still holds, even though the global context has changed beyond recognition since 1977.

The increase in the number of small businesses that internationalize soon after their formation to engage in 'international entrepreneurship' (Zahra 2005) has attracted significant research interest. The paper by Oviatt and McDougall (1994) was particularly influential in drawing attention to the phenomenon. By focusing on the founding entrepreneurs' international competence, vision, and awareness of growth opportunities, Oviatt and McDougall took theories of foreign investment beyond preoccupation with leveraging home-based corporate resources (Autio 2005). By pointing out that international entrepreneurs are able and willing to make strategic choices and take on the risks associated with international expansion—but, because of a poverty of resources, usually adopt low-cost governance mechanisms such as network structures—they drew attention to a whole range of international business activities largely ignored by the mainstream literature on TNCs (Oviatt and McDougall 2005). This emphasis on the scarcity of resources faced by international entrepreneurs leading to a preference for low-cost governance mechanisms, by contrast with larger well-established TNCs following the Johanson and Vahlne (2003) route to internationalization is suggestive of the pattern typically followed by investors from the South. The focus on the international social capital of entrepreneurs and their ability to access and mobilize cross-border resources encourages a reconsideration of the dynamics and potential of private foreign investment from emerging markets. Although Oviatt and McDougall (1994) do not explicitly discuss the role of kinship networks in international entrepreneurship, this is clearly allowed for in their emphasis on low-cost governance mechanisms. In other words, internationalization might not always be 'an uphill struggle' but, rather, might be a 'condition for value creation' (Autio 2005).

By inference, then, the international entrepreneurship literature is optimistic about the growth of FDI from emerging markets for as long as there are entrepreneurs willing to look for opportunities for growth through internationalization. Investments by these entrepreneurial firms, usually family controlled, are rarely recorded as FDI because they are unlikely to be registered as subsidiaries of companies with headquarters in another country. On the other hand, the owners are foreign nationals and many have deep-rooted, if technically informal, cross-border links with other firms. Some might be returning members of the diaspora holding foreign passports. As Nanda and Khanna (2007) demonstrate, diasporas stimulate international entrepreneurship by creating cross-border social networks that serve an important role in helping entrepreneurs to circumvent the barriers to business relations and trade arising from imperfect local institutions in developing countries.

Autio, Sapienza, and Almeida (2000) argue that 'international new ventures' have the inherent 'learning advantages of newness'. They predict that, because the founder-owner is in control, new knowledge is assimilated quickly, and therefore these firms grow much more rapidly than established firms that are more likely to be stifled by bureaucratic decision-making procedures. However, as Zahra (2005) asks, do these new ventures actually have the capacity to absorb and assimilate new knowledge and expertise? If many of these foreign-owned firms do not feature in standard measures of FDI flows estimated using balance of payments statistics, as in the World Investment

Report (UNCTAD 2006), is an important source of economic dynamism missing from accounts of FDI in emerging markets?

A brief overview has been presented of some of the main strands of the literature on FDI. This suggests that firms originating from particular countries are likely, in part, to reflect the particular economic, political, and social histories of those countries. Dunning's (2000) ownership advantages are nurtured in specific business environments. Johanson and Vahlne's (1990) internationalization processes might have generic elements but are also partly contextually determined. Oviatt and McDougall's (1994) concept of international entrepreneurship is highly dependent on social capital formation, and therefore very much influenced by social networks married to business activity (Nanda and Khanna 2007).

The next section of the chapter presents the descriptive statistics relating to the firms investing in fifteen SSA countries from CISA that participated in the UNIDO survey in 2005 (UNIDO 2007). In order to identify the distinctive features of these particular investors, they are grouped and compared with each other and with groupings extracted from the complete survey sample of 1,216 firms. The regional groups used are, again: the North (Europe, North America, and Japan) and three regions of the South: MENA; SSA (excluding South Africa); and Asia (excluding China and India).

Some of the comparisons need to be treated with caution, as the sample sizes are sometimes modest, making more robust analysis very difficult; in particular, the samples are not large enough to control for industry subsectors. However, it is argued that in the absence of better empirical evidence it is useful to examine some of the features of investment flows from particular countries and regions to SSA, and to begin to sketch out their main features. It is hoped that this will encourage further research into the great diversity of FDI in SSA.

RESULTS

Sector and start of operations

At a sectoral level, the major difference between investors from CISA operating in SSA is the importance of the South African services sector and the predominance of manufacturers amongst investors from both China and India. Over 60 per cent of investors from South Africa operate in the services sector, the highest proportion for any country of origin grouping, including the sample of firms from the North (Figure 9.1).

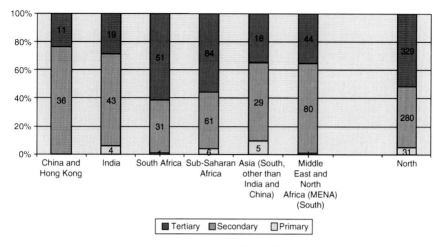

Figure 9.1. *Sectoral composition of investment from different countries and regions*
Source: UNIDO 2007.

At a sub-sectoral level, nearly one-third of Chinese firms manufacture textiles or garments, and a similar proportion of Indian companies manufacture chemicals, plastics, and rubber (Figures 9.2–9.5). The well-documented lack of internationalization of India's garment or textiles industries, largely as a result of past policy interventions by the government of India, stands in contrast to the rest of Asia (Henley 2004). Chinese and other Asian firms are the major exporters (~40 per cent). More than three-quarters of Indian firms, by contrast, only serve the local market (p < 0.001) (Figure 9.6).

The pattern of South African investments most closely matches FDI from the North, with the significant exception of the virtual absence of export-oriented investors from South Africa. The most important manufacturing sub-sector for both is food and beverages (Figures 9.4 and 9.5). Trading companies involved in marketing, sales, and distribution are important for all source countries and regions.

Since the 1980s, a clear shift is visible in the dominance of FDI from the North in SSA (p < 0.001) (Figure 9.7). Older-established firms are mainly from the North, and newcomer firms originate from the South. This is reflected in the average age of firms from the North of 21.6 years, three times older than the average Chinese firm (Table 9.1). Breaking down the population of firms of Southern origin, Chinese firms are the youngest (with an average age of 7 years in 2005) closely followed by firms from elsewhere in Asia (with 7.4 years of operational experience in SSA). Indian and South African firms are on average of similar age (12 years and 13.1 years, respectively (p < 0.005)). While it is unsurprising that South African firms operating

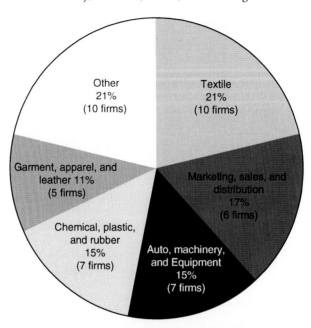

Figure 9.2. *Distribution of investors from China by sub-sector*
Source: UNIDO 2007.

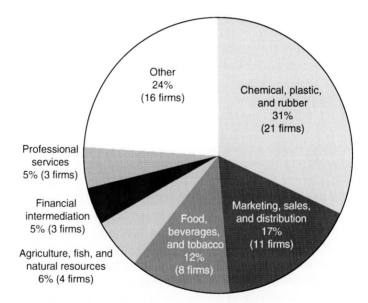

Figure 9.3. *Distribution of investors from India by sub-sector*
Source: UNIDO 2007.

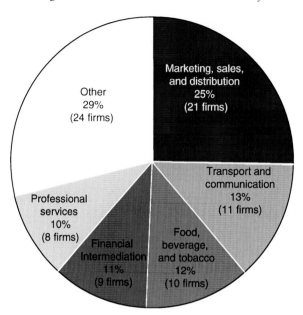

Figure 9.4. *Distribution of investors from South Africa by sub-sector*
Source: UNIDO 2007.

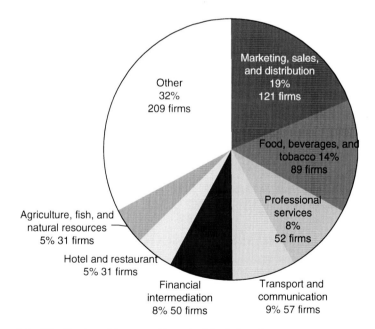

Figure 9.5. *Distribution of investors from the North by sub-sector*
Source: UNIDO 2007.

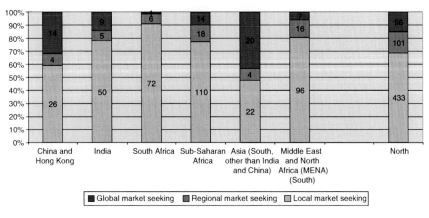

Figure 9.6. *Market orientation of investors*

Source: UNIDO 2007.

in SSA are younger than firms from the North because of exclusion from most of SSA during the apartheid years, it is striking that Chinese firms are on average much younger than both Indian and South African firms. It is also very noticeable that nearly half of South African investors are using acquisitions as a 'catch-up' entry mode in SSA, including taking advantage of privatization opportunities (p < 0.001) (Figure 9.8). This is very different from Chinese investors who overwhelmingly favour a green-field investment strategy.

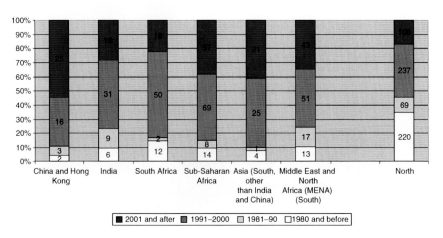

Figure 9.7. *Time period of start of operations*

Source: UNIDO 2007.

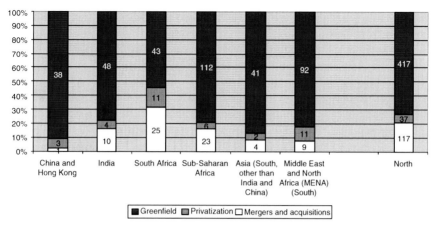

Figure 9.8. *Mode of entry and ownership*

Source: UNIDO 2007.

In the complete UNIDO survey sample (2007: 35), of 1,200 firms, among those that started operations before 1981, 79 per cent originated from the North. This percentage of Northern-origin companies drops steadily and significantly for each subsequent start-up period (p < 0.001). Among companies that started operations after 2000, the proportion of North origin firms is only 37 per cent. It is also noticeable that the decade 1981–90 was a period of very little foreign investment in Africa from any region.

Sales and assets performance

The average firm from the North achieved sales of US$19.0 million from a book value of US$24.7 million and employed 347 people in SSA (Table 9.1). A block of 220 Northern-origin firms that have been operating in SSA for over

Table 9.1. *Characteristics of foreign investment in sub-Saharan Africa (mean values)*

Investor origin	Age (years)	Book value (US$ million)	Sales (US$ million)	Employees
China	7.0	5.39	6.99	657
India	12.0	2.60	2.59	119
South Africa*	13.1	18.1	11.2	200
North	21.6	24.7	19.0	347

Notes: * Excluding MTN Nigeria communication Ltd.

Source: UNIDO 2007.

twenty-five years, many before independence, remains well established in SSA. These firms obtained average sales of over US$34 million from a book value of US$42 million and employed over 600 people in 2004. By contrast, Chinese firms in the sample achieved average sales of US$7 million from a book value of US$5.4 million, yet, although much younger, on average employed 660 people. Indian firms are significantly smaller, achieving sales of US$2.6 million from a book value of US$2.6 million and employing 120 people.

South African firms are more comparable to firms from the North in terms of sales and assets, achieving sales of US$11.2 million from an average book value of US$18.1 million and a workforce of 200. Overall, South African firms are significantly different from those from China and India in terms of size and capital intensity, and their preference for a formal governance structure. Of the South African firms, 80 per cent operating in SSA are formal subsidiaries of a parent company. Indian firms are, on average, the smallest of all groups of firms originating in the South. Perhaps reflecting their size and low level of financial commitment, more than 80 per cent of Indian firms are owner managed firms with no formal organizational links with a corporate headquarters in another country. This also appears to confirm the growing importance of international entrepreneurs in SSA, who are responding to the lowering of trade and investment barriers since the 1990s.

South African firms are 50 per cent more capital intensive than the average firm from the North (US$107,000 of assets per worker compared with US$71,500 and achieving sales per worker of US$96,800 compared with the US$90,100 obtained by the average Northern firm (Table 9.2)) reflecting their

Table 9.2. *Firm performance*

Investor origin		Preceding year's sales per employee (US$)	Preceding year's sales per US$ of book value	Book value per employee (US$)
China	N	37	27	32
	Mean	15,300	2.43	36,900
India	N	58	51	53
	Mean	38,000	3.17	39,700
South Africa	N	72	63	66
	Mean	96,800	3.96	107,000
The North	N	571	487	512
	Mean	90,100	3.63	71,500
Complete sample	N	1011	868	934
	Mean	74,000	3.43	75,500

Source: UNIDO 2007.

increasing focus in the emerging services sector. At the other extreme, Chinese companies have an average book value per worker of just US$36,900 and obtain sales per worker of US$15,300. South African firms, on average, obtain the highest capital productivity in terms of gross sales: 4.0 compared with Northern companies, which achieved 3.6. Labour-productivity figures also confirm that South African investors are ahead of those from the North despite their relative youthfulness.

The productivity of a typical Indian company is better than that of a Chinese company. In terms of sales per dollar of book value and sales per worker, the productivity of a typical Indian company is better than that of a Chinese firm, probably reflecting greater operational experience, but is significantly worse than investments from South Africa or from the North ($p < 0.01$) (Table 9.2).

FIRM GROWTH AND IMPACT ON THE HOST ECONOMY

Performance self-evaluation and sales growth

Investors from South Africa were the most bullish of any source country in their performance self-evaluation; 75 per cent reported their performance over the preceding three years to be in line with, or above, expectations. Indian firms were also positive in their evaluations of investment performance: 68 per cent. Chinese firms, by contrast, were much less sanguine. Nearly half rated their performance as below expectations.

Paradoxically, in terms of sales growth, Chinese firms and firms from elsewhere in Asia (excluding India) experienced very high growth, 48 per cent and 39 per cent during the previous year ($p < 0.004$) (Figure 9.9). These firms evidently have very ambitious sales targets, since many of their self-evaluations of performance are quite negative. It would appear that twenty of these Chinese investors have set themselves ambitious rates of return targets for establishing what are considered high-risk, short-payback operations, mostly export platforms. South African firms, by contrast, achieved sales growth of 18 per cent, while Indian firms obtained sales growth of just 13 per cent. Interestingly, Indian firms' sales targets seemed to be quite modest, yet satisfaction with performance was quite high. By comparison, Northern firms achieved sales growth of 15 per cent.

When firms were asked about their expectations for the ensuing three years, the pattern changed to greater optimism amongst all investors except for Chinese companies, with their expectations of sales growth converging

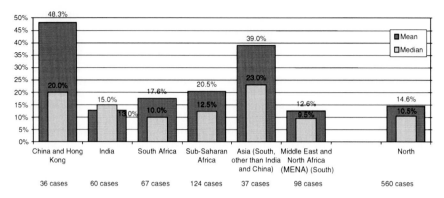

Figure 9.9. *Preceding year's sales growth*

Source: UNIDO 2007.

with the average for the whole sample. Both Indian and South African firms anticipate doubling their sales growth over the ensuing three years (Figure 9.10).

The sub-sectors where sales growth was concentrated in the previous year (2004) are: textiles (50 per cent), garments and leather (42 per cent), and construction (28 per cent), all sub-sectors with high participation by firms from Asia. The ensuing three high-growth sub-sectors—financial services,

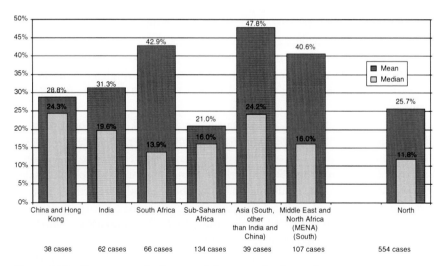

Figure 9.10. *Future annual sales growth (over ensuing 3 years)*

Source: UNIDO 2007.

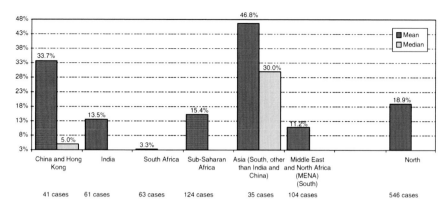

Figure 9.11. *Exports (as percentage of sales)*
Source: UNIDO 2007.

utilities, transport, and communications—attract market-seeking investors from South Africa.

Using more-detailed analysis of high-sales-growth firms, it is apparent that global exporters from China, India, and from elsewhere in Asia achieved 'hyper' growth rates. A third of the sales of the average Chinese company, valued at just under US$1 million per firm, are exported (Figure 9.11). Even this performance is dwarfed by investors from the rest of Asia, which achieved average export sales of 47 per cent of output, valued at US$4.1 million per firm. When asked about the importance of the US African Growth Opportunities Act (AGOA) in encouraging investment in SSA, investors from Asia, including India, considered it to be significant in their decision to invest in manufacturing in SSA.

CAPITAL INVESTMENT

South Africa, with massive investments in MTN-Nigeria of US$1.6 billion, dominated the average of investments over the preceding three years for firms from all countries at US$35 million. Even excluding MTN-Nigeria from statistics for firm-level investments over the preceding three years, South African firms still dominated the average new investment per firm in SSA at US$8.5 million. The next two countries by size of average investment over the preceding three years are Switzerland at US$6.2 million per firm and France at US$4.2 million. The average firm from the North made US$3.1 million of new investment over the same period. By contrast, Chinese firms invested US $1.24 million and Indian firms just US$780,000.

When asked about investment plans over the ensuing three years, the average Chinese firm was forecasting new investment of US$1.44 million. This is similar to new investment by other Asian firms (excluding India) of US $1.35 million. Indian companies, partly reflecting their smaller size, were expecting to invest under US$500,000 per firm. On average, 481 Northern firms were planning to invest US$3.5 million, which is close to their reported investment rate during the previous three years. Clearly, in terms of total capital flows from any region over the preceding three years, firms from the North dominate even though their sales growth is relatively slow. However, with the close correlation between sales and investment confirmed in the overall survey, Southern investors are forecasting moving to close the gap, with average investment per firm of US$3.3 million forecast over the ensuing three years.

In order to evaluate investment levels without the influence of company size and to compare relative growth rates, new investment was analysed as a percentage of the preceding year's sales (Figure 9.12). On average, Southern firms have higher investment rates per dollar of sales; 64 per cent compared with 33 per cent for the average Northern firm. The drivers for this high investment rate, mostly small and medium-sized companies, come from India, SSA, other Asian countries, and, particularly, MENA. Chinese companies plan to remain essentially low-investment, high-employment companies. South African companies, especially in the telecommunication and financial services sectors, have rapidly accumulated assets in SSA and are expanding gross sales from an already large base.

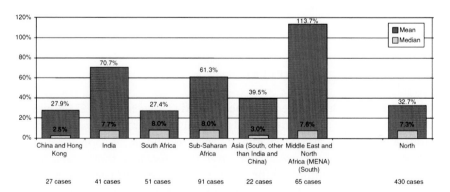

Figure 9.12. *Investment rate over the ensuing 3 years (as percentage of sales)*

Source: UNIDO 2007.

EMPLOYMENT AND WAGES

Chinese employers and investors from elsewhere in Asia (excluding India) manage large labour forces (660 and 580 respectively) compared with an average payroll of 300 for all units from the South and 350 from the North. In terms of employment growth rates, on average, all groupings of Southern firms by origin have been expanding faster than firms from the North (Figures 9.13 and 9.14). South African firms most closely correspond with firms from the North in terms of annual employment growth rates over the preceding three years (12 per cent compared with 10 per cent per annum).

Employment in all Asian firms in the sample, including those from China and India, has grown at significantly faster rates than firms from the North, and is forecast to continue to grow at more than twice the annual average employment growth rate of firms from the North. Again, South African firms forecast that they will follow a similar employment growth trajectory to firms from the North, at 9 per cent per annum. High employment growth firms from Asia are relatively new investors in SSA, concentrated in the garment and textiles sectors and based on export platforms supplying primarily global markets outside Africa. These firms are locating in Madagascar and, to a lesser extent, Kenya, Mozambique, and Tanzania. The Chinese

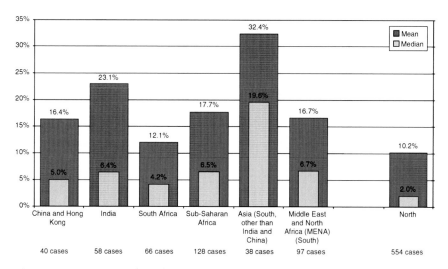

Figure 9.13. *Past annual employment growth (over preceding 3 years)*

Source: UNIDO 2007.

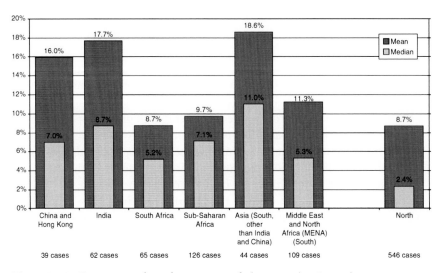

Figure 9.14. *Future annual employment growth (over ensuing 3 years)*
Source: UNIDO 2007.

cluster is particularly strong in Madagascar. By contrast, Francophone West Africa does not appear to be attracting any of the global exporters from Asia.

The pattern of wages per worker is, as might be expected, the obverse of employment growth. South African firms, heavily concentrated in the services sector, pay average wages per worker that are much higher than those paid by Indian or Chinese employers (US$7,400 compared with, respectively, US$2,100 and US$1,100 annually) (p < 0.001) (Figure 9.15). The Northern 'norm' is US$5,900 per worker. In the complete sample of 1,216 companies, at a sub-sectoral level, financial services companies pay average wages of US$11,400. Three other services sub-sectors—transport and communications, professional services, and energy companies—pay, on average, more than US$6,000 annually. The three sub-sectors that on average pay less than US$2,000 are export-oriented, labour-intensive manufacturing concerns—wood products, textiles, and garments. The only host country with a majority of firms participating in the survey that are global exporters is Madagascar, where the average annual wage was US$1,300—the lowest average annual wage of the fifteen survey countries.

In the complete survey sample of 1,216 firms, the most important predictor of wage levels is labour productivity at the firm level. Specifically, in terms of the manufacturing sector, low wages are associated with larger, younger firms. Chinese firms are on average seven years old and employ three times as many

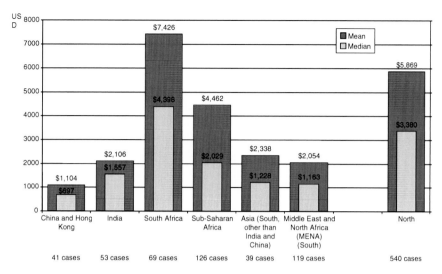

Figure 9.15. *Annual wage per worker (in US$)*

Source: UNIDO 2007.

workers as the average South African company, and more than five times the number of workers employed by the average Indian business.

Another proxy for the quality of human resources is the proportion of graduates in a firm's workforce. South African firms, once more, have a very similar profile to firms from the North, employing 17 per cent of graduates on the payroll. Chinese and Indian firms were similar to each other, employing around 12 per cent of graduates. Interestingly, Chinese and Indian firms also have the highest proportion of expatriates in the graduate workforce (~37 per cent to 40 per cent), while South African firms employ just 23 per cent. Put another way, sixty-eight South African firms employ 171 expatriate graduates, while 138 Asian firms employ 519 expatriates (Figure 9.16).

The employment of expatriates could go some way towards compensating for the perceived lack of expertise available in the local labour market or reflect managerial preference for their own nationals. Whether foreign managements are able to exercise this choice is constrained by work permit regulations and salary cost considerations. The average age of Indian and Chinese firms is younger than firms from the North, so perhaps this is a temporary feature of the employment structures of new arrivals. Over time, these firms might be expected to develop knowledge-transfer mechanisms and greater trust in the competence of local graduate employees. However, family-owned sales and distribution companies, where stock and cash

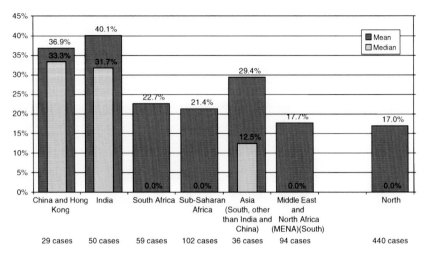

Figure 9.16. *Share of expatriate graduates in university graduates workforce*
Source: UNIDO 2007.

flow control is of major importance, as is interpersonal trust in handling substantial cash-based transactions, might be expected to be particularly slow in making this transition.

CHOICE OF LOCATION

The largest clusters of Chinese firms are located in Madagascar (30 per cent) and Nigeria (25 per cent). However, Chinese firms are the most widely dispersed, with the sample nearly equally distributed between East and West Africa. As might be expected, taking into account historical and cultural ties, two-thirds of Indian firms are concentrated in East Africa, though 20 per cent are located in Nigeria. South African firms are noticeably concentrated in immediate neighbours Mozambique (46 per cent) and Malawi (18 per cent) and the rest of East Africa, with only 8 per cent of investors located in West Africa.

Each foreign investor was asked to comment on the importance of a list of twenty-six location factors for their operation in SSA, and whether each factor had become more positive or negative for their firm over the preceding three years. A ranking was then calculated for each factor for the whole sample of 1,216 firms. This ranking of factors is presented as the numbers in parentheses along the horizontal axis in Figures 9.17–9.20. Thus, economic stability (1),

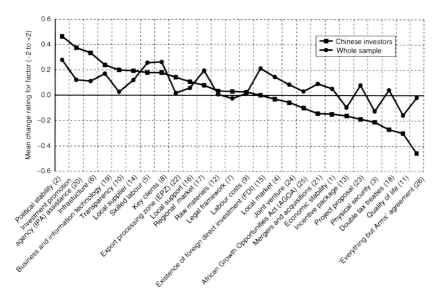

Figure 9.17. *The assessment of Chinese investors of changes in African location factors compared with the assessment of all investors in the sample*

Note: The numbers in parentheses represent the ranking of factors by their importance for the whole sample.

Source: UNIDO 2007.

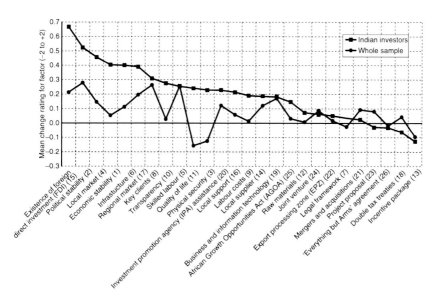

Figure 9.18. *The assessment of Indian investors of changes in African location factors compared with the assessment of all investors in the sample*

Note: The numbers in parentheses represent the ranking of factors by their importance for the whole sample.

Source: UNIDO 2007.

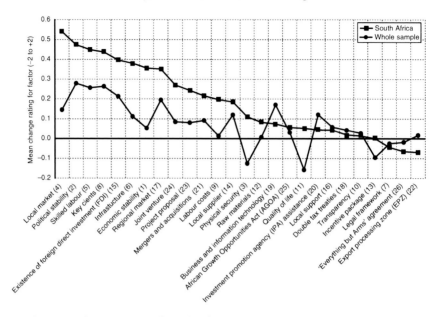

Figure 9.19. *The assessment of South African investors of changes in African location factors compared with the assessment of all investors in the sample*

Note: The numbers in parentheses represent the ranking of factors by their importance for the whole sample.
Source: UNIDO 2007.

political stability (2), and physical security (3) were rated the three most important location factors by the whole sample.

Considering the responses from all investors, the five factors that had improved most in rank order of degree of improvement were: political stability (2), presence of key clients (8), availability of skilled labour (5), existence of other foreign investors in the country (15), and accessibility of regional markets (17). The recognition of the improvement in political stability by investors in SSA is clearly a positive sign.

Only five factors were, on average, considered to have deteriorated over the preceding three years. These were: quality of life (11), physical security (3), incentive package (13), legal framework (7), and taking advantage of the EU 'Everything but Arms' Agreement (EBA) (26). The perceived deterioration in physical security is worrying.

Figures 9.17–9.20 present differences in the perspectives of investors by country of origin contrasted with the complete sample of 1,216 firms. The vertical axis shows the mean rating change for each of the twenty-six factors mapped along the horizontal axis. Figures 9.18 and 9.19 compare

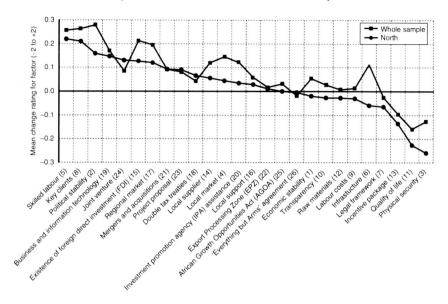

Figure 9.20. *The assessment of Northern investors of changes in African location factors compared with the assessment of all investors in the sample*

Note: The numbers in parentheses represent the ranking of factors by their importance for the whole sample.

Source: UNIDO 2007.

the perceptions of Indian and South African investors with those of the whole sample. Overall, Indian and South African investors are very positive about the investment environment by comparison with the sample as a whole. Most notably, both groups emphasize improvements in political and economic stability, the local market, and infrastructure—factors widely identified as major barriers used to explain SSA's low share of world FDI (Asiedu 2003a; 2003b; 2006; Morisset 2000). Indian and South African investors even acknowledge some improvement in physical security. By contrast, Chinese firms are generally less positive about the investment environment in SSA, with the important exceptions of improvements in political stability and in infrastructure (Figure 9.17).

The perceptions of Northern investors compared to those of the sample as a whole are presented in Figure 9.20. In general, Northern investors are more negative about the investment environment in SSA than the sample as a whole. In particular, they share with Chinese investors a concern for what is perceived as the deteriorating quality of life and physical security in African countries.

DISCUSSION

This chapter has been written on the assumption that it is of value to differentiate between investors on the basis of their country of origin in the South. While this approach does not seem to have been problematic to writers such as Lall and Wells, writing in the 1980s, it is more so in an increasingly globalized world economy where corporations can change their country of registration through a shareholder resolution. Nevertheless, ownership-specific advantages of firms are created in a particular economic context, even if this is sometimes difficult to specify (Filatotchev, et al. 2007). Entrepreneurs, even when they establish stand-alone firms in foreign countries and maintain no formal links with a parent company, exploit the expertise and social capital developed, at least in part, in their country of origin. While identifying origins might be problematic, ascribing causality is even more difficult, not least because of the learning over time involved in undertaking FDI in a specific country. The next section presents a summary of the main features of FDI from South Africa, India, and China in the fifteen SSA countries participating in the UNIDO Survey of 2005 (UNIDO 2007). Investments from the three countries are significantly different from each other.

SOUTH AFRICAN INVESTORS

In general, South African FDI most closely matches that of FDI from the North. Since South African firms entered SSA markets long after Northern transnational corporations (TNCs) had established their operations in traditional fast-moving consumer goods (FMCG) manufacturing, they have tended to spearhead moves into the provision of capital-intensive business services of which MTN is perhaps the archetype. Paralleling Northern investments, South African investors have also made inroads into food and beverages manufacturing. They favour the formal governance structure of a parent company with operating subsidiaries in SSA. There are few stand-alone South African investors. Even fewer firms export.

South African subsidiaries are very capital intensive, have made and plan major future investments over the ensuing three years, and expect sales to double over that period. Although they have hired only a moderate numbers of employees, a high proportion are local graduates and are well paid, reflecting the high productivity achieved. Overall, South African foreign investors are very positive about the location of their operations in SSA, even acknowledging positive improvements in physical infrastructure and local markets.

INDIAN INVESTORS

Perhaps the most distinctive features of Indian-owned firms operating in SSA are that the overwhelming majority are stand-alone, owner managed firms and are, on average, much smaller than Chinese or South African firms. In terms of performance, they are similar in capital intensity to Chinese firms but achieve more than two-and-a-half times the dollar value in sales per employee and 30 per cent more sales per dollar invested. They have been operating in SSA for twelve years, on average. As might be anticipated from their size, they tend to operate in niches in traditional import-substituting sub-sectors such as small-scale chemicals and plastics production, and food and beverages.

Although sales growth was below average over the preceding three years, Indian investors are optimistic about the ensuing three years, expecting to double sales. Reflecting the small average size of firms, investment has been modest in absolute terms, but future investment rates as a proportion of sales are expected to be very high. While, on average, they might employ just 120 people, they have been hiring at twice the rate of South African firms and expect to continue to do so over the ensuing three years. They pay wages of less than one-third of those paid by South African firms, even though the capital productivity and sales per employee gap is somewhat less. Overall, Indian firms are very positive about their firm's location in SSA. In answer to Zahra's (2005) questions about the expertise of international entrepreneurs, it would seem that Indian firms are, indeed, expanding faster than large Northern TNCs operating in SSA, albeit from a much smaller base. Perhaps a better test of their expertise is whether they export and, by that criterion, they are currently failing.

CHINESE INVESTORS

Chinese firms are relatively new arrivals in SSA and are overwhelmingly concentrated in the manufacturing sector, particularly the garments and textiles sub-sectors. They are significantly more export oriented than investors from India and South Africa. The few firms that operate in the services sector market and distribute manufactured goods. About half of Chinese firms are owner-managed operations and half are subsidiaries of small TNCs, with global sales of less than US$200 million.They are significantly more widely dispersed across SSA than firms from India and South Africa, perhaps reflecting their relatively weak business and cultural links to the region. It might also reflect the influence of the Chinese authorities on the outward foreign investment decisions of Chinese TNCs, where the state is a majority shareholder in the parent company (UNCTAD 2006).

A typical Chinese manufacturer is achieving very high sales growth but with modest sales per employee from a large and rapidly expanding workforce. Operations involve moderate capital investment per employee and pay low average wages per employee. Although Chinese firms are expanding their operations very rapidly, they are the least positive among investors from the South about locating in SSA. This perhaps reflects the high growth expectations Chinese firms bring with them from China, where doubling sales every year has not been uncommon.

CONCLUSION

It is rather clear from the activities of CISA investors covered by the UNIDO survey that their motives for establishing operations in SSA are driven primarily by market seeking rather than efficiency considerations (Dunning 1993). Paradoxically, even recently arrived Chinese global exporters are setting up export platforms in East Africa incentivized by third-country trade regimes (mostly the USA and, to a lesser extent, the EU). While Chinese firms might be very focused on efficiency considerations at an operational level, it seems rather unlikely they would locate in Africa without AGOA and EBA. Some, however, might be using outward FDI as a means of escaping from home country institutional constraints (Witt and Lewin 2007). On one level, then, the pattern of FDI from the three countries is definitely not a new phenomenon and follows the well-trodden path of European investment in SSA. Indeed, the density of trading and distribution companies in the population of firms from the major investing countries, whether from the North or the South, seems to confirm the longevity of a very old pattern of trade-driven business relations with SSA.

An interesting topic for further investigation might be the business dynamics of trading companies in SSA as an indicator of whether foreign investors are increasing or decreasing their commitment to Africa (Johanson and

Vahlne 1977). Certainly, the 289 firms covered by the UNIDO survey (mostly from the North, and operational in SSA before 1981) were able to achieve 24 per cent better sales performance per dollar of assets than the overall average of the survey sample as a whole. This suggests that persistence and the accumulation of operational experience over the long run yields higher capital productivity in SSA.

Certainly, the investment and trade policy regimes typically found in SSA today are very different from the protectionist policies prevailing in the 1960s and 1970s that attracted the older generation of Northern investors to SSA. However, the small size of domestic markets (apart from Nigeria) means that there remains limited scope for competition for well-established firms from other local producers. Competition, rather, comes from imports. The ubiquity of FDI from all three countries in the marketing, sales, and distribution services sub-sector is evidence of the significance of import trade. Whether these trading firms progress through the stages proposed by Johanson and Vahlne in 1977, and become committed manufacturers in SSA, or continue as marginal trading outposts of the world's manufacturers, remains to be seen. Unfortunately, a necessary precondition—the development of efficient regional markets in Africa—continues to be hampered by both domestic market conditions and 'between-the-border' factors inhibiting cross-border trade (Broadman 2007).

One question raised indirectly in this chapter that requires further research is the role of corporate governance in initiating and sustaining FDI in SSA. Indian companies are typically owner managed, well-established, but small; however, compared with larger, newer-vintage Chinese firms achieve high levels of capital efficiency and productivity. Is this simply an experience effect or is this due to the superior focus and networking capabilities of Indian family firms that help them cope better with the information asymmetries and opaque business environment found in many SSA countries (Wright, et al. 2006)?

South African investors in SSA, on the evidence of the UNIDO survey (UNIDO 2007) seem to have rapidly established an enviable position in many of the markets they now serve. They have managed to raise—by African standards, at least—large amounts of capital that they have deployed more efficiently than established investors from the North, pay higher wages, employ significant numbers of local graduates, and invest in training their employees. Chinese firms, by contrast, absorb large numbers of workers but invest very little in fixed assets, pay low wages, and spend very little on training. South African investors are relying on the growth of the domestic markets of SSA, the Chinese on preferential access to US and EU markets. In many ways, the last decade has become increasingly benign for all foreign investors in SSA. It will be interesting to observe which of the three countries' investors flourish in the next decade.

REFERENCES

Asiedu, E. (2003a) 'Foreign Direct Investment to Africa: The Role of Government Policy, Governance and Political Instability'. <http://website1.wider.unu.edu/conference/conference-2003-3/conference-2003-3-papers/Asiedu-0708.pdf>.

——(2003b) 'Policy Reform and Foreign Direct Investment to Africa: Absolute Progress but Relative Decline', *Development Policy Review*, 22: 41–8.

——(2006) 'Foreign Direct Investment in Africa: The Role of Natural Resources, Market Size, Government Policy, Institutions and Political Instability', *World Economy*, 29: 63–77.

Autio, E. (2005) 'Creative Tension: The Significance of Ben Oviatt's and Patricia McDougall's Article "Toward a Theory of International New Ventures"', *Journal of International Business Studies*, 36: 9–19.

——H. Sapienza, and J. Almeida (2000) 'Effects of Age at Entry, Knowledge Intensity and Imitability on International Growth', *Academy of Management Journal*, 43: 909–1014.

Broadman, H. G. (2007) *Africa's Silk Road: China and India's New Economic Frontier* (Washington, DC: World Bank).

Dunning, J. H. (1993) *Multinational Enterprises and the Global Economy* (Harlow: Addison Wesley).

——(2000) 'The Eclectic Paradigm as an Envelope for Economic and Business Theories of MNE Activity', *International Business Review*, 9: 163–90.

Filatotchev, I., R. Strange, J. Piesse, and Y.-C. Lien (2007) 'FDI by Firms from Newly Industrialised Economies in Emerging Markets: Corporate Governance, Entry Mode and Location', *Journal of International Business Studies*, 38: 556–72.

Henley, J. S. (2004) 'Chasing the Dragon: Accounting for the Underperformance of India by Comparison with China in Attracting Foreign Direct Investment', *Journal of International Development*, 16: 1039–52.

IMF (1993) *Balance of Payments Manual*, 5th edn (Washington, DC: IMF).

Johanson, J., and J.-E. Vahlne (1977) 'The Internationalization Process of the Firm: A Model of Knowledge Development and Increasing Foreign Market Commitments', *Journal of International Business Studies*, 8: 23–32.

—— ——(1990) 'The Mechanism of Internationalization', *International Marketing Review*, 7: 11–24.

—— ——(2003) 'Business Relationships, Learning and Commitment in the Internationalization Process', *Journal of International Entrepreneurship*, 1: 83–101.

Lall, S. (1983) *Third World Multinationals* (Chichester: John Wiley).

Mathews, J. A. (2006) 'Dragon Multinationals: New Players in 21st Century Globalization', *Asia Pacific Journal of Management*, 23: 5–27.

Moosa, I. A. (2002) *Foreign Direct Investment Theory, Evidence and Practice* (New York: Palgrave Macmillan).

Morisset, J. (2000) 'Foreign Direct Investment in Africa: Policies also Matter', *UNCTAD: Transnational Corporations*, 9: 107–25.

Nanda, R., and T. Khanna (2007) 'Diaspora and Domestic Entrepreneurs: Evidence from the Indian Software Industry'. Working Paper (June) (Cambridge, Mass.: Harvard Business School).

Oviatt, B. M., and P. P. McDougall (1994) 'International New Ventures', *Journal of International Business Studies*, 25: 45–64.

————(2005) 'The Internationalization of Entrepreneurship', *Journal of International Business Studies*, 36: 2–8.

UNCTAD (2006) *World Investment Report 2006* (New York and Geneva: UN).

UNIDO (2007) 'Africa Foreign Investor Survey 2005: Understanding the Contributions of Different Investor Categories to Development; Implications for Targeting Strategies' (Vienna: UNIDO). <http://www.unido.org/index.php?id=o54113>.

Wells, L. T. (1977) 'The Internationalization of Firms from Developing Countries', in T. Agnon and P. Kindleberger (eds), *Multinationals from Small Countries* (Cambridge, Mass.: MIT Press): 133–56.

————(1981) 'Foreign Investors from the Third World', in K. Kumar and M. G. McLeod (eds), *Multinationals from Developing Countries* (Lexington, Mass.: D. C. Heath): 23–36.

————(1983) *Third World Multinational: The Rise of Foreign Investment from Developing Countries* (Cambridge, Mass.: MIT Press).

Witt, M. A., and A. Y. Lewin (2007) 'Outward Foreign Direct Investment as Escape Response to Home Country Institutional Constraints', *Journal of International Business Studies*, 38: 579–94.

World Bank (2006) *Doing Business in 2007: How to Reform* (Washington, DC: World Bank).

Wright, M., I. Filatotchev, R. Hoskisson, and M. Peng (2006) 'Strategy Research in Emerging Economies: Challenging the Conventional Wisdom', *Journal of Management Studies*, 42: 1–33.

Yin, E., and C. J. Choi (2005) 'The Globalization Myth: The Case of China', *Management International Review*, 45 (spec. issue).

Zahra, S. A. (2005) 'A Theory of International New Ventures: A Decade of Research', *Journal of International Business Studies*, 36: 20–8.

10

National Policies to Attract Foreign Direct Investment in Research and Development: An Assessment of Brazil and Selected Countries

Mariana Zanatta, Eduardo Strachman,
Flávia Carvalho, Pollyana C. Varrichio,
Edilaine Camillo, and Mariana Barra

INTRODUCTION

The internationalization of research and development (R&D) by multinational corporations (MNCs) has been thoroughly debated over the few past decades. Initially, the key question concerned the reasons as to why large companies would locate their activities, especially R&D, in other countries rather than remaining in their home economies. Recently, the main issue has become the choices of location made by such companies. Why are some countries preferred at the expense of others? And what are the determining factors that attract intensive foreign direct investment (FDI) in R&D?

The main factors related to the attraction of R&D investments are: an appropriate physical infrastructure for setting up technological facilities; abundance of qualified professionals—mainly scientists and engineers; and proximity to high-level universities and research institutes, appropriate Intellectual Property regimes, and fiscal incentives, among others (UNCTAD 2005a; Zanatta 2006). Therefore, a fundamental consideration for countries competing for MNC R&D investments is the influence and improvement of such factors through effective policies. With this goal in mind, some national policies play a fundamental role in creating, in an articulate and consistent manner, an institutionally appropriate environment, both economically and technologically attractive to such activities.

At present, countries face fierce competition for technological investments. Even though most of these investments go to developed countries, some developing nations are also becoming increasingly important locations for this type of FDI, growing their share (individually or as a group) in MNC R&D investments.[1] China, India, and Brazil, among others, have been competing for these investments and seeking to improve their local features in order to win this battle.

This chapter is part of a broad research project[2] that aims to contribute to the understanding of this general context and to the formulation of public policies that could be effective in fostering MNC technological investments in Brazil, especially in R&D. In this sense, the purpose of this chapter is to examine policies to attract R&D investments in selected countries: China, India, Ireland, Israel, Singapore, and Taiwan. Their choice stems from their success, through effective policy-making, in attracting a significant amount of technological investments, which can be noticed by the number of R&D centres set up in these nations.

The next section describes the methodology applied in the research of selected countries. The chapter continues with a brief description of the theoretical background of R&D FDI attraction, which emphasizes the role of policies in order to benefit more fully from the potential gains of the internationalization of R&D. The subsequent section presents the analysis of each country in order to provide the basis for drawing a comparative overview of the Brazilian case. The chapter goes on to summarize the main findings of the comparative analysis of policies in the selected countries and concludes by presenting final considerations and some critical aspects for successful policy-making in Brazil.

---

[1] Based on Bureau of Economic Analysis data, North American subsidiaries have augmented their R&D expenditures abroad through time. In spite of the increase in absolute terms, developed countries from Europe, Canada, and Japan have lost their share in total expenditures from these firms, dropping from 86.2 per cent in 1994 to 79.7 per cent in 2001. On the other hand, Asian-Pacific countries have increased their share, specifically in R&D expenditures, from 3.4 per cent in 1994 to 11.6 per cent in 2002, reaching a peak of 13.6 per cent in 2001. China has shown a special performance among countries in the region, where American subsidiaries spent 3.1 per cent of total R&D expenditures in 2002, in comparison with 0.05 per cent in 1994. In Singapore, the share has also risen, from 1.4 per cent to 2.8 per cent (Zanatta 2006).

[2] The project 'Policies to Develop Technological Activities in Brazilian MNC Subsidiaries' has been coordinated by Professor Sérgio Queiroz from the Department of Science and Technology Policy of Unicamp and sponsored by FAPESP (the Foundation for Research Support of the State of São Paulo). It consists of the study of activities of Brazilian MNC subsidiaries as well as the examination of policies created by competing nations, including developing countries, to attract these kinds of investments. The originality of the study stems from its analysis of a huge collection of recent data in a broad set of selected countries that create policies with the specific purpose of attracting R&D investments from those companies.

METHODOLOGY

The methodology for this study was developed in the context of a broad research framework; the purpose was to verify the strategies and policy instruments utilized by competing nations in order to attract FDI in R&D. The examples of successful policy tools will provide both the background for a critical analysis of the Brazilian case and guidelines for improving the instruments used to nurture and support R&D activities.

Individual country reports have been elaborated with detailed information on: (i) economic data (GDP, population, per capita income, foreign trade, FDI flows); (ii) science, technology, and industry (S&T&I) data (R&D expenditures, patents, human resource indicators, publications); (iii) a summary of past and recent industrial and S&T&I policies; (iv) institutional structure supporting the S&T&I system; (v) mapping of key programmes and incentive instruments for the development of technological activities by MNCs; and (vi) examples of MNC R&D activities in the country. By so doing, it was possible to identify recent actions undertaken in these countries to enhance their attractiveness to R&D activities, as well as to analyse such policies in the light of a wide economic and technological development trajectory, bearing in mind that strategies for the attraction of FDI are part of a broader national plan and industrial policies.

The criteria used to select the countries for the research sample were the effective results obtained by those nations in attracting FDI in R&D. Selection was achieved through a comprehensive mapping of the main policies and measures established in locations pursuing this specific purpose. Initially, the sample consisted of eleven countries (Australia, Canada, China, Hungary, India, Ireland, Israel, Russia, Singapore, Spain, and Taiwan). Subsequently, other countries also showed the potential to attract FDI in R&D and were therefore included in the sample (Argentina, Chile, Czech Republic, Malaysia, Mexico, and Poland). Thus, including Brazil, the total number of countries analysed was eighteen. However, this chapter is restricted to the analysis of China, India, Ireland, Israel, Singapore, and Taiwan, owing to the fact that they are revealed as the most illuminating cases.

GLOBAL COMPETITION FOR FDI IN R&D
AND ITS DETERMINING FACTORS

Since the 1990s, several nations have had a growing concern with attracting FDI, leading to increasing competition among countries for those investments.

Developing countries are the main competitors in this battle, as several emerging economies have based their strategies for industrialization on MNCs.

When they establish themselves in a host economy, foreign firms accelerate and facilitate the transfer of technology and access to management and marketing strategies from the developed world. That was the case, for instance, in Brazil through import substitution during the process of industrialization. The benefits of FDI to host economies are more than increased productive capacity and enhanced exports; they also materialize themselves in knowledge spillovers, a result of the interaction by MNCs—traditionally owners of state of the art technologies—with a country's production system as a whole.

The presence of technological spillovers from MNC activities is a frequent argument used to sustain favourable views of the attraction of FDI. MNC activities—production, managerial, marketing, or R&D—have a high degree of 'novelty' to the host economy in many cases and therefore should afford innumerable learning opportunities for domestic firms. Currently, not only is the role of MNC firms taken as a key to technological development, but also specific R&D activities carried out in subsidiaries are crucial for the increase of productivity growth and welfare of host economies (UNCTAD 2005a).

In fact, since the 1960s, there have been a considerable number of studies highlighting the benefits of FDI because of technological spillovers, but it was in the 1990s that such studies gained strength. The results, even though different as a consequence of the variety of research methods and of the diverse economic circumstances of host countries, support the hypothesis of higher benefits in terms of technological learning from R&D investments (Fan 2002; Marin and Bell 2003; Reddy 1997). The occurrence of technological spillovers is often linked to certain characteristics of the host economy, such as the level of technological development (which determines the size of the technological gap between local and foreign firms) and human resources capabilities. The accumulation of local capabilities is frequently associated with a better assimilation of the knowledge transferred by foreign firms (Blömstrom and Kokko 2003; Fan 2002).

The internationalization of R&D activities by MNCs, although not new, has been intensified and now incorporates new host countries. In this scenario, developing countries have gained importance as a destination for MNC R&D investments. China has become the main destination in the developing world, while Brazil, India, and Russia have gained favour, outpacing developed countries such as Germany and the UK (EIU 2004; UNCTAD 2005b). Alone, investments from North American MNCs in developing countries have increased ninefold in the period 1989–99, reaching US$2.4 billion (UNCTAD 2005a). In conformity with this is the growing importance of subsidiaries to the innovative activity of developing host countries (Costa and Queiroz 2002). In Brazil, MNCs are responsible for almost half the private R&D expenditures; in Ireland the value exceeds 70 per cent, and in Singapore is around 60 per cent (UNCTAD 2005b).[3]

The driving forces behind global relocation of R&D activities are: increasing global competition, the advance of information and communication technologies and the growing qualification (and costs) of many national systems of S&T&I, together with more favourable environments for investment (UNCTAD 2005a). New opportunities for developing economies that possess abundant and qualified labour forces have also brought a variety of new technologies in sectors such as microelectronics, biotechnology, pharmaceutical, chemicals, and software.

The process of relocation (and relative decentralization) of technological activities enhances the likelihood that emerging economies can benefit from learning through spillovers. As a consequence, several countries have made efforts to improve their economic environment in order to attract FDI, especially that related to R&D. This has been achieved, among other measures, through policies aimed at developing essential factors, such as the supply of human resources, improvement of infrastructure, strengthening of the supply networks, and development of the science-technology bases (UNCTAD 2005b).

Therefore, an effective framework of policies to attract MNC R&D activities must begin by strengthening the institutional structure that supports innovative activities in a country, such as the development of specific human capital capabilities; the increase in research capacity from both private and public sectors; the improvement of intellectual property regimes; and last, but not least, policies to promote a competitive environment for investments, with favourable arrangements for S&T&I (for example, functional tax and incentives systems).

The availability of skilled human capital and adequate facilities for undertaking technologically advanced activities, as well as the state of the art of local technology, are determinants of a greater attractiveness to MNCs to set up their R&D activities offshore. For those reasons, the quality of the educational system of a country is a crucial factor businesses consider in their international expansion (EIU 2004).

Policies to strengthen the R&D infrastructure of host countries not only act positively as a factor to attract technological investments, but they are also part of a broader effort to foster innovation and local development.

---

[3] MNCs do not have the same relevance to R&D in India, as they respond to less than 10 per cent of such activities in that country (UNCTAD 2005b).

The articulation between general (industrial) and specific (FDI promotion) policies becomes a key factor for the effective achievement of those objectives.

Summing up, R&D policies for the promotion of intensive FDI must be addressed in a scenario of growing competition for specific investments, for the reasons already stated. There are several cases of countries that succeeded in attracting significant R&D investment, such as Ireland, Israel, China, Taiwan, and India, who can bring lessons to be applied to the Brazilian scenario. The positive results obtained by some of the developing countries analysed in our sample confirm that well-planned and efficiently conducted policies can attract qualified investments. This, in turn, can enhance the technological capabilities of the host countries. The analysis of successful histories is a useful tool to reflect on the current initiatives carried out with the same aim.

THE ROLE OF MNCS IN THE BRAZILIAN PRODUCTIVE STRUCTURE

The growing share of multinationals in the productive structure of the Brazilian manufacturing industry gives support to the establishment of government measures aimed at fostering a greater contribution of those enterprises to local technological efforts. Moreover, the economic literature stresses the deepening of the internationalization of the productive structure in the 1990s. Of the 500 largest global companies, 405 were operating in Brazil in 2000. The evolution of the share of multinationals among the 500 largest private companies in Brazil is impressive: in 1992, 39 per cent were foreign firms, and in 2000, this share rose to 46 per cent (Hasenclever and Matesco 2000). This evolution also reflects on MNCs' share in the total sales of the 500 largest enterprises. While the group's sales, as a whole, increased 7.7 per cent between 1989 and 1997, MNC sales grew by 10.3 per cent, totalling 50 per cent of all domestic sales (Laplane, et al. 2001; Laplane, Gonçalves, and Araújo 2004).

In the 1990s, the share of foreign firms rose in all Brazilian industrial sectors, especially in capital-intensive sectors and/or in industries with higher technological dynamism (Laplane, et al. 2001; Moreira 1999; Nonnemberg 2003; Rocha and Kupfer 2002)—sectors in which foreign presence was already significant. Rocha and Kupfer (2002), using a sample of 300 firms, show that foreign firms have increased their hegemony in technology diffusion sectors, with 86 per cent of the revenues of such sectors in 1999 (this share was 60 per cent in 1991), while national firms' share shrank from 40 per cent in 1991 to 13.1 in 1999. State enterprises, which held 1 per cent of such revenues in 1991 (as, for instance, Embraer), left those sectors in 1999 as a result of a huge privatization process.

The importance of MNCs in Brazil, as highlighted, justifies the efforts directed to a deeper commitment of these firms to technological activities in Brazil and, since many of such firms are already established in the country, the technological focus of their investments is also a matter of providing for them a favourable economic environment (including S&T&I).

AN ANALYSIS OF SELECTED COUNTRIES: ILLUSTRATIVE CASES

This section analyses each country selected in this study separately, in order to compare their experiences with the Brazilian case. The chosen nations can illustrate the building of a proper institutional setting that can foster MNC technological investments.

China

Since the 1990s, China has stood out from other countries as a major destination of world FDI inflows. In 1994, FDI inflows to China accounted for approximately US$34 billion, reaching US$60 billion in 2004 (UNCTAD 2007). In spite of being a recent example of a rapidly changing economy, current Chinese performance in the attraction of foreign investments, including those in R&D activities, has as its major cause the modernization measures and the recent opening of the country (economic, political, cultural, and so on) to foreign investors, as well as the economic, industrial, and S&T policies that have been implemented since Mao's demise in 1978.

In the beginning of this new era, the four main policy priorities were: industry, agriculture, S&T, and the military sector. Since 1979, China has established a series of bilateral agreements with several countries, including the USA, in order to advance China's technological knowledge and training. In the same year, special economic zones (SEZs) were created. These had a very important role in China's technological catch-up, and also represented the first government attempt to open the country to FDI and foreign technologies (Walsh 2003).

In 1984, the Chinese government further improved those policies, creating new types of economic zones—economic and technology development zones (ETDZs)—for the development of high-tech sectors, with a focus in specific industrial projects and the building of an export-based economy. According to the government, the ETDZs might be seen as launch pads to open up the economy, stir up capital inflows, increase exports, develop high-tech sectors, and support the transformation of regional economies (Invest in China 2003). The results of such policies are evident in the growth of exports of high-tech products from China (Table 10.1).

In 1985, the government announced the 'Decision on Reform of the Science and Technology Management System', which oriented development policies towards industrial technologies, attempting to improve the relationship between R&D potential and the production system in China. This change required the collaboration of research institutions, universities, and firms in order to accelerate both R&D and the commercial application of its results. The government also promoted some new institutional reforms to foster these relationships, such as the creation of the National Natural Science Foundation in 1986, clearly inspired by the American National Science Foundation (NSF). In 1992, the National Engineering Research Centre (NERC) was created; since then, the Ministry of S&T (MOST) have often assessed its activities.

The government also developed important measures to improve general and specific education as well as training, achieving extraordinary outcomes. Since the 1990s, the numbers of scientists and engineers working in S&T activities have grown steadily, from 2.3 million in 1991, with engineers comprising 57.7 per cent of that number, to 3.3 million in 2003, with engineers comprising 68.6 per cent. Such policy measures directed towards

Table 10.1. *China: imports and exports of high-tech products (2000–5) (in US$100 millions)*

	2000	2001	2002	2003	2004	2005
Exports of high-tech products	370.4	464.5	678.6	1,103.2	1,653.6	2,182.5
Share in total exports (%)	14.9	17.5	20.8	25.2	27.9	28.6
Share in industrial manufactured exports (%)	16.6	19.4	22.8	27.3	29.9	30.6
Imports of high-tech products	525.1	641.1	828.4	1,193.0	1,613.4	1,977.1
Share in total imports (%)	23.3	26.3	28.1	28.9	28.7	30.0
Share in industrial manufactured imports (%)	29.4	32.4	33.7	35.1	36.3	38.6

Source: Ministry of Science and Technology of the People's Republic of China (2006).

education and the training of human resources were directly related to the long-run goal of promoting high-tech sectors.

There are also important policies to attract MNC FDI in China by means of several fiscal incentives. Moreover, there are studies on the adoption of lower taxes on MNCs,[4] which can be complemented by special taxes for investments in sectors and/or regions with high priorities.[5] The 'open door' policy for FDI and the creation of the special economic zones have had enormous success in attracting foreign investments and directing them to various regions of China. Not only Shanghai and Beijing are now important national and regional centres for MNC R&D, but also Tianjin and Guangdong have joined this new trend. As is well known, the enormous availability of world-class human and physical resources for S&T activities is a very important factor for the concentration of these investments in those locations, besides the incomparable and growing dimensions of the Chinese domestic market (Serger 2006).

The electronic and telecommunication sectors have recorded huge investments in MNC R&D in China. Motorola is an MNC with very important activities in China, having opened its first office there in 1987. In 1992, the firm set up Motorola China Electronics Ltd in Tianjin. Some authors estimate that at the beginning of 2004 there were 200 MNC R&D centres in China (Von Zedwitz 2004), a total which will doubtless have increased to between 250 and 300 by the time of writing.[6]

India

India has made huge investments in higher education and domestic research institutes since the first years of its independence in the late 1940s. From the 1980s and 1990s, these efforts have brought forth effective results, as shown by

---

[4] The current policies directed toward tax reductions or exemptions mean that MNCs can be exempted from income taxes in the first two years after obtaining the first profits in the country, and they can also receive a reduction of 50 per cent on the same taxes in the three following years. This period is extended to six years in case of high-tech firms. Furthermore, if the firm activities are explicitly directed towards exports, this tax reduction of 50 per cent will persist until these exports comprise more than 70 per cent of the total receipts.

[5] The income taxes in China are 15 per cent in Economic Zones, High-Tech Industrial Zones, and Economic and Technological Development Zones, but 24 per cent in the much more developed and attractive coastal areas and provincial capitals.

[6] According to data from UNCTAD 2005b, these figures are higher than 700 MNC R&D centres. However, some experts consider these figures overblown, since not all formal MNC R&D centres are in full activity; many have only a few engineers representing a formal fulfilment of the requirements of the Chinese government (Serger 2006). Nevertheless, we must stress that 250 to 300 effective MNC R&D centres are an impressive asset for any country in the world.

the extraordinarily rapid development of some high-tech industries and the active role of the Indian diaspora, mainly in the USA, UK, Canada, and Asia (Mitra 2006). Currently, India has the second largest pool of engineers and scientists in the world (only behind the USA). In 1990, there were 339 institutions offering education in engineering in India, admitting 87,000 new students per year. In 2003, this figure increased to 1,208 faculties, with a potential to admit 360,000 new students per year.

An amendment to the Indian Law of Patents, brought into effect in 2002, framed it in accordance with the Trade-Related Intellectual Property Rights (TRIPS) Agreement. Other measures capable of attracting FDI were those aimed at the improvement of interactions between public research laboratories and private firms, making R&D efforts more oriented to commercial outcomes and therefore increasing the records of registered patents within India as well as in the United States Patent and Trademark Office (USPTO).

FDI has been liberalized in India in almost all sectors since 1991, but the Indian government has a clear interest in green-field investments. The geographic localization of FDI is subject to regulations—not being permitted in cities with more than one million inhabitants (with the exception of those previously pointed out as industrial cities and the foci of specific investments). There are also no geographic restrictions to investments in electronics, informatics and telecommunications, printing, and any sectors that do not produce pollution.

Another attempt to attract FDI involved allowing industrial plants to relocate from abroad to India without the need for a licence provided the value of these plants does not exceed US$10 million. The preference is for those plants whose equipment is fewer than ten years old. India has also been promoting trade through the implementation in some regions of special export zones similar to the Chinese special economic zones, as well as through incentives for the creation of export processing zones. One must also stress that there is no discrimination between Indian and foreign corporations, with the exception of some minor restrictions regarding capital expansion (in the case of joint ventures between foreign and Indian corporations) and activities related to equity issues and/or sales.

The Indian government has a series of mechanisms to support R&D, including fiscal exemptions: capital yields as well as capital investments in R&D can receive 100 per cent exemption from income tax; deductions of 125 per cent of taxes are allowed for research with the support of laboratories and/or research or education institutions approved by the government; exemptions can even increase to 150 per cent when spending is made in selected sectors. Firms strongly specialized in R&D are exempt from income taxes for three years, which can be extended to a maximum of ten years. These incentives can be accompanied by accelerated depreciations for equipment produced with domestic technologies, and exemptions for tariffs and taxes on equipment and inputs destined for R&D.

In the pharmaceutical industry, there are many joint initiatives for investment in R&D by MNCs and other parties, resulting in the creation of international marketing networks and research projects in government laboratories, with governmental support and funding.[7] Concomitantly, the modifications in the Patents Law, after the signing of the WTO agreement, put pressure on this industry to avoid mere imitative R&D, despite the inclination of some successful entrepreneurs to innovation activities even before liberalization.

Israel

Israel is an extremely peculiar example of FDI attraction in technological activities, because of its pioneering role in sheltering MNC R&D centres as a consequence of its well-known S&T infrastructure, as well as because of the antiquity of its incentive policies for these kinds of activities. This particularity, as is well known, is caused mostly by the political history of Israel and the Middle East—a region fraught with wars and disputes over territories—but also by the special political and economic relations of Israel with the USA.

This political environment dictated Israeli industrial and S&T policies. Since its independence in 1948 there has always been a need to occupy the frontiers of that small country. National and foreign companies that set up plants and offices in designated locations received the largest incentives. Legislation for the encouragement of capital investment was promulgated in 1950 and is still in force.

Until the mid-1980s, S&T policy was concentrated on the improvement of Israeli defence apparatus, strongly determining the type of domestic industrial activities. That is to say, these measures helped Israel build up and improve its absolute and comparative advantages (Dosi, Pavitt, and Soete 1990). The combination of large public spending on defence, a high participation of people with strong education competencies (also among the immigrant population), and the quest for world-class universities, even before the foundation of the

---

[7] This is the case of the Dr Reddy's Laboratories Ltd DRL, which licensed three molecules for big foreign corporations (two for Novo Nordisk and one for Novartis), with total revenue of US$8 million.

country,[8] contributed to the result that Israel presented, proportionately, the greatest number of scientists and technicians in the world: 140 per 10,000 inhabitants (Ministry of Industry, Trade, and Labour 2005).[9]

Thus, since the first years after its independence, Israel has developed a broad and strong S&T base, mainly in information technologies and in medical equipment. The country even developed its own digital computers in the late 1950s. These developments attracted high-tech corporations from the end of the 1970s, stimulated by the abounding human capital, the elevated demand for sophisticated security products, and by Israel's state-of-the-art industrial complex. In 1974, Intel established a development centre in Israel (the first outside the USA), with an initial investment of just US$300,000 and a team of five employees. However, the corporation now has two manufacturing plants and five R&D centres, with a total of 6,100 employees in Israel. Several processors, including Intel Centrino, were developed in Israel.

By the mid-1970s, R&D incentive measures were extended to foreign high-tech companies and were maintained with few modifications. In 1984, technological activities (of national or foreign companies) were favoured with legislation encouraging capital investment, enlarging the scope of the S&T policies. There are now additional incentives to foreign investors, such as a longer period of tax exemption and reduced interest rates, primarily for those areas near Israel's boundaries. Nevertheless, as Israel now concentrates a great IT technology cluster, the propensity of these high-tech industries to agglomerate has diminished the efficacy of spatial incentives, despite Israel's reduced dimensions.

Finally, other distinguished measures are the incentives for 'start-ups' (many have even been acquired by MNCs) and for the development of venture capital funds (managed, to a large extent, by foreign investors) in an effort to turn these accumulated S&T assets into new companies (the actual focus is biotechnology) rather than merely attracting foreign investment. Many MNCs have been fostered by these pre-competitive investments. Intel, for example, has invested a total sum of US$100 million in twelve 'start-ups'.

---

[8] The Technion Israel Institute of Technology was founded in 1924 in Haifa, and in 1948, the year of Israel's independence, had 680 alumni in a series of faculties, such as civil, mechanical, and electrical engineering; architecture; and city planning. The Hebrew University was founded in April 1925 and in 1947 its 1,200 alumni were distributed in faculties and institutes such as microbiology, chemistry, medicine, agriculture, sciences, humanities, and so on.

[9] A strong presence of highly educated immigrants since before independence and especially since the 1980s contributed to these high shares.

Ireland

Ireland is also known for its pioneering role in building up an active institutional environment in order to attract FDI. In 1949, the Industrial Development Agency (IDA) was established, responsible for attracting and promoting FDI. For a long time, IDA has stood out for its continuous, consistent, and well-implemented industrial policy. Occasional changes in the political scenario do not imply disruptions in the policies implemented by IDA, understood as a long-term goal of the Irish State (Ruane and Görg 1997).

Since the 1950s, Ireland's economy and industry have been undergoing a process of modernization, for which the attraction of MNC investments was a key element. Until the beginning of the 1980s, these policies were fundamentally composed of tax exemptions on profits over exports and government subsidies for investments in plant and capital goods to be used in the production of those exports. Both programmes were changed in 1982 because of a requirement of the European Economic Community (EEC), when those taxes (formerly of 10 per cent, afterwards increased to 12.5 per cent) were modified to taxes on total profits. However, when compared with European standards, these tax percentages were still considerably lower.

Incentive programmes have been improved throughout the years. The Irish government started demanding counterbalance results to its policies, such as an increase in the number of job positions created, in addition to the simple proof of purchase of capital goods. Without complying with these demands, investing companies would not continue to receive governmental incentives (Ruane and Görg 1997). In the 1970s, these policies became more selective, with the government trying to encourage investments and attract MNCs to sectors in which the country could broaden its competitive advantages.

At that time, the government identified the pharmaceutical industry and information and communication technologies (ICTs) as special policy foci, with the USA as the chief source of investments, mostly for industrial clusters. Furthermore, Ireland intended to establish enduring relations between MNCs and domestic corporations, even if national companies would play a secondary role as specialized suppliers of foreign companies. In the 1980s, Ireland started to build up S&T policies, simultaneously trying to improve the performance of domestic companies in comparison with MNCs (Hayward 1995). Since then, several research centres have been established in Ireland, principally in ITC and agriculture. Consequently, government disbursements in S&T increased 74 per cent in real terms between 1980 and 1993.

After 1992, the Irish government emphasized the strengthening of the National System of Innovation (NSI), starting to give preference to finance investments in technological capabilities. Moreover, it tried to give increasing support to investments in national companies,[10] considered insufficient when compared to those for MNCs. Ireland also started to give some tax exemptions to qualified people in S&T, in order to prevent a 'brain drain'. In the 1990s, it also stimulated capital goods, medical equipment, and technology industries as well as sectors related to life sciences (biotech, bio-engineering, and so on), besides the traditionally underscored ITC and pharmaceutical industries.[11]

Taiwan

Taiwan has some relevant economic and technology indicators to be illustrated. Its GDP has been growing around 5 per cent per year since the end of the 1990s, despite the decrease registered in 2001. In 2002, its pace of growth was recovered owing to the implementation of the National Development Plan.

Since the 1950s, national R&D expenses have gradually increased and reached 2.5 per cent of GDP in 2005, mainly incurred by the private sector (60 per cent) and concentrated in engineering areas (see Table 10.2). In this sense, it is worth noticing the outstanding number of graduate and expatriate engineers who return to Taiwan to fill the growing demand for specialized

Table 10.2. *R&D Expenditures: selected countries, 2000–5 (as percentage of (GDP))*

	2000	2001	2002	2003	2004	2005
Brazil	1.01	1.05	1.00	0.97	0.91	—
China	0.90	0.95	1.07	1.13	1.23	1.34
India	0.86	0.82	0.80	0.79	0.77	—
Ireland	1.13	1.10	1.10	1.16	1.20	—
Israel	—	4.77	4.74	4.46	4.43	4.50
Singapore	1.89	2.11	2.15	2.12	2.24	2.36
Taiwan	2.06	2.08	2.20	2.35	2.44	2.52

Source: Elaborated by the authors based on OECD 2007.

[10] Through Enterprise Ireland, an agency specially directed to domestic firms.
[11] In 2002, Ireland was the first exporter of intermediary and final pharmaceutical products in the world, selling €34 billion abroad. Out of fifteen of the largest pharmaceutical MNCs in the world, thirteen are in Ireland, some of them with very important R&D projects. GlaxoSmithKline, for instance, will make its Irish branch its world centre for nanotechnologies. On the other hand, we must stress that the Irish federal government also spends €1 billion in R&D on that sector.

human resources, mainly in technological parks such as Hsinchu (created in 1979), a locus of attraction of MNC technological activities.

Taiwan demonstrates that overcoming difficulties related to its geographical restrictions and its political history was a result of well-structured and continuing economic and industrial policies. In this sense, Taiwan's exports reflect its national priorities towards economic development and strategic industrial policy. The country has become a world leader in high-tech products, especially in the electronic and petrochemical sectors (Table 10.3). These positive international results are the consequence of more than three decades of national development strategy oriented towards exports (Breznitz 2005). For these results, national policies were based on public research institutes and on the incentive to develop small and medium-sized firms, which account for the major share of businesses in Taiwan.

National policies in Taiwan have a strong selectivity. Industrial policy is focused on strategic sectors such as semiconductors and biotechnology, implementing a permanent monitoring process of the potential growing sectors. MNCs do not receive any different treatment and there is some evidence that national companies might benefit from the linkages with foreign firms, which also share technological learning mechanisms with local agents. In this sense, incentives are offered for businesses to develop R&D activities, human resources training, and the acquisition of new technologies.

In 2002, a national policy focused on the attraction of MNC R&D and business centres was implemented which resulted in the attraction of twenty-three of these facilities to Taiwan. Among the companies were Ericsson, Dell, and IBM, which are keeping an eye on the relative importance of these centres within their global corporations. Ericsson's centre is one of the four major

Table 10.3. *Taiwan: products that ranked within the world's three largest producers, 2006*

First place worldwide		Second place worldwide		Third place worldwide	
Product	% (*)	Product	%	Product	%
1. Mask ROM (1)	91.4	1. Glass fibre (1)	37.0	1. Small and medium-sized TFT-LCD panel (1)	14.6
2. Foundry (1)	66.7	2. OLED panel (1)	25.9	2. PCB (1)	14.0
3. IC testing (1)	60.3	3. IC substrate (1)	25.7	3. PTA (2)	13.8
4. Optical disc (2)	53.0	4. DRAM (1)	25.0	4. Nylon fibte (2)	10.5
5. IC Packaging	47.8	5. IC design (2)	21.2	5. PU leather (2)	6.7

Notes: *Taiwan's market share; (1) = production value; (2) = production volume.

Source: *Taiwan Statistical Data Book* (2007).

regional company centres in Asia specializing in third-generation communication technologies. Dell's R&D centre produces approximately half of the notebooks and providers for the entire corporation, with thirty new designs. The 'IBM Series Taiwan Development Centre' is IBM's first centre outside the USA to perform activities related to innovation and interaction of local development with the global corporation platforms.

Singapore

Over the past few years, Singapore has exhibited a conspicuous economic performance, with average economic growth rates of 6 per cent. Regarding technological development, the changes are even more significant. The share of R&D expenditures on GDP climbed from 0.3 per cent in 1980 to 2.3 per cent in 2005 (Wong and Ho 2005) (see also Table 10.1).

Since the 1960s, measures to liberalize trade and attract FDI have been key tools used to change this scenario. The government has undertaken efforts to highlight the strategic geographical localization of the country as a trade centre and to develop telecommunication and transport networks in order to attract foreign investments. The late independence of Singapore in 1965 has not limited its economic performance, as its national planning and the adoption of FDI policy focused on labour-intensive activities (the radio and TV industry), essential pillars of the first period of the national economic development process (Koh and Wong 2003).

In the early 1980s, with the growing regional competition, the government abandoned the strategy of attracting low-cost investments and started targeting high-value-added investments. To achieve this aim, several programmes were implemented to turn Singapore into an IT reference point in the East Asian region.[12] From the middle of this decade onwards, efforts can be seen towards the diversification of the sectors benefited by FDI, including the service sector (Coe 1999).

Singapore's FDI experience has some similarities with the Irish case owing to the political effort and the constitution of an investment promotion agency (IPA) dedicated to leverage the kind of investments to be developed in the country.[13] Under the auspices of the Economic Development Board (EDB),

---

[12] National Computer Board 1980 and National Computerization Plan 1981 illustrate this goal.
[13] Some authors cite Ireland and Israel as direct competitors for the attraction of technological FDI. Thus, global competition for investments has been stimulating Singapore's government to seek cost reductions associated with the undertaking of investments; however, recent studies describe the country as one of the most expensive business centres of the Asian region.

FDI has been continually entering the country. The board is responsible for conducting national industrial policy based on the concession of incentives to develop its IT industry. It is now aiming to consolidate a biomedical sector in Singapore. Concomitantly, the government has conducted policy focused on the development of a chemical cluster, which ranks as the third most important sector in the manufacturing industry of the nation (Xinhua News Agency 2006). Another initiative is to foster links with local companies, promoting outsourcing activities, or improving extension services.

The main goal of national policies has been to implement initiatives that could contribute to industrial and technological growth, and the consequent improvement of national competitiveness. The objective is to assure a safe and efficient environment for foreign investments. The array of incentives, created mainly to support MNCs, has been materialized in the increase of the pattern of established investments and the differentiation of Singapore compared with its competitors. Some authors highlight the flexibility and agility of the national government's response as fundamental factors of this successful model. Nevertheless, the local industry tends to be fragile and some initiatives are being implemented to support this national actor. During the 1990s, various efforts were made to strengthen Singapore's technology infrastructure in an attempt to consolidate small and medium-sized companies that originated from spin-offs (Wong and Ho 2005).

Recently, Singapore stands out for its service exports and the emergence of biomedical sciences (comprising pharmaceutical, medical devices, biotechnology, and health care services) (Helble and Chong 2004). Besides MNCs, the country has attracted new research talents through some strategic programmes. The stimulus to innovation in technology can be seen in 'Science and Technology Plan 2010', the government plan announced in 2006 aimed at increasing national R&D expenditures to 3 per cent of GDP by 2010.

Brazil

Taking into account the international cases previously presented, the Brazilian experience is analysed considering its own efforts to attract MNC technology investments. Brazil has historically been receptive to FDI inflows. In the post-Second World War period, MNCs assumed a decisive role in Brazilian industrial structure by providing its dynamics in several sectors. From the mid-1950s onwards, with the 'Plano de Metas'[14] (1956–61), Brazil's national

---

[14] Targets Plan.

industries developed advanced sectoral chains, and MNC subsidiaries became a determinant part of this structure.

In the international context, American MNCs, followed by European companies, were at that time in the process of internationalizing production. Domestic private and state capital was added to foreign capital, comprising the foundation of Brazilian 'heavy' industrialization.

At the beginning of the 1970s, Brazil was already one of the most internationalized economies in the world and MNC subsidiaries accounted for one-third of total industrial production. From 1974 and 1980—the period from the National Development Plan II to PND II (the second and last heavy industrialization plan effectively implemented in all Brazilian history)—the federal government adopted a more selective policy approach based on sectoral targets, conditioning the entrance of MNC investments to certain desired economic benefits. Until then, policy regarding the attraction of FDI had been generic and oriented to maintaining a favourable environment for foreign investments but without predefined priorities. During the PND II, FDI attraction became conditioned to sectoral specialization as part of a broader national industrial policy—focused on basic inputs and capital goods—mainly due to trade imbalances (Nonnemberg 2003).

The 1980s were characterized by an inflection in the Brazilian FDI pattern, with a strong decrease of foreign investments inflows: Brazilian share in world FDI inflows declined from 0.9 per cent (1982–6) to just 0.2 per cent (1987–91). The main limiting factor was the unfavourable economic environment, with a generalized recession in economic activity and investments owing to uncertainties caused by the external debt crisis and the ensuing high inflation.

In the 1990s, FDI inflows began to return to the country, as a result of the commercial liberalization, privatization, and deregulation processes that took place in that period. The amount of foreign investment increased from US\$1.3 billion in 1993 to US\$32.8 billion in 2000 (the highest in Brazilian history). In 2006, US\$18.8 billion of FDI inflows entered in Brazil (BCB 2006). However, these economic structural changes were not accompanied by coordinated instruments of industrial policy; simultaneously, there was no explicit policy to attract FDI aimed at quantitative and qualitative changes in the national industrial structure; that is, in order to obtain competitive gains.

The Brazilian institutional structure of FDI attraction also presents many flaws. Other countries have institutions and organizations (at regional or national levels) clearly responsible for both promoting themselves abroad and attracting investments to their territories. In Brazil, this structure was created for a short time (1999–2002) by the so-called 'Investe Brasil', which has now ceased. Brazil is one of the few countries without an agency to support these goals and to coordinate with the federal and/or state governments (Ricupero and Barreto 2007). Today, Brazilian initiatives to promote FDI are quite timid and uncoordinated; such as APEX-Brasil (the Brazilian Trade and Investment Promotion Agency, which is oriented mainly towards the promotion of exports) and RENAI (the National Network of Investment Information, which works as an information vehicle about investment opportunities in Brazil and about how to accomplish them).

The presence of IPAs is taken as an important factor in the attraction of investments, as they might influence decisions by enterprises on where to invest, contributing to the creation of a positive image of the country abroad. The recent outbreak of IPAs worldwide, as has been already shown, is evidence of their significant role in the attraction of FDI as well as of the fierce worldwide competition for such investments (Morriset 2003; Zanatta, Costa, and Filippov 2006).

The lack of coordination among federal government institutions to formulate and implement FDI policy in Brazil, including FDI in R&D, is quite apparent. As Suzigan and Furtado (2007: 19) highlight, 'the problem of technology and industrial policy institutions is precisely not to have sufficiently and coherently accompanied the industrial and the science and technology development [in Brazil]'. Therefore, the current institutional structure, uncoordinated and fragmented in different government levels, is inadequate. This signals the need to create new instruments that link the existing institutions and the current industrial policy measures, including those directed towards FDI, chiefly in R&D (and also the development of new policies and/or—probably more important—new agencies), in a more centralized and connected governance structure.

Among the recent policy measures that might have some effect on the attraction of FDI to R&D activities is the Innovation Law (Law 10.973/04). This legislation establishes incentives for innovation, interactions with the public (universities and research institutes) and private sectors, as well as the concession of financial resources to the productive sector, under the guise of subsidies, finance, or partnerships. It is aimed at the development of innovation in products and processes (Zanatta 2006). However, this initiative is very recent and its effectiveness is dependent on a long-term evaluation.

In addition, recent legislation (Law 11.196)[15] reduces the Industrialized Products Tax (IPI, a value-added tax) in the presence of acquisitions of R&D equipment and also allows an accelerated depreciation of the related capital goods. However, most firms do not use these legal instruments in their R&D

---

[15] This law has been modified by Law 11.487, which includes new incentives for technological innovation, and changes the rules related to accelerated amortization of R&D investments.

activities, and are even unaware of their existence. Thus, while these initiatives could have significant results, in the long term it is necessary to disseminate and maintain them throughout several governments, as happens in the most successful countries analysed in our research.

Brazil has also displayed impressive progress in its building up of human resources: in 2006, the numbers of people holding an MSc or PhD were around 40,000 and 10,000, respectively (Capes 2006). Nevertheless, this qualified workforce is not absorbed by the private sector, remaining strongly concentrated in the academic area, probably justifying the efforts of the Innovation Law to increase the interaction between the public and private sectors.

A COMPARATIVE ANALYSIS OF THE SELECTED COUNTRIES[16]

Throughout the analysis, one can notice common elements in some national policies, indicating a relevant regional element of this analysis. In this way, some countries were aggregated according both to their geographical region and to similarity in characteristics, as can be seen in Table 10.4.

One can observe that selected Asian countries (China, Singapore, and Taiwan) have long-term, continuing, and articulated policies that influence national economic and industrial development. These policies are also select-ive, in terms of both corporate activities (R&D) and industrial sectors (tech-nology intensive). Israel and Ireland have similar policy characteristics, consequent on their success in attracting R&D-intensive FDI. Table 10.5 summarizes some of the main policies towards specific R&D investments in the countries studied.

Finally, Brazil, except for the long-term policies, is nearer to the experiences of Latin American countries such as Argentina, Mexico, and Chile. This is to say, the favourable characteristics described were not observed in its policies as well as in the effective results of FDI in R&D. In this sense, the evidence provided by the present analysis is that disarticulated policies and the absence of a defined focus (sectoral or corporate activities) seem to be less effective in attracting MNC R&D activities.

---

[16] For a more accurate comparison among China, India, and Brazil, see Zanatta and Queiroz 2007, which was elaborated in the context of Zanatta 2006 (Unicamp PhD diss.).

Table 10.4. *Characteristics of policies attracting foreign direct investment (FDI), selected countries*

Countries/ regions	Long term	Continuity	Consistency	Selectivity	
				Corporate activities	Industrial sectors
Asia	Less than 30 years	Existent	High	Existent, with effective results on attracting R&D investments	Pharmaceutical, biotechnology, and information and communication technologies
Brazil	More than 30 years	Non-existent	Low, macroeconomic policy opposes industrial and FDI policy objectives	Non-existent	General FDI. PITCE:* capital goods, semiconductors, pharmaceuticals, and software
Israel, Ireland	More than 30 years	Existent	High	Existent, with effective results on attracting R&D investments	Pharmaceutical, biotecnology and information and communication technologies

Notes: *Industrial, technological, and foreign trade policy.
As a methodological issue it is worth stressing the qualitative character of the systematization above, mainly regarding the results of attraction of FDI in R&D. The relevance and originality of this exercise relays on the attempt to systematize information collected in a vast array of sources for each of the selected countries, trying to establish similarities and differences among them.

Source: Elaborated by the authors based on the comparative analysis of the selected countries.

CONCLUSION

Based on the analysis of selected countries, it was possible to stress that selectivity and continuity, together with the articulation (interconnections and flexibility) of national policies, are fundamental factors in building up an attractive environment for MNC R&D activities, as they signal a steadfast compromise of the national governments with regard to technological activities.

Some of the international experiences studied stress the strategic role assumed by policies in order to promote FDI and industrial and technological activities. Ireland, for example, has created a governmental structure responsible for its industrial policy under the auspices of the IDA, which had carried

Table 10.5. *Main policies directed at multinational corporation (MNC) R&D investments*

Country	Policy description	Since
China	R&D is a requirement for some FDI. Technological parks benefit from tax exemptions in R&D activities. Imports of equipments for technology-intensive activities are tax free.	2000s
India	Fiscal exemptions of up to 150%; focus on selected sectors. Investments are exempt from income tax.	1991
Israel	Focus on high-value-added and high-tech sectors—especially biotechnology. Funding of up to 50% of R&D projects of foreign or domestic firms, vis-à-vis royalties payments of 2%–3% of sales revenues of related products.	1970s
Ireland	Focus on high-tech sectors; preferred financing of technological investments. Incentives granted via IDA.	1990s
Taiwan	Industrial policies focused on semi-conductors, displays, and biotech, with no differentiation between capital origins.	late 1970s
Singapore	Focus on high-value-added investments; active role of IPA to pursue such investments. Development of industrial clusters.	1980s
Brazil	Innovation law—incentives to partnerships, concession of financial resources to innovative activities. PITCE—(industrial, technological, and foreign trade policy) has, as its guidelines, innovation, technological development, industrial modernization, foreign markets competitivity, higher-scale and productive capacity. Strategic (high-tech) sectors are a priority.	2004

out this function for over fifty years. This is the main reason why Irish industrial policy is recognized for its consistency and continuity.

Generally, the analysis of these countries permitted identification of the most important factors in attracting MNC R&D activities and the policies that influence these factors, showing that each country has both advantages and handicaps when compared with others. Ireland and Israel, for instance, stand out for the continuity and selectivity of their FDI policies, including in R&D activities. For a similar reason, India, Taiwan, and Israel are well known for their high-quality S&T infrastructure, with technology institutes and world-class universities. China and India are known for their abundant technically and scientifically well-trained workforce, and for the strong commitment of their governments to the augmentation and improvement of human resources. The effectiveness of these factors is conditioned by many economic, political, social, and historical events, and also by the coordination of these elements with S&T&I policies.

One could say that there is no easy recipe for countries to follow—increasingly, the developing ones—in order to participate more actively in this process of worldwide R&D dissemination. The competition and attraction of these technological activities comprise many factors in complex and previously undetermined systems. Thus, a general recommendation to those countries interested in winning the competition for R&D-intensive FDI is to improve the factors of attraction with continuous, consistent, and well-developed policies, strongly connected to their industrial strategy.

The analysis of international experiences also reveals the extent to which Brazil is still handicapped in the global competition for technology FDI. Table 10.6 shows numbers of recent R&D projects by MNCs in the selected countries: Brazil attracted less R&D investment in a number of projects. The absence of an investment promotion agency, which could act in a coordinated manner with other policies, is evidence (at least, currently) of the lack of priority regarding such issues. Brazil needs more focused and selective FDI policies in terms of sectors and activities, with higher priorities and support. The countries described provided evidence that their governments have selective FDI policies—mainly in the IT, pharmaceutical, and biotech sectors. In this sense, despite some recent initiatives towards innovation and R&D investments in Brazil—such as the Innovation Law—one notices the absence of state policies that are definitely committed to the continuity and coordination of those policy measures.

Summing up, Brazil is still lacking two important elements with which to attract FDI in R&D: coordinated governmental actions and institutions responsible for this attraction. Despite the fact that Brazil has made strong

Table 10.6. *R&D projects by multinational corporations (MNCs), selected countries*

Country	Number of R&D projects	Some firms investing in R&D
China	416	Nokia, Microsoft, Intel, Nortel, Motorola
India	635	Microsoft, Intel, Cisco, GM, GE, ABB, Ericsson, Adobe, Google, Texas Instruments, Alcatel-Lucent, Nokia
Israel	12	Intel, IBM, Siemens, Motorola, AMAT, HP, Microsoft, General Electric, BMC Software, Unilever, SAP
Ireland	55	Microsoft, Motorola, Ericsson, Pfizer, GlaxoSmithKline
Taiwan	56	HP, Dell, Microsoft, IBM, Intel, Life Sciences CoE, Honeywell, Dupont, Sony, Atotech, NEC, Alcatel, GlaxoSmithKline, Ericsson
Singapore	86	Eli Lilly, Novartis, BASF, Intel, General Electric, GlaxoSmithKline, Bosch, Sony
Brazil	28	Motorola, Freescale, Bosch Johnson & Johnson, Whirlpool, General Motors, Fiat, Ford, Voith Siemens, Siemens

Source: Locomonitor database.

advances in its human resource policy—registering significant increases in numbers of MSc- and PhD-qualified personnel, as well as in international scientific publications—this qualified workforce still seems to be out of touch with regard to the needs of the private sector. It is essential to reinforce scientific, technological, and engineering competences, for these qualifications are crucial inputs to the innovation processes and thus to the strategic decisions of MNCs.

REFERENCES

BCB (Banco Central do Brasil) (2006) 'Boletim do Banco Central'. <http://www.bcb.gov.br/?BOLETIMHIST>.

Blömstrom, M., and A. Kokko (2003) 'The Economics of Foreign Direct Investment Incentives'. NBER Working Paper 9489 (Cambridge, Mass.: NBER).

Breznitz, D. (2005) 'Development, Flexibility and R&D Performance in the Taiwanese IT Industry: Capability Creation and the Effects of State-industry Co-evolution', *Industrial and Corporate Change*, 14: 153–87.

Capes (Coordenação de Aperfeiçoamento de Pessoal de Nível Superior) (2006) 'Estatísticas de Pós-graduação'. <http://ged.capes.gov.br/AgDw/silverstream/pages/frPesquisaColeta.html>.

Coe, N. M. (1999) 'Emulating the Celtic Tiger? A Comparison of the Software Industries of Singapore and Ireland', *Singapore Journal of Tropical Geography*, 20: 36–55.

Costa, I., and S. Queiroz (2002) 'Foreign Direct Investment and Technological Capabilities in Brazilian Industry', *Research Policy*, 31: 1431–43.

Dosi, G., K. Pavitt, and L. Soete (1990) *The Economics of Technical Change and International Trade* (London: Harvester Wheatsheaf).

EIU (Economist Intelligence Unit) (2004) 'Scattering the Seeds of Invention: The Globalisation of Research and Development', *The Economist*. <http://graphics.eiu.com/files/ad_pdfs/RnD_GLOBILISATION_WHITEPAPER.pdf>.

Fan, E. X. (2002) 'Technological Spillovers and Foreign Direct Investments: A Survey'. ERD Working Paper Series 33 (Manila: Asian Development Bank).

Hasenclever, L., and V. R. Matesco (2000) 'As Empresas Transnacionais e o seu Papel na; Competitividade Industrial e dos Países: O caso do Brasil', in P. M. Viega, *Globalização: o Brasil e os desafios da globalização*, 11th edn (Rio de Janeiro: Relume Dumará): 161–92.

Hayward, S. (1995) 'Developing Ireland: Institutional Innovation and Technology Policy since the Mid-1980s'. Dublin. mimeo.

Helble, Y., and L. C. Chong (2004) 'The Importance of Internal and External R&D Network Linkages for R&D Organisations: Evidence from Singapore', *R&D Management*, 34.

Hobday, M. (1995) 'East Asian Latecomer Firms: Learning the Technology of Electronics', *World Development*, 23.

Hsu, J. (1997) 'A Late Industrial District? Learning Network in Hsinchu Science-based Industrial Park in Taiwan', PhD diss., Department of Geography, University of California at Berkeley. <http://www.geog.ntu.edu.tw/Introduction/member/teacher/jinnyuh/papers/chap2.pdf>.

Hsu, C.-W., and H.-C. Chiang (2001) 'The Government Strategy for the Upgrading of Industrial Technology in Taiwan', *Technovation*, 21: 123–32.

Invest in China (2003) 'Advantages and Characteristics of State Economic and Technological Development Zones'. <http://www.fdi.gov.cn>.

Ministry of Industry, Trade, and Labor (2005) 'Israeli Economy at a Glance', *Planning, Research and Economic Administration* (Aug.).

Koh, W., T. H. Wong, and P. K. Wong (2003) 'Competing at the Frontier: The Changing Role of Technology Policy in Singapore's Economic Strategy' (Dec.). mimeo. <http://ssrn.com/abstract=626342>.

Laplane, M., F. Sarti, C. Hiratuka, and R. Sabatini (2001) 'Empresas Transnacionais no Brasil nos anos 90: Fatores de Atração, Estratégias e Impactos', in D. Chudnovsky, *El Boom de Inversión Extranjera Directa en el MERCOSUR* (Buenos Aires: Siglo XXI de Argentina Editores).

——J. Gonçalves, and R. D. Araújo (2004) 'Efeitos de Transbordamento de Empresas Estrangeiras na Indústria Brasileira (1997–2000)'. NEIT (Campinas: Institute of Economics, Unicamp: State University of Campinas). mimeo.

Lee, W. Y. (2005) [2000] 'O Oapel da Oolítica Científica e Tecnológica no Desenvolvimento Industrial da Coréia do Sul', in L. Kim and R. R. Nelson, *Tecnologia, aprendizado e inovação: as experiências das economias de industrialização recente* (Campinas: Editora da Unicamp): 365–93.

Marin, A., and M. Bell (2003) 'Technology Spillovers from Foreign Direct Investment (FDI): An Exploration of the Active Role of MNC Subsidiaries in the Case of Argentina in the 1990s', Druid Summer Conference 2003, 'Creating, Sharing and Transferring Technology', Copenhagen, 12–14 June. <http://www.druid.dk>.

Ministry of Science and Technology of the People's Republic of China (2006) S&T Statistics. <http://www.most.gov.cn/eng/statistics/2006/index.htm>.

Mitra, R. M. (2006) 'India's Potential as a Global R&D Power', in Magnus Karlsson (ed.), *The Internationalization of Corporate R&D: Leveraging the Changing Geography of Innovation* (Östersund: Swedish Institute for Growth Policy Studies (ITPS)): 267–306.

Moreira, M. M. (1999) *Estrangeiros em uma economia aberta: impactos recentes sobre produtividade, concentração e comércio exterior* (Rio de Janeiro: BNDES).

Morisset, J. (2003) 'Does a Country Need a Promotion Agency to Attract Foreign Direct Investment? A Small Analytical Model Applied to 58 Industries'. World Bank Policy Research Working Paper 3028 (Apr.).

Nonnemberg, M. J. B. (2003) 'Determinantes dos Investimentos Externos e Impactos das Empresas Multinacionais no Brasil: As Décadas de 70 e 90', Texto para Discussão 969 (Rio de Janeiro: IPEA).

OECD (2007) OECD Factbook: Economic, Environmental and Social Statistics. <http://titania.sourceoecd.org/vl=7250511/cl=14/nw=1/rpsv/fact2007/>.

Reddy, P. (1997) 'New Trends in Globalization of Corporate R&D and Implications for Innovation Capability in Host Country: A Survey from India', *World Development*, 25: 1821–37.

Ricupero, R., and F. A. Barreto (2007) 'Importância do Investimento Direto Estrangeiro do Brasil no Exterior para o Desenvolvimento Socioeconômico do País', in A. Almeida, *Internacionalização de empresas brasileiras: perspectivas e riscos* (São Paulo: Elsevier/Fundação Dom Cabral).

Rocha, F., and D. Kupfer (2002) 'Structural Changes and Specialization in Brazilian Industry: The Evolution of Leading Companies and the M&A Process', *Developing Economies*, 40: 497–521.

Ruane, F., and H. Görg (1997) 'Reflection on Irish Industrial Policy towards Foreign Direct Investment'. Trinity Economic Paper Series 97/3.

Saxenian, A. (2001) 'Transnational Communities and the Evolution of Global Production Networks: The Cases of Taiwan, China and India'. East-West Center Working Papers 37. <http://www.eastwestcenter.org/stored/pdfs/ECONwp037.pdf>.

Suzigan, W., and J. A. Furtado (2007) 'Institucionalidade da política industrial e tecnológica: problemas, desafios e propostas'. Article presented to the second Brazilian Congress of Innovation in Industry (Congresso Brasileiro de Inovação na Indústria), São Paulo.

UNCTAD (2005a) 'Globalization of R&D and Developing Countries'. Proceedings of the expert meeting, Geneva (Jan.).

——(2005b) 'World Investment Report 2005: Transnational Corporations and the Internationalization of R&D' (New York and Geneva: UN).

——(2007) 'Rising FDI into China: The Facts behind the Numbers'. UNCTAD Investment Brief 2. <http://www.unctad.org/en/docs/iteiiamisc20075_en.pdf>.

von Zedwitz, M. (2004) 'Managing Foreign R&D Laboratories in China', *R&D Management*, 34: 439–52.

Walsh, K. (2003) *Foreign High-tech R&D in China: Risks, Rewards, and Implications for US–China Relations.* Henry L. Stimson Center. <http://www.stimson.org/tech-transfer/pdf/FrontMatter.pdf>.

Wong, P. K., and Y. P. Ho (2005) 'Knowledge Sources of Innovation in a Small Open Economy: The Case of Singapore'. Druid Summer Conference 2005, 'Dynamics of Industry and Innovation: Organization, Networks and Systems', Copenhagen, 27–9 June. mimeo. <http://www.druid.dk>.

Xinhua News Agency (2006) 'Singapore Stresses Talent, Innovation, R&D in Developing Chemicals Industry' (17 Apr.).

Zanatta, M. (2006) 'Políticas brasileiras de incentivo à inovação e atração de investimento direto estrangeiro em pesquisa e desenvolvimento', PhD diss., Institute of
Geosciences, Unicamp: State University of Campinas.

——I. Costa, and S. Filippov (2006) 'Foreign Direct Investment: Key Issues for
Promotion Agencies'. UNU-MERIT Policy Brief 10.

——and S. Queiroz (2007) 'The Role of National Policies on the Attraction and
Promotion of MNEs', *International Review of Applied Economics*, 21: 419–36.

11

Foreign Direct Investment and Trade in the Southern African Development Community

Henri Bezuidenhout and Wim Naudé

INTRODUCTION

The growing trend towards globalization and regionalization of economies has led to the increased importance of international capital flows. Foreign direct investment (FDI) has become a major source of capital flows in many developing nations. The study of the impacts, causes, and economic relationships of FDI has gained in popularity in the last decade (Naudé and Krugell 2007). There is substantial agreement that FDI can contribute to economic growth and can result in technology transfers to developing countries (Asiedu 2001; Borenstein, de Gregorio, and Lee 1998; Lim 2001; Naudé and Krugell 2007).

In Africa, the potential contribution that FDI can make is significant. The New Partnership for Africa's Development (NEPAD) initiative determined that Africa requires about US$64 billion annually in capital to be able to generate the growth of 7 per cent per annum that is needed to achieve the Millennium Development Goals (MDGs). Historically, Africa is the region in the world most marginalized in terms of attracting FDI. Sub-Saharan Africa (SSA) only attracted an average of US$7 billion annually from 1995 to 2001 (US$2.9 billion if Angola, Nigeria, and South Africa are excluded). This amounts to an average of only 1.5 per cent of total world FDI (Asiedu 2004a; UNCTAD 2005b).

Africa's failure to attract sufficient inflows of FDI is undoubtedly because it is a high-risk environment for private capital, owing to various institutional and geographical features (Asiedu 2006; Naudé and Krugell 2007), as well as various 'anti-growth policy syndromes' that have depressed investment (Fosu and O'Connell 2006). In the recent past, an increasing number of African countries have embarked on economic reform programmes and initiatives to address these negative features of the policy and institutional environment. Perhaps the most important of these measures are aimed at trade reform, and both unilateral as well as multilateral initiatives have been taken to liberalize trade (Owhoso, et al. 2002: 408). The expectation is that trade liberalization will improve the openness of African economies, with benefits to growth coming from more trade (rising exports and the ability to acquire imported inputs for manufacturing production) and FDI (Morriset 2000). In particular, the belief exists that more trade owing to trade liberalization will have a determining and positive complementary impact on FDI.[1] Greenaway, Sapsford, and Pfaffenzeller (2007: 206) claim that 'the more open is the trade policy the greater is the economy's gravitational attraction to foreign capital'. They also find evidence from a sample of seventy-seven developing countries over the period 1990–2000 that FDI contributes to growth in open economies but not closed ones (ibid. 208).

In this chapter, we investigate the empirical evidence on the link between trade and FDI in Africa. We do so by focusing on the Southern African Developing Community (SADC),[2] a multilateral trade initiative, rather than on single countries or on the cross-African case. The reasons for this are twofold. First, SADC represents the most developed region of SSA and is economically the largest contributor to the African economy (SADC 2006). Its relatively large (in the African context) internal market can be seen as offering a growing market for foreign investors as well as a 'springboard' for trade with the rest of SSA (Owhoso, et al. 2002: 412).[3] The SADC aims to establish a Customs Union by 2010. Given the potential for trade diversion owing to the relatively large size of one dominant economy (South Africa) (Carrère 2004; Sandrey 2006), understanding the potential impact of trade on FDI might be important for the way in which regional integration is managed. Second, regional integration has been increasing throughout the developing world in recent times (Baldwin 2006). The pertinent question is whether the

---

[1] Indeed, despite Africa's poor historical record in terms of attracting FDI, there has been relatively good progress over the past decade or so, with the FDI stock in Africa rising from US$26 billion in 1990 to US$187 billion in 2005 and with Africa's share of FDI to developing countries increasing from 4.7 per cent to 6.3 per cent over the same period (UNCTAD 2006a).

[2] SADC, established in 1992, consists of fourteen countries, including Angola, Botswana, the Democratic Republic of Congo, Lesotho, Madagascar, Malawi, Mauritius, Mozambique, Namibia, South Africa, Swaziland, United Republic of Tanzania, Zambia, and Zimbabwe. South Africa alone accounts for more than 75 per cent of SADC's total GDP.

[3] It can also be mentioned that the economic literature on SADC as a regional free trade area is relatively small compared with the much larger economic literature on the West and Central African CFA 'Franc' zones.

resulting growing intra- and inter-regional trade contribute to more FDI? The evidence from SADC could be instructive to other countries and groupings considering trade liberalization and regional integration as strategies to obtain greater FDI.

In the next section, a brief review of the recent literature on FDI and its determinants in Africa is given, with an emphasis on recent discussions on the relationship between trade and FDI. The subsequent section sets out the methodology (an adapted gravity model based on Bos and Van de Laar 2004 and Borrmann, Jungnickel, and Keller 2005) including a discussion of the data used. The chapter goes on to present the results of the empirical study and then offers concluding remarks.

THE RECENT LITERATURE

In this section, we discuss the recent literature on the relationship between trade and FDI and summarize the findings from recent studies on the determinants and effects of FDI in Africa. We point out that although important progress has been made in understanding the reasons for the low levels and growth of FDI to Africa the recent literature has not dealt adequately with the relationship between trade and FDI in Africa.

The relationship between trade and FDI has recently been the subject of some scrutiny in the literature. Mekki (2005) pointed out that the reason for this increasing scrutiny is owing to the fact that, traditionally, theories of FDI and trade have different origins and aims. Trade theory tries to explain why countries trade with one another whereas FDI theory tries to explain why firms produce abroad and invest in particular countries. As a consequence, various studies have attempted to integrate FDI into trade theory, for example: Brainard 1993; Dunning 1981; Eaton and Tamura 1994; Fontagné and Pajot 1997; Helpman 1984; Helpman and Krugman 1985; Horstmann and Markusen 1992; Markusen 1983; Markusen 1995; and Markusen and Venables 1995. These studies have concluded that, on the one hand, FDI generates complementary trade flows of finished goods while, on the other hand, they suggested that FDI and trade can act as substitutes for finished goods, but be complementary for intermediate goods (Blonigen 2001; Head and Ries 2001; Swenson 2004). Empirical evidence from Tunisia finds that FDI inflows and trade are indeed complementary for the manufacturing sectors of the economy, but are substitutes for some primary sectors (Mekki 2005).

Other empirical studies found that where FDI takes place in the production of a specific good, exports in the same good declined but exports for inter-mediate goods used in the production process of the same product rose significantly (Blonigen 2005; Head and Ries 2001; Swenson 2004).

A number of studies also find empirical evidence that FDI and trade are correlated. Jensen (2002) finds that FDI inflows have a positive influence on the technological base of Polish exports. Alguacil and Orts (2002) find a positive relationship between FDI outflows and exports from Spain. Pontes (2004) concludes that, for high levels of trade costs, FDI and trade act as complements and otherwise as substitutes. The OECD (2002) finds that, among their member countries, FDI levels are strongly correlated with trade and trade openness. However, they only treat FDI as a determinant of trade. The OECD (2005) confirms that the long trend among OECD member states is that FDI is becoming more trade intensive as a result of MNEs establishing global production networks and business-to-business value chains. The World Bank (2004) finds that, in general, Asian FDI inflows are increasingly affected by openness to trade and flows to export orientated economies. Fontangé and Pajot (1997) find that for France, Sweden, the USA, EU, and Japan the traditional trade theory of FDI acting as a substitute does not hold and that trade and FDI mostly act as complements. Repkine and Walsh (1998) examine the industrial output of Bulgaria, Hungary, Poland, and Romania during the first six years of the post-Communist era. They found that FDI induced vertical waves of EU-oriented output where non-EU output mostly collapsed.

Jun and Singh (1996) argue for bi-directional causality between FDI in-flows and exports for developing countries. They conclude that greater export orientation will attract more FDI. Liu, Burridge, and Sinclair (2002) find empirical bi-directional causality between growth, FDI inflows, and trade in China but only one-way causality to imports. Aizenman and Noy (2005) apply various statistical techniques and find strong bi-directional linkages between FDI flows and trade on an international level, differentiating only between developed and developing countries.

In conclusion, it can be said that no clear conclusion is reached on the complementary or substitutionary link between trade and FDI. The literature indicates that the linkage is dependent on the specific case.

As far as SSA is concerned, there have been comparatively few studies on FDI, leading Owhoso, et al. (2002: 408) to note that 'the African continent has been ignored in academic studies of FDI'. Although this is a somewhat strong statement (there is a small, but increasing literature on FDI in Africa—see Table 11.1), it is the case that, with a single exception, not one

Table 11.1. *Recent foreign direct investment (FDI) studies on Africa*

Authors	Description of main findings/focus
Asiedu 2002	The marginal benefit from increased openness to trade is less successful for sub-Saharan Africa. Africa is therefore different and policies that proved successful elsewhere might not be equally successful in Africa.
Asiedu 2004a	Sub-Saharan Africa has attracted more FDI due to policy reforms, but has a declining share of global FDI.
Asiedu 2004b	In order to realize the employment benefits of FDI, sub-Saharan Africa needs to attract FDI in non-natural resource industries and host countries need to improve their infrastructure and human capital stocks.
Asiedu 2006	From a study using panel data for twenty two African countries, finds that natural resources and a large domestic market are important determinants of FDI and that macroeconomic policies are also significant.
Basu and Srinivasan 2002	Studies the determinants of FDI in Africa and argues that these can be classified according to four categories: natural resources, specific locational advantages, policies towards FDI, and economic reforms.
Goldstein 2004	Political instability (high perceived risk) is a key limitation on FDI to Southern Africa, despite the region's potential.
Jenkins and Thomas 2002	Africa's negative international image of political and economic instability has a severe impact on the whole continent and a concerted effort to improve stability will also improve FDI inflows.
Mhlanga 2007	The determinants of FDI to SADC are studied using project-level data. It is found that market size, colonial ties, and proximity of the investing country are the major determinants of FDI to SADC.
Morisset 2000	Countries with attractive investment environments were able to attract a significant share of FDI. Therefore, aggressive liberalization and strong economic growth will lead to an increased level of FDI.
Naudé and Krugell 2007	Geography does not have a direct influence on FDI flows to Africa and neither market-seeking nor resource-seeking FDI seems to dominate. Political stability proved to be a significant determinant of FDI, which indicates that good institutions are important.
Ng 2007	Studies the link between FDI and productivity in fourteen sub-Saharan Africa countries and finds only limited evidence that FDI inflows contribute to higher productivity in Africa.
Seetanah and Khadaroo 2007	Investigates the relationship between FDI and growth in the case of thirty-nine African countries over the period 1980–2000. Finds that FDI has a positive and significant effect on growth. However, the contribution of FDI to growth is less than that of domestic private and public investment, and also less than in non-African countries.
Te Velde 2002	Two issues of concern regarding FDI and Africa are (a) that sub-Saharan Africa attracts only a small share of total FDI flows; and (b) that it is hotly debated whether FDI really leads to economic and social development in Africa. The focus is on what host countries can do to influence FDI.

of the existing studies considered the relationship between trade and FDI in Africa.[4]

Some key publications to have focused on FDI in Africa in recent times are summarized in Table 11.1. From Table 11.1, it can be seen that the recent literature on FDI in Africa points to the need in African countries for improvements in human capital, infrastructure, political stability, and appropriate macroeconomic policies.

These studies on FDI to Africa omitted to take into consideration the possible relationship between FDI and trade, the exception being Asiedu (2002), who found that the marginal benefit to FDI from increased openness to trade is marginally significant for SSA. Apart from this finding, however, it would appear that the relationship between trade and FDI is not well understood in Africa. As has been pointed out, greater openness to trade and rising trade could lead to higher inflows of FDI. For Africa, such a relationship could be important in view of (i) African economies' greater openness to trade, following more and more countries' adoption of trade liberalization programmes and regional integration schemes; and (ii) the greater desire amongst African countries to further regional integration and trade (as seen, for instance, in objectives of the African Union, NEPAD, and regional trade agreements such as SADC).

METHODOLOGY

Modelling approach

We use an adapted gravity model (Bos and Van de Laar 2004). It is derived from Newton's gravity equation that holds that the gravitational pull between two objects is directly and positively related to their mass and the distance between the objects acting as a restraint (Borrmann, Jungnickel, and Keller 2005).

The application in economics implies that an economic flow between two economic entities will depend on their respective economic sizes and the distance between them. Distance can be represented as physical distance or a psychological restraint or encouragement to do business (ibid.). For FDI, it can also be stated that gravity, in general, refers to the forces that work to

---

[4] Most studies of FDI in Africa focus on the determinants of FDI to Africa (Ng 2007: 5).

bring actual FDI flows in line with expected FDI flows (Bos and Van de Laar 2004).

The general gravity formula states that the attractive force between objects i and j can be defined as:

$$F_{ij} = G \frac{M_i M_j}{D_{ij}^2} \qquad (11.1)$$

where

- F_{ij} is the attractive force
- M_i and M_j are the masses
- D_{ij} is the distance between the two objects
- G is a gravitational constant.

If these principles are applied in order to explain FDI in terms of trade it can be written as:

$$FDI_{ij} = A_{ij} \frac{X_i X_j}{Dist_{ij}} \qquad (11.2)$$

where

- FDI_{ij} is the flow in FDI from home country i to host country j
- X_i and X_j are the respective export totals of i and j
- $Dist_{ij}$ is the distance between home country i to host country j
- A_{ij} is a constant.

When transformed into a linear equation using logs, it can be written as follows:

$$\ln\ FDI_{ij} = \beta_0 + \beta_1 \ln\ X_i + \beta_2 \ln\ X_j - \beta_3 \ln\ Dist_{ij} + \varepsilon_{ij} \qquad (11.3)$$

(With β_0 simple constant, ϵ_{ij} the error term, β_1 and β_2 are positive.)

The coefficient for the distance term need not be negative. The outcome is reflected in whether distance is a deterrent for FDI or a magnet. $Dist_{ij}$ represents a vector of variables that represent distance. Theory will also dictate that, in the case of resource seeking FDI, the imports of the home country will determine FDI rather than exports.

During the estimation process, three models are investigated. Each model builds upon, and is an extension of, the previous one. The strategy entails, first, modelling data at an aggregate level and then gradually expanding the model to include individual home and host countries. The first model, Model 1 (covering 1973–2004), a single equation regression, serves as a preliminary investigation into the data and is done at an aggregate level. In

Model 2 (covering 1974–2004), Model 1 is expanded to include the export totals of the major trading partners of SADC as separate variables. Model 2 is also a single equation regression. Both Models 1 and 2 give an indication as to the viability and validity of using the adapted gravity approach. With positive results in the first two models, a panel regression is carried out for the SADC countries and their most important trading partners in Model 3 (covering 1989–2004). A Granger causality test is also carried out on the stacked FDI inflow and SADC export variables.

Variables and data

The variables and data used in Models 1–3 are described in Table 11.2.

Other variables were also tested but proved not to be significant. They included the Transparency International corruption perception index (Transparency International 2006); the World Bank good governance indicators (World Bank 2006a); trade balances, current account balances, various trade variables, tourist arrivals, number of commodities traded on debts owed from the UNCTAD *Handbook of Statistics* (UNCTAD 2006b); IMF exchange rates (IMF 2006); and internet connectivity figures from the World Bank development indicators (World Bank 2006b).

The equations in Model 1 and Model 2 are estimated for aggregate SADC, while the panel in Model 3 contains the stacked data for individual SADC countries. SADC consists of Angola, Botswana, the Democratic Republic of Congo, Lesotho, Madagascar, Malawi, Mauritius, Mozambique, Namibia, South Africa, Swaziland, Tanzania, Zambia, and Zimbabwe (SADC 2006). Six more countries could conceivably be included in SADC, in the long term. They are Burundi, Comoros, Kenya, Rwanda, Seychelles, and Uganda. For the purposes of this chapter, they are included as their trade and geographic locations are completely intertwined with SADC. FDIs from South Africa in other SADC countries are not taken into consideration. Although increasingly important for SADC, outward FDI from South Africa, China, and India in Africa is a relatively recent phenomenon (Henley, et al.: Chap. 9 of this volume). The scope of the study covers 1989 to 2004 and thus the relationship with these countries cannot as yet be adequately empirically investigated.

For Model 3 distance is calculated from the individual SADC countries' capitals to the trading partners' capitals.

Table 11.2. *List of variables used in final estimations*

Variables used	Description	Source
Model 1		
SADCFDI	Total FDI inflows to Southern African Development Community.	UNCTAD 2006a.
SADCExports	Total trade exports of Southern African Development Community to the developed world.	UNCTAD 2006b.
MajorExports	Total trade exports of the major developed countries to the rest of the world.	UNCTAD 2006b.
MajorExportstoAfrica	Total trade exports of the major developed countries to Africa.	UNCTAD 2006b.
Distance	Distance from South Africa to the UK is used because in the aggregate data single equation distance is a constant.	Distances were calculated with the infoseek.com distance calculator. It uses coordinates from the US Geological survey to calculate distance between two points on the world globe.
Dummy1	Dummy variable with values of 1 in 1979, 1985, 1990, and 1994; otherwise 0. These years were years in which Southern African Development Community experienced political turmoil.	Own calculations.
Model 2		
SADCFDI	Total FDI inflows to Southern African Development Community.	UNCTAD 2006a.
SADCExports	Total trade exports of Southern African Development Community to the developed world.	UNCTAD 2006b.
USExports, UKExports, JapanExports	Total trade of the major individual trading partners (the USA, UK, and Japan) to Africa.	UNCTAD 2006b.
Distance	Distance from South Africa to the UK is used because, in the aggregate data single equation, distance is a constant.	Distances were calculated with the infoseek.com distance calculator. It uses coordinates from the US Geological survey to calculate distance between two points on the world globe.

(continued)

Table 11.2. Continued

Variables used	Description	Source
Model 3		
Dummy2	Dummy variable with values of 1 in 1976, 1979, 1985, 1990, and 1994; otherwise 0. These years were years in which Southern African Development Community experienced political turmoil.	Own calculations.
FDIinflows	Stacked variable of the FDI inflows to the respective Southern African Development Community countries.	UNCTAD 2006a.
ExportsSADC	Stacked variable of the value of merchandise exports of the respective Southern African Development Community countries.	UNCTAD 2006b.
ExportsUS, ExportsUK, ExportsGermany, ExportsFrance, ExportsItaly, ExportsJapan	Total trade of the individual trading partners to Africa.	UNCTAD 2006b.
DistanceUS, DistanceUK, DistanceGermany, DistanceFrance, DistanceItaly, DistanceJapan	A stacked variable of distance from the respective Southern African Development Community countries to their individual trading partners the USA, UK, Germany, France, Italy, and Japan.	Distances were calculated with the infoseek.com distance calculator. It uses coordinates from the US Geological survey to calculate distance between two points on the world globe.
Dummy3	Stacked dummy variable that is 1 in years of political instability and natural disasters in the respective Southern African Development Community countries. It takes on 0 in other years.	Crudely constructed by using the brief historical overviews of the individual SADC countries and years of instability as given in the CIA 2006 and *Encyclopaedia Britannica* 2006.

EMPIRICAL RESULTS

In this section, the results of the empirical analysis are presented, discussed, and interpreted. The results were obtained as outlined in the previous section and consist of the individual results of the three specified models.

Model 1

Table 11.3 shows the final results of Model 1. Total exports of the developed world are limited to their exports to Africa only. A dummy variable (Dummy 1) is introduced. Dummy 1 is 0 except for 1979, 1985, 1990, and 1994, where it is 1. These years were of great consequence for the SADC region as they represent (i) the end of the Rhodesian conflict in 1979; (ii) the debt freeze of South Africa in 1985; (iii) significant political changes announced in South Africa, Tanzania, Mozambique, and Kenya in 1990; and the changes in South Africa in 1994. It explains why the variable is significant at the 5 per cent level. The explanatory variables are 'lagged' for one period and finally an AR(2) term proves to be highly significant at the 5 per cent and 1 per cent levels. All these changes bring about significant change in the estimation results. The 'Total exports of the developed world' variable is the only variable that is insignificant even at the 10 per cent level.

Because Model 1 is a preliminary investigation, no further investigation nor a more in-depth statistical analysis is carried out. The facts that the SADC export variable is significant at the 1 per cent level, and the distance variable is also significant at the 10 per cent level, clearly indicate that relationships as set out in the adapted gravity model do exist within the data. This warrants further investigation.

Table 11.3. *Model 1 results*

Dependent variable: LOG(SADCFDI)
Method: Least squares (sample: 1973–2004)

Variable	Coefficient	t-statistic	Probability
LOG(SADCExports(Lag1))	3.972	5.064	0.000*
LOG(ExportstoAfrica(Lag1))	−1.353	−1.482	0.151
LOG(Distance)	−1.867	−2.023	0.053*
Dummy1	−0.543	−2.486	0.020*
AR(2)	0.635	5.641	0.000*
R^2			0.837
Adjusted R^2			0.811
Akaike info criterion			2.043
Schwarz criterion			2.276
Durbin–Watson statistic			1.604

Model 2

In Table 11.4, the results are shown for Model 2. Total export of the trading partners is limited to exports to Africa only, as suggested by Model 1. A dummy variable, Dummy 2, which is an expansion of Dummy 1 from Model 1, is also included. The years of 1977 and 1983 are added as having a value of 1 to 1979, 1985, 1990, and 1994 to take into account (i) the Angolan and Rhodesian conflicts of 1977; (ii) the aftermath of the Soweto riots of 1976; and (iii) the severe droughts and food shortages that occurred in the region in 1983. All variables except EU exports and distance, which once again form the constant term, are significant at the 1 per cent level. Owing to some missing values, the sample size is reduced from 1974 to 2004.

All test results indicate a satisfactory fit but, because of fears of multicollinearity and unit roots, further investigation into the accuracy of the equation is needed. The total exports variables are all subject to concurrent global economic trends and could lead to multicollinearity and also unit roots in the residuals that could bias the estimation results. Table 11.5 gives the test results for the model and its residuals. It should be noted that all tests confirm a good fit.

Model 2 finds a statistically significant relationship between FDI inflows to SADC and trade. Specifically, the results show that a complementary relationship exists between exports from SADC and FDI and between imports from the USA (USExports) and FDI to SADC. The negative coefficients on LOG(UKexports) and LOG(Japanexports) would suggest, at this stage, substitution between SADC imports from these countries and FDI inflows.

Table 11.4. *Model 2 results*

Dependent variable: LOG(SADCFDI)
Method: Least squares (sample: 1974–2004)

Variable	Coefficient	t-Statistic	Probability
LOG(SADCExports)	2.702	7.601	0.000*
LOG(USexports)	3.096	5.531	0.000*
LOG(UKexports)	−2.402	−2.541	0.018*
LOG(Japanexports)	−2.483	−6.502	0.000*
LOG(Distance)	0.056	0.179	0.860
Dummy2	−1.003	−14.324	0.000*
R^2			0.965*
Adjusted R^2			0.958*
Akaike info criterion			0.528*
Schwarz criterion			0.808*
Durbin–Watson statistic			1.607

Table 11.5. *Model 2: regression diagnostics*

Summary of test results		
Ramsey RESET test	F-statistic	0.048
	Log likelihood ratio	0.063
White heteroskedasticity test	F-statistic	0.912
	Obs*R^2	20.085
Breusch–Godfrey Serial Correlation LM test	F-statistic	0.062
	Obs*R^2	0.168
ARCH test	F-statistic	0.893
	Obs*R^2	0.929
Normality tests	Jarque–Bera	0.781
	Jarque–Bera probability	0.677
	Skewness	0.080
	Kurtosis	2.226
Unit root tests	Augmented Dickey–Fuller test statistic	−4.844
	Augmented Dickey–Fuller test probability	0.001
	Phillips–Perron test statistic	−4.844
	Phillips–Perron test probability	0.001
Forecast tests	Mean absolute error	0.268
	Mean absolute percentage error	4.360

Political instability in 1976 appears to be significant and has a negative impact on FDI inflows. In Table 11.4, the coefficient on the distance variable is, however—contrary to expectations—insignificant.

As mentioned in previous sections, there are some questions as to whether trade causes FDI or whether FDI causes trade. Most evidence for developed

Table 11.6. *Causality test for foreign direct investment (FDI) and exports in Southern African Development Community (SADC)*

Pairwise Granger causality tests	Sample: 1970–2005	
Lags: 1	Obs	523
Null hypothesis	F-Statistic	Probability
ExportsSADC does not Granger Cause FDIinflows	37.199	0.000
FDIinflows does not Granger Cause ExportsSADC	1.530	0.217
GDP does not Granger Cause FDIinflows	42.747	0.000
FDIinflows does not Granger Cause GDP	14.946	0.000
GDP does not Granger Cause ExportsSADC	15.4581	0.000
ExportsSADC does not Granger Cause GDP	28.5061	0.000

countries suggests that FDI causes trade, with little FDI being caused by trade. Therefore, it is pertinent to examine the causality between trade and FDI in SADC before doing the panel estimations. Table 11.6 shows the results of a Granger causality test that was done on the stacked series of FDI inflows to the individual SADC countries and the stacked value of merchandise exports. The test was repeated with various lagged options but always gave the same result. The test indicates that, in the specific case of the twenty countries included in the analysis, exports from SADC (Granger) cause FDI to SADC.

Model 3

Model 3 consists of six panel estimations using the gravity specification. Estimations were done for a different trading partner, while the panel represents the variables for the twenty SADC countries. Table 11.7 shows the final estimation results for the panel estimations of the twenty SADC countries with the six major trading partners.

In the case of the USA and UK, all variables are significant at the 1 per cent level except the total trade of the USA and UK with Africa. These are also the only two equations where the constant was significant. For France and Germany, all variables were significant at the 1 per cent level. For France, however, an AR (1) term was also significant. Italy mostly shares results with France and Germany but the total export of Italy variable is only just not significant at the 10 per cent level. In the equation for Japan, only the SADC exports and the political stability dummy variable, Dummy 3, are statistically significant.

SADC exports are significant throughout the estimations and this confirms the result of the Granger causality test. It should be noted that the coefficient of SADC exports for all the estimations is nearly on a one to one basis. This implies that for every 1 per cent increase in SADC exports there is an almost 1 per cent increase in FDI.

The large negative and mostly significant coefficients on distance and 'Dummy3' for most equations indicates, first, that the SADC countries are geographically very distant to their trading partners, and that, second, perceived political instability matters for FDI. The overall measures of fit are mixed and fluctuate between rather mediocre fits for the USA and the UK to overall good fits for Germany, France, and Italy. Panel unit root tests indicate that no unit root is present but normality tests indicate that normality cannot be assumed for the residuals. This is attributed to the severe fluctuations in the data, which coincide with periods of political instability.

Table 11.7. *Model 3 results*

Dependent variable: LOG(FDIinflows)

Method: Panel GMM EGLS (cross-section weights) (sample: 1989–2004)

Variable	USA	UK	Germany	France	Italy	Japan
Constant	58.59 (3.55)	36.67 (2.2)				
LOG(ExportsSADC)	0.88 (11.04)	0.96 (8.66)	0.91 (17.47)	0.88 (12.57)	0.92 (14.66)	0.91 (12.35)
LOG(Export*)	−0.13 (−0.20)	−0.82 (−0.69)	1.12 (2.59)	1.36 (2.37)	0.93 (1.65)	−0.45 (−0.65)
LOG(Distance*)	−6.21 (−4.26)	−3.45 (−3.67)	−1.32 (−3.04)	−1.62 (−2.66)	−1.16 (−2.04)	0.25 (0.38)
Dummy3	−3.77 (−6.47)	−4.22 (−4.79)	−3.39 (−11.96)	−3.2 (−7.3)	−2.63 (−7.7)	−3.24 (−5.65)
AR 1 Term	0.27 (3.63)	0.315 (4.27)	0.33 (6.14)	0.36 (5.11)	0.36 (5.09)	
			Weighted statistics			
R²	0.599	0.453	0.625	0.720	0.854	0.712
Adjusted R-squared	0.591	0.443	0.621	0.716	0.852	0.707
Durbin–Watson statistic	1.936	1.951	1.329	1.976	2.029	1.975
J-statistic	0.076	0.000	6.584	3.032	3.382	0.618
			Unweighted statistics			
R²	0.529	0.327	0.571	0.698	n./a	0.687
Sum² Residual	696.427	976.573	632.501	463.594	n./a	481.931
Durbin–Watson statistic	1.859	1.869	1.232	1.977	n./a	1.951

Notes: t-statistic in parenthesis.

In periods of substantial fluctuations, there is possible over- or underestimation of the actual value. This is more significant for the figures of Burundi than for the other countries. This problem could be addressed by amending the dummy variable. It is, however, not advisable because the fluctuations should be seen as the inability of the gravity specification to capture all the relevant variables that explain FDI inflows or the inability of a dummy variable to explain the effects of political instability completely. Other variables outside the scope of the gravity specification might be effective in explaining the fluctuation observed in the residuals. Country-specific evaluation might deliver other results because they are not obtained as the overall error that includes the joint series of country residuals. In future research, the specification can be opened up to include other variables that might explain the fluctuations more clearly. In a country-specific evaluation, other results might also be obtained. Both of these suggestions fall outside the scope of this chapter.

The final conclusion from Table 11.7 is that the general trend in FDI inflows is significantly explained in the estimation by SADC exports, distance, and political instability. The insignificance of US, UK, and Japanese exports to SADC suggests a possible lack of complementarities between SADC imports and FDI inflows from these countries, in contrast to the complementarities in both exports and imports to and from Germany, France, and Italy.

CONCLUDING REMARKS

In a recent assessment of policies needed to lift African countries out of their poverty trap, Sachs, et al. (2004: 150) placed a high priority on regional integration, stating that 'Regional integration will raise the interest of potential foreign investors by increasing the scope of the market.' In this chapter, we focused on the SADC and asked whether, in these countries, a relationship exists between trade and FDI. In so doing, the contribution of this chapter was threefold. First, we contributed to the growing literature on FDI in Africa. Second, we contributed towards understanding the relationship between trade and FDI in Africa, which has so far been neglected in the literature. Third, our results are of interest to countries in Africa considering regional integration as a strategy to raise economic growth through greater openness to trade.

Using an adapted gravity model, our results are insightful as they suggest a more complex relationship between FDI inflows to SADC and SADC exports than may have been expected. For instance, the export variables for home countries indicated mixed results, with the USA, UK, and Japan having insignificant and negative coefficients. In contrast, Germany, France, and

Italy had positive significant coefficients but insignificant constant values. The complementary role between home exports and host FDI inflows thus clearly depends on the nature of the underlying trading relationship. In addition to these results, we also established that distance and political instability have a significant and negative impact on FDI.

From these results the following policy recommendations can be made. First, trade liberalization remains important in Southern Africa for attracting more FDI through its beneficial impacts on exports from the region (Edwards and Alves 2006; Mengistae and Patillo 2004). Second, further regional integration within SADC needs to ensure that trade diversion losses from traditional trading partners such as the EU and the USA be minimized; however, given the general strong relationship between exports and FDI, further regional integration might increase the 'proximity' of countries to their export destination markets, especially in the case of the many landlocked countries in SADC. Indeed, this could also benefit landlocked countries such as Burundi, Rwanda, and Uganda, which are currently not members. Third, growing trade within SADC as a result of regional integration might lead to growing investment from South Africa in the region, given the country's proximity to its other SADC partners. The country is already the third largest single investor in other SADC countries in dollar values (Mhlanga 2007: 9). Finally, greater efforts will need to be made within SADC to limit the negative impacts and 'neighbourhood effects' that political instability can exert on FDI. The region's apparent inability to contribute solutions to the ongoing crisis in Zimbabwe could ultimately be costing the whole region in terms of FDI.

REFERENCES

Aizenman, J., and I. Noy (2005) 'FDI and Trade: Two-way Linkages?' National Bureau of Economic Research Working Paper 11403 (June).

Alguacil, M. T., and V. Orts (2002) 'A Multivariate Cointegrated Model Testing for Temporal Causality between Exports and Outward Foreign Investment: The Spanish Case', *Applied Economics and Fundacion de Estudios de Economia Aplicada*, EEE50.

Asiedu, E. (2001) 'On the Determinants of Foreign Direct Investment to Developing Countries: Is Africa Different?' *World Development*, 30: 107–19.

——(2004a) 'Policy Reform and Foreign Direct Investment in Africa: Absolute Progress but Relative Decline', *Development Policy Review*, 22: 41–8.

——(2004b) 'The Determinants of Employed of Affiliates of US Multinational Enterprises in Africa', *Development Policy Review*, 22: 371–9.

——(2006) 'Foreign Direct Investment in Africa: The Role of Natural Resources, Market Size, Government Policy, Institutions and Political Stability', *World Economy*, 29: 63–77.

Baldwin, R. E. (2006) 'Multilateralising Regionalism: Spaghetti Bowls as Building Blocks on the Path to Global Free Trade', *World Economy*, 29: 1451–518.

Basu, A., and K. Srinivasan (2002) 'Foreign Direct Investment in Africa: Some Case Studies'. IMF Working Paper WP/02/6 (Washington, DC: IMF).

Blonigen, B. A. (2001) 'In Search of Substitution between Foreign Production and Exports', *Journal of International Economics*, 53: 81–104.

——(2005) 'A Review of the Empirical Literature on FDI Determinants'. National Bureau of Economic Research Working Paper 11299 (Apr.).

Borenstein, E., J. de Gregorio, and J.-W. Lee (1998) 'How Does Foreign Direct Investment Affect Economic Growth?', *Journal of International Economics*, 45: 115–35.

Borrmann, C., R. Jungnickel, and D. Keller (2005) 'What Gravity Models Can Tell Us about the Position of German FDI in Central and Eastern Europe'. Hamburg Institute of International Economics Discussion Paper 328 (Aug.).

Bos, J. W. B., and M. Van De Laar (2004) 'Explaining Foreign Direct Investment in Central Europe: An Extended Gravity Approach'. Research Memoranda 041, Maastricht: METEOR, Maastricht Research School of Economics of Technology and Organization.

Brainard, S. L. (1993) 'A Simple Theory of Multinational Corporations and Trade with a Trade-off between Proximity and Concentration', National Bureau of Economic Research Working Paper 4269 (Feb.).

Carrère, C. (2004) 'African Regional Agreements: Impact on Trade With or Without Currency Unions', *Journal of African Economies*, 31: 199–239.

CIA (Central Intelligence Agency) (2006) World Factbook. <https://www.cia.gov/cia/publications/factbook/index.html>.

Dunning, P. (1981) *International Production and the Multinational Enterprise* (London: George Allen & Unwin).

Eaton, J., and A. Tamura (1994) 'Bilateralism and Regionalism in Japanese and US Trade and Direct Foreign Investment Patterns', *Journal of the Japanese and International Economies*, 8: 478–510.

Edwards, L., and P. Alves (2006) 'South Africa's Export Performance: Determinants of Export Supply', *South African Journal of Economics*, 74: 473–500.

Encyclopaedia Britannica (2006) <http://www.britannica.com>.

Fontagné, L., and M. Pajot (1997) 'How Foreign Direct Investment Affects International Trade and Competitiveness: An Empirical Assessment'. CEPII Working Document 97–17.

Fosu, A. K., and S. A. O'Connell (2006) 'Explaining African Economic Growth: The Role of Anti-growth Syndromes', in *Annual Bank Conference on Development Economics 2006* (Washington, DC: World Bank).

Goldstein, A. (2004) *Regional Integration, FDI and Competitiveness in Southern Africa* (Paris: OECD).

Greenaway, D., D. Sapsford, and S. Pfaffenzeller (2007) 'Foreign Direct Investment, Economic Performance and Trade Liberalization', *World Economy*, 30: 197–210.

Head, K., and J. Ries (2001) 'Overseas Investment and Firm Exports', *Review of International Economics*, 9: 108–22.

Helpman, E. (1984) 'A Simple Theory of International Trade with Multinational Corporations', *Journal of Political Economy*, 92: 451–71.

——and P. R. Krugman (1985) 'Market Structure and Foreign Trade', in *Increasing Returns: Imperfect Competition and the International Economy* (Cambridge, Mass.: MIT Press).

Horstmann, I. J., and J. R. Markusen (1992) 'Endogenous Market Structure in International Trade', *Journal of Economics*, 32: 109–29.

IMF (2006) 'The World Economic Outlook for September 2006'. <http://www.imf.org/external/pubs/ft/weo/2006/02/data/index.aspx>.

Infoplease Distance Calculator (2006). <http://www.infoplease.com/atlas/calculate-distance.html>.

Jenkins, C., and L. Thomas (2002) 'Foreign Direct Investment in Southern Africa: Determinants, Characteristics and Implications for Economic Growth and Poverty Alleviation' (Oxford and London: CREFSA, London School of Economics/CSAE). mimeo.

Jensen, C. (2002) 'Foreign Direct Investment, Industrial Restructuring and the Upgrading of Polish Exports', *Applied Economics*, 34: 207–17.

Jun, K. W., and H. Singh (1996) 'The Determinants of Foreign Direct Investment in Developing Countries', *UNCTAD: Transnational Corporations*, 5: 67–105.

Lim, E. (2001) 'Determinants of, and the Relation between, Foreign Direct Investment and Growth: A Summary of Recent Literature'. IMF Working Paper WP/01/175.

Liu, X., P. Burridge, and P. J. N. Sinclair (2002) 'Relationships between Economic Growth, Foreign Direct Investment and Trade: Evidence from China', *Applied Economics*, 34: 1433–40.

Markusen, J. R. (1983) 'Factor Movements and Commodity Trade as Complements', *Journal of International Economics*, 14: 341–56.

——(1995) 'The Boundaries of Multinational Enterprises and the Theory of International Trade', *Journal of Economic Perspectives*, 9: 169–89.

——and A. J. Venables (1995) 'Multinational Firms and the New Trade Theory'. NBER Working Paper 5036 (Cambridge, Mass.: NBER).

Mekki, R. (2005) 'The Impact of Foreign Direct Investment on Trade: Evidence from Tunisia'. Paper presented at 4th Annual Conference of the European Economics and Finance Society, 'Economic and Financial Issues in an Enlarged Europe', Coimbra, Portugal, 19 May.

Mengistae, T. C., and C. A. Pattillo (2004) 'Export Orientation and Productivity in Sub-Saharan Africa', *IMF Staff Papers*, 51: 327–53.

Mhlanga, N. (2007) 'Understanding Foreign Direct Investments to the Southern African Development Community (SADC): An Analysis Based on Project-Level Data'. Paper presented at the UNU-WIDER Conference, 'Southern Engines of Global Growth: China, India, Brazil and South Africa', Helsinki, 8 Sept.

Morisset, J. (2000) 'Foreign Direct Investment in Africa: Policies also Matter', *UNCTAD: Transnational Corporations*, 9: 107–25.

Naudé, W. A., and W. F. Krugell (2007) 'Investigating Geography and Institutions as Determinants of Foreign Direct Investment in Africa using Panel Data', *Applied Economics*, 39: 1223–34.

Ng, T. H. (2007) 'Foreign Direct Investment and Productivity: Evidence from Sub-Saharan Africa'. unpub. (Vienna: UNIDO).

OECD (2002) *Foreign Direct Investment for Development* (Paris: OECD).

——(2005) *International Investment Perspectives* (Paris: OECD).

Owhoso, V., K. C. Gleason, I. Mathur, and C. Malgwi (2002) 'Entering the Last Frontier: Expansion by US Multinationals to Africa', *International Business Review*, 11: 408–30.

Pontes, J. P. (2004) 'A Theory of the Relationship between Foreign Direct Investment and Trade', *Economics Bulletin*, 6: 1–8.

Repkine, A., and P. P. Walsh (1998) 'European Trade and Foreign Direct Investment U-shaping Industrial Output in Central and Eastern Europe: Theory and Evidence'. IMF Working Paper WP/98/150.

Sachs, J. D., J. W. McArthur, G. Schmidt-Traub, et al. (2004) 'Ending Africa's Poverty Trap', *Brookings Papers on Economic Activity*, 1: 117–240.

SADC (Southern African Development Community) (2006). Website. <http://www.sadc.int>.

Sandrey, R. (2006) 'Trade Creation and Trade Diversion Resulting from SACU Trading Agreements'. tralac (trade law centre for southern Africa) Working Paper 11/2006. <http://www.tralac.org>.

Seetanah, B., and A. J. Khadaroo (2007) 'Foreign Direct Investment and Growth: New Evidences from Sub-Saharan African Countries'. Paper presented at the Centre for the Study of African Economies Conference, 'Economic Development in Africa', Oxford, 20 Mar.

Swenson, D. L. (2004) 'Foreign Investment and Mediation of Trade Flows', *Review of International Economics*, 12: 609–29.

te Velde, D. W. (2002) *Foreign Direct Investment for Development: Policy Challenges for Sub-Saharan African Countries* (London: Overseas Development Institute).

Transparency International (2006) Website. <http://www.transparency.org>.

UNCTAD (United Nations Conference on Trade and Development) (2005a) *Economic Development in Africa: Rethinking the Role of Foreign Direct Investment*. UNCTAD/GDS/AFRICA/2005/1 (Geneva: UNCTAD).

——(2005b) World Investment Report, FDI Indicators. <http://www.unctad.org/Templates/WebFlyer.asp?intItemID=3489andlang=1>.

——(2006a). Website. <http://www.unctad.org/Templates/Page.asp?intItemID=3198&lang=1>.

——(2006b) Handbook of Statistics. <http://www.unctad.org/Templates/Page.asp?intItemID=1890>.

World Bank (2004) 'Foreign Direct Investment in Developing Asia', *Asian Development Outlook Part 3* (Washington, DC: World Bank).

——(2006a) 'Good Governance Indicators'. <http://www.worldbank.org/wbi/governance>.

World Bank (2006b) 'World Development Indicators'. <http://web.worldbank.org/WBSITE/EXTERNAL/DATASTATISTICS/0,,contentMDK:20899413~pagePK:64133150~piPK:64133175~theSitePK:239419,00.html>.

Index

ACFTA 128
African economic reform
    programmes 264
African FDI studies 266–8
African tariff/non-tariff barriers 208
African trade liberalization 264
AfrIPANet 209
AFTA (Asian Free Trade Area) 117
AGOA (African Growth Opportunities
    Act) 221, 232
agricultural subsidies 53
anti-growth policy syndromes 263
apartheid 44, 46
ASEAN 117, 128–9
Asian Dragons 114, 117
Asian economies, emerging 14–138
Asian Tigers 114

balance of payments 33
Bangladesh exports 133
Barra, Mariana 236–59
Bernanke-Gertler effect 182
Bezuidenhout, Henri 3, 263–79
Bhutto, Benazir 53
BIS banks 195, 197
Blanchard, O. 68
Brazil
    APEX-Brasil (Brazilian Trade and
        Investment Promotion Agency) 254
    area 45
    assets 152–8
    balance of payments 33, 187–92
    BIS debt 197, 198
    capital account liberalization
        (CAL) 143, 145, 146–7, 172–204
    capital flows 144, 172–204
    capital outflow liberalization 143–70
    Carta-Circular No.5 (CC5) 146, 147
    corporations 151

current account balance 33–4, 187, 188
demographic characteristics 18–19
economic causation 21–3
economic characteristics 45–8
economic growth 14, 17–19, 20, 23–9,
    44, 172
economic mechanisms 21–3
economic performance 1, 2
education 54
effect on developing countries 26–9,
    36–7
effect on industrialized countries 25–6
effect on world economy 23–4
as emerging economy 39, 44
end-use restriction 150
energy consumption 24
as engine of growth 20
exchange rates 23, 183–7, 190, 203–4
as export market 2
exports 17, 27, 30, 188
FDI (foreign direct investment) 1, 3–4,
    32–3, 144, 158–62, 165–70, 253, 256
Fiex (*Fundos de Divida Externa*) 146
foreign aid by 36–7
foreign capital inflows 23
foreign debt 192–9, 203
foreign exchange reserves 34–6, 192
foreign portfolio debt 163–4, 166–8
foreign portfolio equity 166
foreign portfolio equity assets 162–3
in the future 16–19
in G20 40
GDP growth rates 172
GDP per capita 11–19
and global output 84
government policy 254
government spending 187–92
gross capital formation (GCF) 35
gross domestic savings (GDS) 35

Brazil (*cont.*)
 heavy industrialization 253
 household surveys 105–9
 imports 30
 income per capita 99, 100
 individuals and financial outflow 151
 Innovation Law 254
 institutional investors 151
 interest rates 23, 199–201
 international finance 33–7
 international investment 31–3
 international migration 37–8
 international trade 30–1
 Investe Brasil 253
 investment 3–4, 146–7, 189, 190, 191,
  see also FDI
 inward direct investment 189
 inward portfolio investment 191
 IPAs 254
 IPT (Industrialized Products Tax) 254
 liabilities 152–8
 manufacturing 27–9
 microeconomic data 173–4
 and MNCs 241, 252–5, 258
 National Development Plans 253
 national policies 255–9
 as net creditor 193
 net direct investment 189
 outward direct investment 190
 outward portfolio investment 191
 in the past 10–11
 place in world economy 9–21
 population 10–11, 12, 45
 portfolio equity 166
 in Quad 40
 R&D expenditure 249
 R&D investments 237, 239, 240, 241,
  252–5, 258
 real-wage constraint 45
 RENAI (National Network of Investment Information) 254
 reserves 152–8
 share of world GDP 10
 skilled workforce 255, 258–9

 slavery 45–6, 47
 stock market 202
 targets plan (Plano de metas) 252–3
 tax law 254
 unemployment 46
 and world economic crisis 4–5
 and WTO 40, 52
  see also East Asian Crisis
Bretton Woods 179, 180
BRIC *see* Brazil; China; India; Russia
Britain
 economic growth 21
 as engine of growth 19
 household surveys 105–9
 R&D investment 239
Bussolo, Maurizo 2, 77–112

Camillo, Edilaine 236–59
capital account liberalization 143, 145,
  150, 172–204
capital controls 177–80
capital investment 221–2
Carvalho, Flávia 236–59
CGE model 79, 82, 97
Chaponnière, Jean-Raphael 2, 114–38
China
 ACFTA 128
 agriculture 89, 91–3, 110, 116
 area 45
 and ASEAN 128–9
 assets 152–8
 balance of payments 33, 57, 187–92
 bilateral trade with Vietnam 126–8
 BIS debt 197, 198
 border dispute with India 53
 budgetary expenditure 69, 70, 71
 capital account liberalization
  (CAL) 143, 145, 150, 172–204
 capital flows 144, 172–204
 capital investments 58, 221–2
 capital outflow liberalization 143–70
 capital/output ratios 62, 63
 Christian group 54
 and clothing quotas 115